Christian Worship

Christian Classics Revived

The Publishers endeavor herein to make reaccessible to Researchers, Academics & Libraries worldwide Reproduced Editions of such rare and time-honored publications which continue to stand out for their cultural & historical importance, over the years. In this Series we'll focus on Christian Faith & Living vis-à-vis topics like Literature & Poetry, Indigenous Philosophizing, Ethical response towards Agriculture, Health & Healing, Science & Technology, Ecofeminist Theology, Sociological approach towards Human Rights, Law & Politics, Arts, History of Ideas, Ancient Civilizations, Cultural Contiguity, Religious Cosmologies & Mysticism, Footsteps of famous Theologians, World Peace & Harmony, Global Capitalism, Network Marketing, Cybertheology, Population & Demographics, Epigraphic Studies, Contextualized Education, and many others. We welcome your comments on our this effort and further suggestions for taking up any such scholarly titles, having gone in oblivion, befitting Classic Works of glorious and legendary writers on Christian Studies.

Christian Classics Revived - 10

Christian Worship

Revealing the Divine

Evelyn Underhill
Fellow of King's College, London

CWI
Christian World Imprints™

Christian World Imprints(TM)
Christian Publishing & Books from India
H-12 Bali Nagar, **New Delhi-110015**
info@christianworldimprints.com
www.ChristianWorldImprints.com
Phone: +91 11 25465925

ISBN 13: 978-93-5148-068-6 ISBN 10: 93-5148-068-2

Cataloging in Publication Data--DK
Courtesy: D.K. Agencies (P) Ltd. <docinfo@dkagencies.com>

Underhill, Evelyn, 1875-1941, **author.**
Christian worship : revealing the divine / Evelyn Underhill.
pages cm. -- (Christian classics revived ; 10)
Reprint.
ISBN 9789351480686
ISBN 9351480682

1. Worship. 2. Public worship. 3. Liturgics. I. Title. II. Series: Christian classics revived ; 10.

DDC 248.3 23

Originally published as *Worship*.

Printed at Replika Press Pvt. Ltd.

SANCTUS, SANCTUS, SANCTUS
DOMINUS DEUS SABAOTH
PLENI SUNT CŒLI ET TERRA GLORIA TUA,
HOSANNA IN EXCELSIS

Come del suo voler gli angeli tuoi
    fan sacrificio a te, cantando Osanna,
    cosi facciano gli uomini de' suoi.

DANTE: *Purg.*, *xi.* 10–12.

All worship was to him sacred, since he believed that in its most degraded forms, among the most ignorant and foolish of worshippers, there has yet been some true seeking after the Divine, and that between these and the most glorious ritual or the highest philosophic certainty, there lies so small a space that we may believe the Saints in Paradise regard it with a smile.

ELIZABETH WATERHOUSE: *Thoughts of a Tertiary.*

GENERAL INTRODUCTION

THE Editors of this series are convinced that the Christian Church as a whole is confronted with a great though largely silent crisis, and also with an unparalleled opportunity. They have a common mind concerning the way in which this crisis and opportunity should be met. The time has gone by when "apologetics" could be of any great value. Something more is needed than a defence of propositions already accepted on authority, for the present spiritual crisis is essentially a questioning of authority if not a revolt against it. It may be predicted that the number of people who are content simply to rest their religion on the authority of the Bible or the Church is steadily diminishing, and with the growing effectiveness of popular education will continue to diminish. We shall not therefore meet the need, if we have rightly diagnosed it, by dissertations, however learned, on the interpretation of the Bible or the history of Christian doctrine. Nothing less is required than a candid, courageous and well-informed effort to think out anew, in the light of modern knowledge, the foundation affirmations of our common Christianity. This is the aim of every writer in this series.

A further agreement is, we hope, characteristic of the books which will be published in the series. The authors have a common mind not only with regard to the problem but also with regard to the starting-point of reconstruction. They desire to lay stress upon the value and validity of religious experience and to develop their theology on the basis of the religious consciousness. In so doing they claim to be in harmony with modern thought. The massive achievements of the nineteenth and twentieth centuries have been built up on the method of observation and experiment, on experience, not on abstract *a priori* reasoning. Our contention is that the moral and spiritual experience of mankind has the right to be considered, and demands to be understood.

Many distinguished thinkers might be quoted in support of the assertion that philosophers are now prepared in a greater measure than formerly to consider religious experience as among the most significant of their data. One of the greatest has said, "There is nothing more real than what comes in religion. To compare facts such as these with what is given to us in outward existence would be to trifle with the subject. The man who demands a reality more solid than that of the religious consciousness, seeks he does not know what."[1] Nor does this estimate of religious experience come only from idealist thinkers. A philosopher who writes from the standpoint of mathematics and natural science has expressed the same thought in even more forcible language. "The fact of religious vision, and its history of persistent expansion, is our one ground for optimism. Apart from it, human life is a flash of occasional enjoyments lighting up a

[1] F. H. Bradley, *Appearance and Reality*, p. 449.

mass of pain and misery, a bagatelle of transient experience."[1]

The conviction that religious experience is to be taken as the starting-point of theological reconstruction does not, of course, imply that we are absolved from the labour of thought. On the contrary, it should serve as the stimulus to thought. No experience can be taken at its face value ; it must be criticised and interpreted. Just as natural science could not exist without experience and the thought concerning experience, so theology cannot exist without the religious consciousness and reflection upon it. Nor do we mean by " experience " anything less than the whole experience of the human race, so far as it has shared in the Christian consciousness. As Mazzini finely said, " Tradition and conscience are the two wings given to the human soul to reach the truth."

It has been the aim of the writers and the Editors of the series to produce studies of the main aspects of Christianity which will be intelligible and interesting to the general reader and at the same time may be worthy of the attention of the specialist. After all, in religion we are dealing with a subject-matter which is open to all and the plan of the works does not require that they shall delve very deeply into questions of minute scholarship. We have had the ambition to produce volumes which might find a useful place on the shelves of the clergyman and minister, and no less on those of the intelligent layman. Perhaps we may have done something to bridge the gulf which too often separates the pulpit from the pew.

[1] A. N. Whitehead, *Science and the Modern World*, p. 275.

Naturally, the plan of our series has led us to give the utmost freedom to the authors of the books to work out their own lines of thought, and our part has been strictly confined to the invitation to contribute, and to suggestions concerning the mode of presentation. We hope that the series will contribute something useful to the great debate on religion which is proceeding in secret in the mind of our age, and we humbly pray that their endeavours and ours may be blessed by the Spirit of Truth for the building up of Christ's Universal Church.

PREFACE

THIS study of the nature and principles of Worship, and the chief forms in which they find expression in Christianity, is not the work of a liturgical expert, and is not intended as a handbook to that difficult science. My object has been rather to explore those primary realities of man's relation to God which our devotional action is intended to express. Worship is here considered in its deepest sense, as the response of man to the Eternal: and when we look at the many degrees and forms of this response, and the graded character of human religion, its slow ascent from primitive levels and tendency to carry with it the relics of its past, we need not be surprised that even within the Christian family there is much diversity in the expressive worship which is yet directed towards a single revelation of the Divine.

The first part of this book studies the fundamental characteristics of Christian worship. First its objective, theocentric yet incarnational temper, and the way and degree in which ritual, symbol, sacrament and sacrifice must and do enter into it; and next, the many strands which are gathered up and expressed in its Eucharistic action, and the need and complementary function within the Divine Society of its corporate and personal aspects. The descriptive and historical studies in Part II are merely intended to illustrate these principles, as embodied in the chief types of cultus; and show from various angles the response of man to God as it comes to flower within Christianity.

Some of the friends and fellow-students who have read

these chapters have been inclined to blame me for giving too sympathetic and uncritical an account of types of worship which were not their own. It has been pointed out to me that I have failed to denounce the shortcomings of Judaism with Christian thoroughness, that I have left almost unnoticed primitive and superstitious elements which survive in Catholic and Orthodox worship, that I have not emphasized as I should the liturgic and sacramental shortcomings of the Protestant sects. But my wish has been to show all these as chapels of various types in the one Cathedral of the Spirit; and dwell on the particular structure of each, the love which has gone to their adornment, the shelter they can offer to many different kinds of adoring souls, not on the shabby hassocks, the crude pictures, or the paper flowers. Each great form of Christian cultus is here regarded, to use an Ignatian simile, as a "contemplation to procure the love of God": for its object is to lead human souls, by different ways, to that act of pure adoration which is the consummation of worship.

The fact that each of these types has its particular shortcomings, that each tends to exaggerate one element in the rich Christian complex at the expense of the rest, that all are liable to degeneration and are seldom found in their classic purity, is merely what our human contingency would lead us to expect. Yet in spite of all this, in every form of worship—even the least adequate—the positive element, man's upward and outward movement of adoration, self-oblation and dependence, exceeds in importance the negative element which is inevitably present with it. For the positive element is always a response to some aspect of Reality, some incitement of God, however dimly understood and imperfectly obeyed. The negative element is the effect of our creaturely situation; immersed in the world of things, yet endowed with a certain capacity for the world of eternity. Thus a certain confusion between the sensible signs by means of which we worship and the supra-sensible truths they represent, attends all man's efforts to embody the deep and delicate realities of his spiritual life. Therefore in each type of worship here studied, I have tried to find these realities, and bring them into relief; to interpret as much as I am able, and to criticize as little as I can. It is only too easy to recognize and denounce the barbarous aspects of sacrifice, or the magical tendencies which dog sacramental religion; but this simple exercise tells us nothing worth knowing about worship. What matters is the fact that under these unpromising appearances we can discern the humble beginnings of man's response to the attraction of God; the birth of Faith, Hope, and Charity.

The writing of this book was first suggested to me by my friend, the Dean of St Paul's. It owes much to his encouragement and advice; and also to the help of many others, not all of whom can be named here, but without whose support I could hardly have ventured to explore territories, in some of which my position is little better than that of a sympathetic tourist. My debt of gratitude and that of my readers is particularly great towards those specialists who have put their expert knowledge so willingly and generously at my disposal, and found time to read and criticize the chapters dealing with the subjects they have made their own. Thus Dr W. O. E. Oesterley has read the chapter upon Jewish Worship, and Dr Nicolas Zernov the section dealing with the Orthodox Church. Here too, as elsewhere, I owe much to help from my dear and kind friend, Bishop W. H. Frere, C.R., whose work is an inspiration to all who dare to write of worship; and also to enlightening conversations with the Bishop of Gibraltar, the Rev. Father Sergius Boulgakoff, the Rev. Father Dmitri, and fellow members of the Fellowship of St Alban and St Sergius. Archdeacon Leslie Owen most kindly read and criticized the chapters on Personal Worship and on the Beginnings of Christianity, which have greatly benefited by his suggestions. To another old friend, the Rev. Dr Maltby, I owe the settling of several points concerning contemporary Methodism; and to the Rev. John Baird, of the Old Cathedral, Aberdeen, valuable help and criticism in regard to my account of Scottish Presbyterian worship. The footnotes indicate, though far from adequately, the extent of my obligations to previous writers. Finally, my warmest thanks are due to the three friends—Mrs. R. V. Vernon, Miss Lucy Menzies and Miss Margaret Cropper—who have accompanied the making of this book with that keen and constant interest which is one of the greatest helps any writer can receive. In all its parts it owes much to their constructive criticisms and suggestions; and still more perhaps to their unfailing support.

E. U.

NOTE TO THE SECOND EDITION

THIS edition is identical with the first, except for the correction of misprints and verbal errors. For the detection of most of these I have to thank the kind heart and eagle eye of Bishop W. H. Frere. Friendly and generous critics have pointed out that I have failed to discuss either the worship of the Plymouth Brethren or of the Salvation Army; and that these have each their peculiar contribution to make to the Christian complex. With this I entirely agree; but the types chosen for study in Part II were intended chiefly as illustrations of general principles. Selection was inevitable; and does not involve any value judgment in respect of those forms of worship which are left undescribed.

E. U.

Epiphany, 1937.

CONTENTS

CHAPTER V

CHAPTER VI

CHAPTER VII

CHAPTER VIII

CHAPTER IX

PART II

CHAPTER X

CHAPTER XI

CHAPTER XIV

CHAPTER XV

PART I

CHAPTER I

THE NATURE OF WORSHIP

WORSHIP, in all its grades and kinds, is the response of the creature to the Eternal: nor need we limit this definition to the human sphere. There is a sense in which we may think of the whole life of the Universe, seen and unseen, conscious and unconscious, as an act of worship, glorifying its Origin, Sustainer, and End. Only in some such context, indeed, can we begin to understand the emergence and growth of the spirit of worship in men, or the influence which it exerts upon their concrete activities. Thus worship may be overt or direct, unconscious or conscious. Where conscious, its emotional colour can range from fear through reverence to self-oblivious love. But whatever its form of expression may be, it is always a subject-object relationship; and its general existence therefore constitutes a damaging criticism of all merely subjective and immanental explanations of Reality. For worship is an acknowledgment of Transcendence; that is to say, of a Reality independent of the worshipper, which is always more or less deeply coloured by mystery, and which is there first. As Von Hügel would say, it is "rooted in ontology": or, if we prefer the witness of a modern anthropologist, even on primitive levels it at least points to man's profound sense of dependence upon "the spiritual side of the unknown".[1]

So, directly we take this strange thing Worship seriously, and give it the status it deserves among the various responses of men to their environment, we find that it obliges us to

[1] R. R. Marett, *Sacraments of Simple Folk*, p. 26.

take up a particular attitude towards that environment. Even in its crudest form, the law of prayer—indeed the fact of prayer—is already the law of belief; since humanity's universal instinct to worship cannot be accounted for, if naturalism tells the whole truth about life. That instinct means the latent recognition of a metaphysical reality, standing over against physical reality, which men are driven to adore, and long to apprehend. In other words it is the implicit, even though unrecognized Vision of God—that disclosure of the Supernatural which is overwhelming, self-giving, and attractive all at once—which is the first cause of all worship, from the puzzled upward glance of the primitive to the delighted self-oblation of the saint. Here, the human derived spirit perceives and moves towards its Origin and goal; even though that perception shares the imperfections and uncertainties of the temporal order, and is often embodied in crude and mistaken forms. Here man responds to the impact of Eternity, and in so doing learns the existence of Eternity; accepting his tiny place in that secret life of Creation, which consists in the praise, adoration, and manifestation of God. That is to say, he achieves his destiny.

These words, of course, are written from the standpoint of Christian Theism. Such a view of worship implies a developed religion; but it is a function of developed religion to speak for and interpret the inarticulate convictions of the race. It is possible to regard worship as one of the greatest of humanity's mistakes; a form taken by the phantasy-life, the desperate effort of bewildered creatures to come to terms with the surrounding mystery. Or it may be accepted as the most profound of man's responses to reality; and more than this, the organ of his divine knowledge and the earnest of eternal life. Between these two extreme positions, however, it is difficult to find a firm resting place for the mind. Nor has the religious man any choice. He is bound to take worship seriously, and ever more seriously with the deepening of his own spiritual sense. It points steadily towards the Reality of God: gives, expresses, and maintains that which is the essence of all sane religion—a theocentric basis to life. "The first or central act of religion is *adoration*, sense of God, His otherness though nearness, His distinctness from all finite beings, though not separateness—aloofness—from them."[1]

It is true that from first to last self-regarding elements are mixed with human worship; but these are no real part of it. Not man's needs and wishes, but God's presence and incitement, first evoke it. As it rises towards purity and leaves egotistic piety behind, He becomes more and more the only Fact of existence, the one Reality; and the very meaning of Creation is seen to be an act of worship, a devoted proclamation of the splendour, the wonder, and the beauty of God. In this great *Sanctus*, all things justify their being and have their place. God alone matters, God alone Is—creation only matters because of Him. "Wherein does your prayer consist?" said St John of the Cross to one of his penitents. She replied: "In considering the Beauty of God, and in rejoicing that He has such beauty."[2]

Such disinterested delight is the perfection of worship. Yet we cannot limit the word to that small group of souls capable of this effect of Charity, or even to those activities which it is usual to class as "religious". Though we find at its heart the adoring response of spirit to Spirit, its periphery is great enough to include all the expressive acts and humble submissions of men, if they are given a Godward orientation. The great outbursts of unshakable certitude and adoring love which we find upon the lips of the Saints stand up like Alpine peaks in the spiritual landscape of humanity. But

[1] F. von Hügel, *Selected Letters*, p. 261.
[2] Given by E. Allison Peers, *Works of St. John of the Cross*, Vol. I, p. xxxvi.

the lower pastures, the deepest valleys and darkest forests, even the jungles and the swamps, are all part of the same world ; depend on the same given heat and light, the same seasonal vicissitudes. Each in its own way responds to that heat and light, and under its incitement brings forth living things. We shall not understand the mountain by treating it in isolation ; nor do justice to the lower levels unless we also remember the heights. " God," says St John of the Cross again, " passes through the thicket of the world, and wherever His glance falls He turns all things to beauty."[1]

Worship, then, at every level, always means God and the priority of God ; however thick the veils through which He is apprehended, and however grotesque the disguise He may seem to wear. Through and in a multitude of strange divinities and along lowly channels suited to the lowliness of man, the " outpouring of the Incomprehensible Grandeur," as Dionysius the Areopagite says, goes on. We in our worshipping action are compelled to move within the devotional sphere, with all its symbolic furniture, its archaic survivals, its pitfalls, its risks of sentimentalism, herd-suggestion, and disguised self-regard. But the mighty Object of our worship stands beyond and over against all this in His utter freedom and distinctness. " Can " and " cannot ", " is " and " is not " must not be predicated of Him, without a virtual remembrance that these words merely refer to our limited experience and not to God as He is in Himself. If this contrast is forgotten, we shall never understand the religious scene and the strange objects with which it is bestrewn. There is no department of life which asks from those who study it so much humble sympathy, such a wide, genial, unfastidious spirit, or so constant a remembrance of our own limitations as this ; nor one in which it is more necessary to remember the wholesome reminder of the psychologist that we ourselves, however apparently civilized,

[1] *The Spiritual Canticle*, stanza 5.

are still possessed of a primitive subconsciousness which is nowhere more active than in the practices of our religion.

If the first point about worship is its theocentric character, if its reference be always to "the Absolute and Eternal, standing beyond the present and the past",[1] there follows from this the obvious truth that man could never have produced it in his own strength. It does not appear spontaneously from within the created order, and cannot be accounted for in terms of evolution. Strictly speaking, there is no such thing as "natural religion": the distinction which is often drawn between "natural" and "revealed" faith is an artificial one, set up by theologizing minds. That awed conviction of the reality of the Eternal over against us, that awareness of the Absolute, that sense of God, which in one form or another is the beginning of all worship, whether it seems to break in from without, or to arise within the soul, does not and cannot originate in man. It comes to him where he is, as a message from another order; God disclosing Himself to and in His creation "by diverse portions and in diverse manners" conditioned by the limitations of the humble creature He has made. It is, in fact, a Revelation, proportioned to the capacity of the creature, of something wholly other than our finite selves, and not deducible from our finite experience: the splendour and distinctness of God. Therefore the easy talk of the pious naturalist about man's approach to God, is both irrational—indeed plainly impudent—and irreverent; unless the priority of God's approach to man be kept in mind.

In this respect worship stands alone, and cannot be equated with man's other discoveries of, and reactions to, his rich and many-levelled environment. In all these, he is pressed by the needs and perils of his situation, or by the prick of his own desires, first to exploration and then to precarious adjustments with this or that aspect of a changing

[1] Nicolas of Cusa, *The Vision of God*, cap. 10.

world. But in his worship, he is compelled as it were in spite of himself to acknowledge and respond to a Wholeness, a Perfection already fully present over against him—something, as St Augustine says, "insusceptible of change". This contrast between the successive and the Eternal lies at the root of all worship, which ever looks away from the transitory and created to the Abiding and Increate; not because this august Reality consoles or succours men, not because worship enriches and completes our natural life, but for Its own sake. Here even the deep religious mood of dependence and of gratitude must give priority to the fundamental religious mood of adoration. Where it is emptied of this unearthly element, this awestruck and creaturely sense of the Holy and Immortal, worship loses its most distinctive characteristic. The Seraphic hymn gives its very essence: "Holy! holy! holy! Lord God of hosts, heaven and earth are full of thy glory. Glory be to thee, O Lord Most High." That is worship.

It is true that this holy Reality is at first recognized by man in a very imperfect and distorted way; and acknowledged in acts which may bear little apparent resemblance to the practices which we regard as religious. Yet already these acts have the distinctive mark of worship. They point beyond the world and natural life, to an independent Object of adoration.[1] That Transcendent Object, even though conceived as the Cause of all natural good, and present in and with the natural scene, yet speaks to man from a realm that exceeds and stands over against all natural good; and may incite him to deeds and renunciations which sharply oppose the interests of his natural life,

[1] It is probable, says Professor J. B. Pratt (*The Religious Consciousness*, p. 262), that the earliest form taken by the genuine religious sense was "a feeling for that indefinable, impersonal, all-pervading power which the Iroquois call *Orenda*, the Algonquins *Manitou*, the Sioux *Wakonda* and the Melanesians *Mana*, but which, under whatever name, is conceived as the ultimate source of power, the controller of happiness, the determiner of destiny."

and have no meaning save in so far as they point beyond the world. As man develops, its attraction and its pressure are more and more realized in contrast to those natural interests. And at last in the Saint (without whose existence worship can never be understood) the revealed Reality fills the horizon and becomes the sole object of love; so that even though God gave nothing of Himself to the soul, yet the soul must give the whole of itself to Him.

It follows from this that worship and prayer, though their relation be so close, and their overlapping so frequent, must never be treated as equivalents. For worship is essentially disinterested—it "means only God"—but prayer is only in some of its aspects disinterested. One offers, the other asks. "What shall I say, my God, my Holy Joy!" exclaims St Augustine. There is the voice of worship. "Without thy visitation I cannot live!" says Thomas à Kempis. There is the voice of prayer. It is true that throughout the history of religion there has always been a mingling of motives; fear and anxiety, over against the all-powerful Unknown, expressed in propitiation and demand, are inevitable elements of the primitive response; and have endured to affect the whole religious history of the race. But as the genuine religious impulse becomes dominant, adoration more and more takes charge. "I come to seek God because I need Him," may be an adequate formula for prayer. "I come to adore His splendour, and fling myself and all that I have at His feet," is the only possible formula for worship. Even on the crudest levels, it has in it the seed of contemplation, and points towards self-loss.

Thus worship will include all those dispositions and deeds which adoration wakes up in us, all the responses of the soul to the Uncreated, all the Godward activities of man. Because it sets the awful Perfection of God over against the creature's imperfection, it becomes the most effective cause of "conviction of sin", and hence of the soul's penitence and purification; here disclosing its creative and transfiguring power. So, too, that strange impulse to sacrifice and unlimited self-abandonment, which is the life-blood of religion, is an expression of the worshipping instinct, and has no meaning except in relation to a supernatural goal. When we consider how unnecessary religious action is to man's physical well-being—how frequently, indeed, its demands run counter to his material advantage—yet how irresistible is its attraction for awakened souls, we can hardly doubt that here in this mysterious intercourse which we know from the human side as "worship", there is disclosed to us a deep purpose of the Eternal Will, and a path is opened along which our conditioned spirits can move out towards the Absolute Life.

Yet having said this, so rich and complex are those spiritual currents which penetrate and surround us, and so firm the refusal of Spirit to fit into the neat categories of thought, that we are bound to qualify the stress upon Transcendence by an acknowledgment of the many strands which enter into the worshipping life; the many paths along which God makes His approach to man, and stirs man to respond to His attraction. We are not Deists. Our worship is of a God Who acts, a Living One Who transcends what seem to us to be His laws, and has a definite relation with His creatures; One, too, who works in the depths of our being, and is self-revealed through His action in history and in nature, as well as in the soul.

> "In the phenomena of worship", says Will, "we see two currents of life meet, one proceeding from the transcendent Reality, the other flowing from the religious life of the subject; one descending, the other ascending. These two currents are not only to be recognized in the sacramental and sacrificial aspects of worship—the descending current includes all forms of revelation, the ascending, all forms of prayer. Nor does the mutual action of the two currents exclude the primacy of the

Divine action; for this is manifest not only in the descending current of the Word, of Revelation, and of sacramental action, but also in its immanent action within the life of souls."[1]

The acknowledgment of our total dependence on this free action of God immanent and transcendent, is therefore a true part of worship. It follows that, wherever the envisaged end is not man's comfort, security, or personal success, but His glory and purpose, the more perfect doing of His Will, then the prayer of petition itself—e.g. for the graces of the spiritual life, the rescue and sanctifying of individuals, or the victory of good causes—becomes a true "hallowing of the Name".[2] In fact the trustful and child-like demand is itself an act of homage, in so far as it has the colour of adoration: "The eyes of all wait on thee, O Lord; and thou givest them their meat in due season." As the spiritual life develops, so this sense of the priority of the Divine action, the total dependence of the derived spirit on the Absolute Spirit, deepens; and God, working with and in His creature, though often secretly and in disguise, is recognized as the only author of all the supernatural actions of the soul.

This, if at one end worship is lost in God and is seen to be the substance of Eternal Life, so that all our attempts to penetrate its mystery must end in acknowledgment of defeat; at the other end, it broadens out to cover and inform the whole of man's responses to Reality—his total Godward life, with its myriad graded forms of expression, some so crude and some so lovely, some so concrete and some so otherworldly, but all so pathetic in their childishness. Here we obtain a clue to the real significance of those

[1] Robert Will, *Le Culte*, Vol. II, p. 552. (condensed).

[2] Thus the Eucharistic prayer of preparation, "Cleanse the thoughts of our hearts by the inspiration of thy Holy Spirit, that we may perfectly love thee and worthily magnify thy holy name," is both supplication and worship; since its declared object is the greater glory of God.

rituals and ceremonies common to almost every creed, which express the deep human conviction that none of the serial events and experiences of human life are rightly met, unless brought into relation with the Transcendent: that all have more than a natural meaning, and must be sanctified by reference to the unseen Powers. Hence the solemn rites which hallow the achievement of adolescence, the blessings of ruler, traveller, bride and bridegroom, the churching of women, ceremonial care for the dead. All these, together with the benediction of house, fields, food, instruments of labour, or badges of service, are to be regarded as acts of worship: for they refer to God as a distinct yet present Reality, and acknowledge His hallowing action and unlimited claim. So, too, the adoring recognition of God in and through nature—in so far as this is not the mere sentimental enjoyment of a pious pantheism—may be a real part, though never the whole, of a worshipping life; for in such a case the visible world, or some aspect of that world, becomes a sacramental revelation of an invisible Reality. Also that total and selfless devotion to the interests of truth or of beauty, which is the impelling cause of the scholar's or the artist's career, has a religious character, and is in essence a response to revelation: for worship has not reached its term until it knows God as "no less truly the ultimate Source, Sustainer and End of perfect Beauty and of utter Truth than of complete Goodness and of purest Self-Donation".[1] Yet all these would lose significance and fall to the natural level, were they not lit up and interpreted by the richer and more costly expressions of man's instinct for God: the long strange history of sacrifice, the dedicated life, and all those "useless" austerities and renunciations which so greatly vex the practical mind. For in these we see in its intense form the human soul's acknowledgment of an obligation to the hidden Perfect; the generous and

[1] F. von Hügel, *Eternal Life*, p. 392.

disinterested—even though uncomprehended—response of the creature to the secret claim and incitement of God. The crude form which this response has often taken should not blind us to its cardinal importance for an understanding of the spiritual situation of man.

And next, if human worship be essentially theocentric, creaturely, disinterested, the humble and graded response of man the finite to the generous and graded self-revelation of the Infinite God, it requires beyond all this a further character; already inherent in its creatureliness. That is, it must have embodiment, concrete expression. Man, as we know him, is embodied spirit; even though all that is involved in this mysterious relationship be veiled from us. He lives under conditions of time and place. Nothing is fully realized by him, or becomes really fruitful for him, until it has been submitted to these limitations; which indeed govern all his thought. His desires and convictions do not become actual until expressed in words or deeds, even though this expression is seldom adequate; and the more fundamental the interest, the stronger is the impulse to expression. His desire for God, his secret drive towards God, is no exception to this law. He is beset by the conviction that he must do something about it here and now; and do it at his own cost. "The primitive," says Dr. Marett, "encounters the divine stimulus here, there and anywhere, within the contents of an experience in which percepts play a far more important part than concepts."[1] His worship begins as a spontaneous reaction to this stimulus; and this reaction always takes the form of something which must be done.

This is why, in every human society which has reached even a rudimentary religious consciousness, worship is given its concrete expression in institutions and in ritual acts: and these institutions and acts become in their turn

[1] R. R. Marett, *Faith, Hope and Charity in Primitive Religion*, p. 109.

powerful instruments, whereby the worshipping temper is taught, stimulated, and maintained. The painted cave of those prehistoric worshippers of an unknown God who were "simple-minded enough to give of their best to the supra-sensible powers",[1] the Pagan temple, the Christian cathedral, are all expressions of the same fundamental human need to incorporate, make visible, the spirit of worship; to lavish skill, labour, and wealth on this most apparently "useless" of all the activities of man. So, too, the ritual chant, with its accompaniment of ceremonial movement and manual acts, is found to exert a stabilizing influence at every level of his religious life. And when this costly and explicit embodiment is lacking, or is rejected where once possessed, and the Godward life of the community is not given some sensible and institutional expression within the social complex, worship seldom develops its full richness and power. It remains thin, abstract, and notional: a tendency, an attitude, a general aspiration, moving alongside human life, rather than in it.

It is true that worship, when thus embodied, loses—or seems to lose—something of its purity; but only then can it take up and use man's various powers and capacities, turning the whole creature towards the Eternal, and thus entering the texture of his natural as well as his supernatural life. Certainly, it is here that we encounter the greatest of the dangers that accompany its long history; the danger that form will smother spirit, ritual action take the place of spontaneous prayer, the outward and visible sign obscure the inward grace. But the risk is one which man is bound to take. He is not "pure" spirit, and is not capable of "pure" spiritual acts. Even though in his worship he moves out towards absolutes, and in and through that worship absolutes are revealed to his soul, it is at his own peril that he leaves the world of sense behind, in his

[1] *Op. cit.*, p. 156.

approach to the God Who created and informs it. This humbling truth must govern all his responses to Reality.

And more than this, the prevenient God, Who is the cause and object of his worship, comes to man and awakens him where he is, and is discovered by him first in the mysterious movements of nature. Here, in this infant-school of the emerging human spirit, the Unconditioned meets him under his own conditions; and is disclosed to him in the degree in which he can bear it, embodied in a measure in the finite realities of the surrounding world of sense. He must therefore be found, served, and acknowledged in and through that finite world of sense, which is the appointed sphere of our activity: in time, by means of history and historic institutions, and in space by means of sacred objects and ceremonial acts. Only in so far as man's worship is thus firmly rooted in the concrete here-and-now of our common experience, and accepts the conditions imposed by that experience, will it retain its creaturely quality and develop its full richness and life-changing power. It is, too, from within such embodied adoration, not in defiance of it, that individual worship emerges and develops best: for great realities, as Von Hügel has pointed out, "though invisible, require for their vivid apprehension an imaginative pictorial embodiment";[1] and only when thus vividly and realistically apprehended, will they fully evoke our worship, and enter the texture of our life.

The demand and action of religion are and must be on man as he is: a social, sensuous, and emotional creature keenly aware of his visible environment, but only half aware of the unseen. Therefore that revelation, that awakening disclosure of the spaceless God which is the cause of worship, must come to us in space, the reality and attraction of His eternity must be experienced in time, if they are indeed to enter and transform our experience.

[1] *The Mystical Element of Religion*, Vol. I, p. 177.

His workings within history and His approach to men through man, must be recognized as a true part of His action, and a true disclosure of His Being; and hence as occasions of our grateful adoration, no less compelling than those glimpses of eternity, which are sometimes vouchsafed to us. This is why the power and passion of religion, the incitement to worship, are largely realized in and through "tradition and institution, in which we invariably find a most strong insistence on the here-and-now, upon a particular place and a particular time":[1] and why the Christian revelation—"God manifest in the flesh"—is unique in its power of evoking worship and love. Here the historical embodies the metaphysical, and presents the deep mysteries of Eternal Life to us in a way that we can apprehend. This humble acceptance of our situation must also govern our participation in those symbolic acts and traditional rites which man has brought forth within his natural environment, to bridge the gap between sense and soul, and support and express the spirit of worship.

All this will need further exploration as we go on. But already at this point the Christian can discern how deep-rooted in the necessities of our situation, and how far-reaching in their implications, are the great truths which rule his own religious life. Looking with reverence at this universal fact of worship, he will recognize, even in its humblest beginnings and strangest embodiments, some of the implicits of his faith. For first it means and seeks God alone. It is the complete fulfilment of the First Commandment. And next, if this Commandment is to be recognized and obeyed by the creature, it requires a self-revelation of that Absolute God within time; and His inciting and quickening Spirit ever at work within the Creation which He has made for Himself. It begins in fact, beyond time, in a movement of the Eternal Charity, an utterance of the Word. And on

[1] Von Hügel, *The Reality of God*, p. 158.

man's side, being what he is, worship is a responsive act which involves his whole nature and therefore requires social and sensible embodiment; in visible and historical institutions which shall be entirely dedicated to adoring communion with the Unseen Perfect, and in symbolic objects and deeds which are often crude and always inadequate, yet the necessary means of religious self-expression in men. So those deep realities which the Christian knows as God, Christ, Spirit, Grace, Church, and Sacrament are already found in many ways and under many disguises, wherever man the worshipper lifts his eyes towards the "spiritual side of the unknown".

And last, though in worship the movement—often slow and halting—is yet on the human side simply and wholly Godwards, and this transcendental, self-oblivious undemanding temper must never be discredited or ignored, there remains the question of the effect upon man himself of this deep action of the soul. Why are we called and pressed to it? Is it, ultimately, for our sake? How does it enter into the creative plan?

First, perhaps, we are called to worship because this is the only safe, humble, and creaturely way in which men can be led to acknowledge and receive the influence of an objective Reality. The tendency of all worship to decline from adoration to demand, and from the supernatural to the ethical, shows how strong a pull is needed to neutralize the anthropocentric trend of the human mind; its intense preoccupation with the world of succession, and its own here-and-now desires and needs. And only in so far as it is released from this petty subjectivism, can it hope to grow up into any knowledge of the massive realities of that spiritual universe in which we live and move. It is the mood of deep admiration, the meek acknowledgment of mystery, the humble and adoring gaze, which makes us capable of this revelation. Worship, then, is an avenue which leads the creature out from his inveterate self-occupation to a knowledge of God, and ultimately to that union with God which is the beatitude of the soul; though we are never to enter on it for this, or any other reason which is tainted by self-regard. We see in its first beginnings man's emerging recognition of the Living Will which is the cause of all his living; and the gradual deepening and widening of this recognition, in diverse ways and manners, till at last all ways and manners are swallowed up in a self-giving love. By this door and this alone, humanity enters into that great life of the spiritual universe which consists in the ceaseless proclamation of the Glory of God.

Thus worship purifies, enlightens, and at last transforms, every life submitted to its influence: and this not merely in the ethical or devotional sense. It does all this, because it wakes up and liberates that "seed" of supernatural life, in virtue of which we are spiritual beings, capable of responding to that God Who is Spirit; and which indeed gives to humanity a certain mysterious kinship with Him. Worship is therefore in the deepest sense creative and redemptive. Keeping us in constant remembrance of the Unchanging and the Holy, it cleanses us of subjectivism, releases us from "use and wont" and makes us realists. God's invitation to it and man's response, however limited, crude or mistaken this response may be, are the appointed means whereby we move towards our true destiny.

Only in so far as this adoring acknowledgment of Reality more and more penetrates his life, does man himself become real; finding within himself the answer to the great Eucharistic prayer, "Make us living men!" and entering by way of unconditioned self-oblation upon the inheritance of Eternal Life. Each separate soul thus transfigured by the spirit of selfless adoration advances that transfiguration of the whole universe which is the Coming of the Kingdom of God. Further discussion of this august theme lies outside the scope of the present work; yet it is well to remind ourselves that worship, though the whole man of sense and spirit, feeling, thought, and will, is and must be truly concerned in it, is above all the work of that mysterious "ground" of our being, that sacred hearth of personality, where the created spirit of man adheres to the increate Spirit of God.

CHAPTER II

RITUAL AND SYMBOL

I

HERE then is Man, the half-animal, half-spiritual creature; living under the conditions of space and time, yet capable of the conscious worship of a Reality which transcends space and time. He has certain means at his disposal for the expression of this worship, this response to besetting Spirit; and again and again he tends, at every level of development, to use these means—which indeed are forced on him by his situation, and by his own psychological characteristics. Of these, the chief are (1) Ritual, or liturgic pattern; (2) Symbol or significant image; (3) Sacrament, in the general sense of the use of visible things and deeds, not merely to signify, but also to convey invisible realities; and (4) Sacrifice, or voluntary offering—a practice too far-reaching in its importance, and too profound in its significance for brief definition here.

All these sensible signs of supra-sensible action appear, in a rudimentary form, wherever man begins to respond in adoration to God. Combined in various ways and degrees, they are the chief elements of Cultus, or the agreed embodiment of his worship. As such both their character and their origin are of great importance to us. For in the first place, the object of Cultus being real communion between Man and God, its formal constituents must be of a kind which further, support, and express this communion. It is set "between the Unseen and the Seen". On the one hand it must be adapted to the psychological nature of the worshipping subject, making the fullest possible contact with his imaginative and sensitive life. But on the other hand, it must embody and express the substance of that Divine revelation which invites man's adoring response. It is conditioned at one and the same time by psychological and metaphysical necessities, and is to be judged by the perfection with which its twofold function is performed; opening a door through which Mystery approaches the creature, and the creature moves out in response.

And in the next place, though our chief concern as religious men and women is not the lowly origin, but the mature development and significance of our practices—still, there are characteristics of that maturity which are better understood by a reference to the infancy of faith. Since we are thoroughly historical creatures, brought forth by God in time and space, and developing under the fostering guidance of the Spirit, we ought not to be afraid to seek in the past the origin and perhaps some of the meaning of many of our methods of worship; still less should we be anxious to discard them, because they testify to that common humanity which we share with primitive men. It is surely mere arrogance to insist that with angels and archangels we laud and magnify the Holy Name, whilst disdaining the shaggy companions who come with us to the altar of faith: having already, indeed, discerned that altar in a darkness which we have left behind, and given costly offerings to the unknown God whom we so coldly serve. The primitive, sensitive to the mysterious quality of life, worshipping by gift and gesture, and devising ritual patterns whereby all the faculties of his nature and all the members of his group can be united in common action towards God, still remains a better model for human worship than the speculative philosopher or the solitary quietist: for he accepts his situation humbly instead of trying to retreat from it. Those who are prevented by spiritual snobbery from appreciating this fact, will never achieve real understanding of their own religious experience; or give it the right context within the historical experience of the race.

When we take together the four chief elements of Cultus—that is to say, the deliberate activity in which man expresses his worship—at once we see that Ritual, Symbol, Sacrament, and Sacrifice have certain common characteristics. First, they possess a marked social quality. They all make it possible for men to do things together. Hence their almost world-wide diffusion does not support Dr Whitehead's definition of religion, as "what the individual does with his own solitariness".[1] On the contrary, the most characteristic means of human worship are precisely those which the solitary does not require: namely the agreed symbols, and the established formulas and rites, which make concerted religious action and even concerted religious emotion possible, and so create the worshipping group. Certainly the religious vitality of this group and its proceedings must depend in the last resort on the spiritual sincerity and action of the individuals composing it: personal and social action must co-operate all the time. It is only too easy for the best and most significant cultus to lose spiritual content when it is not a vehicle for the worship of spiritual men. Then it declines from religion to magic, and from a living worship to a ceremonial routine, in which the exact recitation of the accepted formula or the correct performance of the ordained act is held to satisfy the full obligations of religion. But this tendency, so perpetually attacked by the Hebrew prophets, and Christian reformers, is inseparable from a method of expression which is forced upon man by his own social and psychological characteristics.

Next, Ritual, Symbol, Sacrament, and Sacrifice all have

[1] *Religion in the Making*, p. 16.

a twofold quality, which closely parallels our human situation. In their living state they have an outside and an inside; a visible action and an invisible action, both real, both needed, and so closely interdependent that each loses its true quality if torn apart; for indeed an idolatry which pins religion to abstract thoughts and notions alone is not much better than an idolatry which pins it to concrete stocks and stones alone. Either of these extremes are impoverishments, which destroy the true quality of a full and living cultus; wherein spirit and sense must constantly collaborate, as they do in all the significant acts and experiences of men. Man, incited by God, dimly or sharply conscious of the obscure pressure of God, responds to Him best not by a simple movement of the mind; but by a rich and complex action, in which his whole nature is concerned, and which has at its full development the characters of a work of art. He is framed for an existence which includes not only thought and speech, but gesture and manual action; and when he turns Godward, his life here will not be fully representative of his nature, nor will his act of worship be complete, unless all these forms of expression find a place in it. His religious action must be social, as well as personal; rhythmic and ceremonial, as well as interior and free. It must link every sense with that element of his being which transcends and co-ordinates sense, so that the whole of his nature plays its part in his total response to the Unseen. Therefore those artistic creations, those musical sounds and rhythmic movements which so deeply satisfy the human need for expressive action, must all come in; and the most ancient and primitive levels of our mental life be allowed to co-operate in our acts of adoration, no less than those more recent achievements of the race on which we prefer to dwell.

"It is," says Dr Frere, "a form of blindness, not common sense, that prevents a man from recognizing

> that behind ceremonies there lie realities—principles, doctrines, and states or habits of mind. No one can hope to judge fairly of matters of ceremonial who does not see that the reason why they cause such heat of controversy is that they signify so much."[1]

Indeed as ritual worship develops in depth and beauty it is seen more and more that its rhythmic phrases and ceremonies, its expressive movement, dialogues, concerted outbursts of praise, are all carrying something else: the hidden supernatural action of the group or church by which the ritual is being used.

Ritual, Symbol, Sacrament, and Sacrifice are therefore more, not less valid expressions of the Spirit of Worship, because they belong at one and the same time to the world of sense and the world of spirit: for this is the actual situation of the amphibious creature by whom these means have been devised and used. Taking from that sensible world which surrounds us—and of which alone we have direct experience—finite realities, to which they attach religious significance, and which can therefore be used for the conveyance of infinite truths, all these perform the essential office of welding the world of things into human worship. The obvious dangers of materialism and æstheticism and the constant invitation to a relapse into more primitive religious conceptions and practices, which wait on all external and stylized expressions of worship, must never be allowed to obscure this truth. These dangers, it is true, perpetually assert themselves, and provoke a reaction towards Puritan ideals. The iconoclast, the Cistercian, the Protestant reformer, the Quaker, the Plymouth Brother, stand each in their different ways for that ever renewed revolt from external elaboration towards austerity and "inwardness"—that constant re-discovery of the inadequacy of all images and all means—

[1] W. H. Frere, *The Principles of Religious Ceremonial*, p. 9.

which corrects the excesses of ritual worship and is a necessary constituent of the Mind of the Church. There is a deep religious truth in that awed sense of the "otherness" and utter transcendence of the spiritual, and horrified perception of the hopelessness—even profanity—of all attempts to represent it, which underlies this trend to an imageless and unembodied worship. It finds its supreme expression in the *Via Negativa* of the mystic; where every affirmation, every imaginative embodiment is rejected in favour of that which "can be loved but not thought".

In spite of all this, however, it is not really possible for human creatures to set up a watertight compartment between visible and invisible, outward and inward worship. The distinction which we commonly make is arbitrary, and merely means that which is or is not visible from the human point of view. Indeed, since we can only think, will, and feel in and with a physical body, and it is always in close connection with sense-impressions received through that body that our religious consciousness is stirred and sustained, it follows that we can hardly dispense with some ritual act, some sensible image, some material offering, as an element in the total act of worship, if that act of worship is to turn our humanity in its wholeness towards God. The mysterious feeding of spirit upon Spirit is made more not less real by the ritual meal which drives home the practical truth of our creaturely dependence. The self-oblation in which adoring love culminates, must find some costly act, however inadequate, by which it can be expressed; as human love is truly—however inadequately—expressed in spontaneous gifts and gestures, which would seem absurd enough to those who had no clue to their meaning. Here those who look with either horror or contempt on physical austerities miss the point, and set up an un-Christian contrast between body and soul. Thus it is that for millions of Christians the ritual service and the symbolic gesture—even the amulet and the food-taboo—are essential constituents of the cultus; vehicles by means of which genuine worship is expressed. The pilgrimage, the healing spring, and the votive shrine still play their part. Nor should we dismiss all this too breezily as "mere superstition". It is rather a naïve expression of the deep conviction that God acts, in particular ways, and asks of man a particular response.

Further, cultus has its subjective and reflex importance; in that it tends to evoke and stabilize the mental and emotional state which it is meant to express. Here at least the James–Lange law has a direct application to facts. As those who deliberately smile are rewarded by an increase of cheerfulness, so those who deliberately kneel are rewarded by an increase in worshipping love. Hence symbolic gestures, verbal formulas, and sacramental acts, in spite of the soul-deadening quality which may so easily invade them once they are accepted as substitutes for the movement of the heart, are—when used and valued rightly—impressive as well as expressive in effect. It is an important function of cultus to educate and support the developing spirit of worship, by presenting to the senses of the worshipper objects intimately connected with his faith, or carrying strong devotional suggestion, and leading him out along these paths towards the invisible Reality. It is true that in its highest reaches worship becomes an act of pure love; but never for man an act stripped of all contingency. Because of the unity of our being, sensible stimulation of eye and ear, or even of taste, touch, and smell, can give supra-sensible suggestions to us and awaken, nourish, and deepen the worshipping sense; and the exclusive spirituality which rejects these homely aids merely defeats its own ends. So, too, the faithful repetition of appropriate acts can deepen our understanding of the realities they are intended to convey. Moreover, such repetition creates appropriate paths of discharge; and sets up those habits of worship within which the attention can concentrate on the deeper realities of our spiritual situation. Thus Maréchal, in his beautiful description of the old peasant telling her beads by the cottage hearth, says most truly:

> The monotony of these repetitions clothes the poor old woman with physical peace and recollection; and her soul, already directed on high, almost mechanically, by her habitual gesture of drawing out the rosary, immediately opens out with increasing serenity on unlimited perspectives, felt rather than analysed, which converge on God. . . . What does it matter, then, if the humble *orante* does not concern herself with living over again the exact meaning of the formula she is repeating? . . . often she does better, she allows her soul to rise freely into a true contemplation, well worn and obscure, uncomplicated, unsystematized, alternating with a return of attention to the words she is muttering, but building up in the long run *on the mechanical basis they afford* a higher, purified, personal prayer.[1]

Habit and attention must therefore co-operate in the life of worship; and it is a function of cultus to maintain this vital partnership. Habit alone easily deteriorates into mechanical repetition, the besetting sin of the liturgical mind. Attention alone means, in the end, intolerable strain. Each partner has his weak point. Habit tends to routine and spiritual red-tape; the vice of the institutionalist. Attention is apt to care for nothing but the experience of the moment, and ignore the need of a stable practice, independent of personal fluctuations; the vice of the individualist. Habit is a ritualist. Attention is a pietist. But it is the beautiful combination of order and spontaneity, docility and freedom, living humbly—and therefore fully and freely—within the agreed pattern of the cultus and not

[1] J. Maréchal, *Studies in the Psychology of the Mystics*, Eng. trans., p. 158.

in defiance of it, which is the mark of a genuine spiritual maturity and indeed the fine flower of a worshipping life. Thus it is that the Litany and Rosary have an enduring value which their critics will never understand. The liturgical use of the psalter has fed the inner life of many a saint: and the Jews' daily repetition of the *Shema*,[1] the Christians' ritual use of the Lord's Prayer, and the Moslems' of the First *Sura*,[2] are all justified by psychology no less than by religion. They evoke, deepen, and maintain that obscure sense of God which is the raw material of worship; and because of their inexhaustible meaning, serve the devotional needs of worshippers of every type. This depth of devotional significance is indeed the distinctive characteristic of genuine liturgical material; so that souls at every level and stage of development can find in it a disclosure of the supernatural, a stimulus to adoration, and a carrying-medium for their prayer. Unlike the spiritual literature intended for personal use, which may be either elementary or advanced, the genuine cultus, in its rites, its symbols, and its sacraments, is required to be both at once. It is, as Dante held that great poetry must be, "polysemous"; uniting many degrees of meaning from the most obvious to the most mystical, within one single form.[3] Only thus indeed can it fulfil its true office, and make concerted religious action possible. Christian history is also in this sense polysemous. True on the factual level, it is also a sacramental presentation of higher truth—the mysterious realities of the supernatural life.

[1] Deut. vi. 4–9; xi. 13–21; Numbers xv. 37–41.

[2] Praise be to God, Lord of the Worlds! the Compassionate, the Merciful, the King on the Day of Judgment! Thee only do we worship, and to Thee do we cry for help. Guide us on the right path; the path of those to whom Thou has been gracious, not of those with whom Thou art angry, or those who go astray.

[3] "Be it known that the sense of this work is not simple, but on the contrary it may be called polysemous, that is to say, of more senses than one." *Epistle to Can. Grande.* Cf. also *Convivio*, II, 7.

When man enters the world of worship, he enters a world which has many of the characteristics of an artistic creation. Much crude and unedifying controversy would die away, were this fact commonly admitted: and the poetry and music which enter so largely into expressive worship were recognized as indications of its essential character. The true Object of our worship cannot be directly apprehended by us. "No man hath seen God at any time". The representative pattern, the suggestive symbol, the imaginative projection too—all these must be called into play and their limitations humbly accepted if the limited creature is to enter into communion with the Holy and so develop his capacity for adoring love. But the difficulty of our situation is this: none of these devices will be effective unless the worshipper takes them seriously, far more seriously indeed than in their naked factualness they deserve. This is the element in expressive worship which is so puzzling to those who stand outside it. Why, for instance, this devout contemplation of a rather bad picture, or punctual recitation of a rather silly prayer? Why this wholesale and unexamined use of a metaphorical language which reveals under analysis so many irrational references; or this acceptance of the obvious and charming creations of religious fancy—the crib, the crowned Madonna, the guardian angel—as representative of religious fact? Why, too, this discipline, this ceremonial care over the distribution of the simple Eucharistic elements? The answer is that in each case a sensible sign has been accepted as the representative of a supra-sensible Reality, in order that it may bridge the gap between the sensible and spiritual worlds: and it will only do this, in so far as the worshipper is willing to give it royal or at least vice-regal rank. The necessity is one which presses hardly upon intellectuals. For they see, with more or less clearness, the symbolic or phantasmic character, the doubtful origin of that "carrying medium" which the less sophisticated mind easily accepts as a literal reality. They are aware of the temptation to regression involved in its uncritical use; and so, cannot employ it in the same whole-hearted way. Thus they are brought up against the paradox, that whereas it is here, in these most deep and solemn of all his actions, that man in proportion to his greatness of soul will struggle for truth; yet it is precisely here, that truth in the direct sense eludes him. He is compelled by his own limitations to accept symbol, phantasy, and the workings of the creative imagination, as vehicles of his communion with God.

All this becomes more tolerable, if we allow worship to be a concern of the whole man; and realize—as careful inspection compels us to do—the inevitable presence of phantasy in all our embodiments, whether religious or secular, from best to worst. Even the Godward life is not exempt from the laws which govern our mental activity. It would seem to be a true function of the imagination to weave a garment for God. Strong beliefs, as Dr Inge has reminded us, express themselves in vivid imagery. "We know that some of our beliefs are symbolical and mythical, but we do not thank our friends for reminding us of it in season and out of season".[1] The soul in this world passes its life among pictures; and we need not be too proud to admit that much which is accepted as fact by primitive worship stays on as poetry and image in cultus of a more developed type. The line between the two is seldom sharply defined; indeed it cannot be without some injustice either to the naïve or the instructed worshipper. Moreover, the devotional mind easily tends to construct imaginative embodiments of the Object of its worship; and erect these into objects of faith. Much Christian prayer is addressed in the first instance to these imaginative embodi-

[1] *God and the Astronomers*, p. 299.

ments:[1] but in proportion to its purity it will pass through and beyond them, as a movement of the human towards the Absolute Love. So long, therefore, as the religious image or formula contains nothing which conflicts with our highest intuitions, and so long as it can create for those who use it a true path of spiritual discharge, it may well be the wiser as well as the humbler part to accept this disconcerting element in our common situation whilst safeguarding personal sincerity. For nothing in the cultus has absolute value for itself alone. Its value lies first in its suggestive quality, its power to express or evoke the mysterious; and next in the span of reference, which can make it a carrying medium for religious apprehensions of many degrees of development, and unite in one adoring action worshippers of many different types. Here on every level phantasy is bound to play a part, and sometimes as it seems to impatient transcendentalists a major part. Yet even its most childish creations are shot through with the golden light of worship; the effort of man as he is, from within the mental world he has created, to respond to the unseen Love.[2]

" I cannot in thinking it over," says Von Hügel, summing up in an illuminating passage the problems created and the discriminations required by this symbolic and oblique character of cultus:

> "find other than two great principles and facts. . . . There is the *sacramental principle,* the waking up of spirit under the stimulus of sense, and this comes, I take it, simply from our soul-and-body compoundness. And

[1] I hesitate to give examples; but at least the element of phantasy —indeed mythology—in the developed cultus of the Blessed Virgin must be obvious to anyone who tries to measure the distance between her status as given in the New Testament and the motto above her basilica at Lourdes —" Par Marie à Jésus ". Yet even this apparent capitulation to the myth-making faculty has been justified as the devotional expression of a theological truth, and may become the means of a genuine approach to God in souls of a certain type; a fact which should not surprise any good Platonist.

[2] Compare cap. IX, p. 176.

then there is the *principle of the community*, of sharing our religion, and of getting it deep and tender through sharing it, with every kind of educated, semi-educated and uneducated fellow-believer. This latter need and life very certainly involve endless patience with and indeed sympathy with, the sacramental principle applied as far as ever it will go ".[1]

II

We can now go on to consider the chief elements of expressive worship: and first the nature of ritual. A religious ritual is an agreed pattern of ceremonial movements, sounds, and verbal formulas, creating a framework within which corporate religious action can take place. If human worship is to be other than a series of solitary undertakings, some such device is plainly essential to it. We cannot do things together without some general agreement as to what is going to be done; and some willing subordination to accepted routine.

Ritual, like drill, is therefore primarily justified by necessity. But there is much more involved in it than this. It utilizes, as Dr Whitehead has pointed out, that general tendency of living creatures to repeat their actions and thereby re-experience the accompanying emotion,[2] which also lies at the origin of the drama and the dance. Indeed, it is hardly necessary to insist on the dramatic character of great religious ceremonies, Christian and non-Christian alike; or the powerful influence of rhythmic speech and movement, as a stimulant of corporate emotion. David dancing before the Ark " with all his might " represents an important and enduring form of religious expression. Psychologically, therefore, ritual tends by means of appropriate sounds and gestures to provoke the repetition of a

[1] *Selected Letters*, p. 357.

[2] A. N. Whitehead, *Religion in the Making*, p. 20.

given religious attitude which can be shared by all taking part in the rite. Its greatest creations—e.g. the Eucharistic liturgy—are sacred dramas, in which the mystery of salvation is re-enacted and re-experienced by the worshipping group. So, too, the congregational litany or hymn, the procession, the corporate act of penitence or praise, acts as a powerful stimulant to the religious feeling of the worshippers. It gives them something to do, and also incites them to do it: again exhibiting its kinship with the dance. For, as we must abandon ourselves to the dance, lose ourselves in it, in order to dance well and "learn by dancing that which is done"; so with the religious rite. We can never understand it without taking part in it; moving with its movement, and yielding to its suggestions. In genuine ritual, as Dr Marett says, the tune counts for a great deal more than the words. Moving and speaking to a measure and rhythm, the more deeply impressive because familiar and loved, we not only catch enthusiasm, but are able to carry on when enthusiasm fails. Social action reinforces our unstable fervour. Giving ourselves with humility to the common worship, we find that this common worship can rouse our sluggish instinct for holiness, support and enlighten our souls. Nor must we be too quick in assuming that improvement in the ritual of worship always consists in the triumph of words over tune; for we are concerned with an action and an experience which transcend the logical levels of the mind, and demand an artistic rather than an intellectual form of expression. Even the great liturgic value of the psalter does not entirely depend on the spiritual truths which the psalmists convey: but at least to some extent on that peculiar quality in poetry, which tends to arouse and liberate the transcendental sense.

In its first emergence, ritual appears as a stylized religious emotion. Spontaneous cries of joy, outbursts of praise, entreaty, self-abasement, seem to represent the earliest response of man to the incitement of God: and these by repetition gradually acquire the sanctions of a rite. The constant "Hear my ringing cry!" of the Hebrew psalmist, and the "Alleluia!" of the Christian, have a long ancestry of which they need not be ashamed: reaching back indeed to the inarticulate sounds by which the most primitive peoples are found to express the emerging spirit of worship. The transition from the common cry to the common utterance and movement is almost inevitable. Thence it is but a step to the conviction that this agreed routine of sense, sounds, and action alone is truly valid, and carries its own guarantees.

At this point the rite assumes, for good or evil, a life and authority of its own; and with it that propensity to become the master instead of the servant of devotion, which is the vice of ceremonial worship. For the immense power of custom and habit—in other words, of tradition—is nowhere more strongly felt than in religious ritual. Here that tendency for any ordered series of acts to crystallize and assume a fixed character, to which even in daily life our whole psychological make-up inclines us, is seen in an extreme form. Departure from the ordained routine always produces a feeling of discomfort, and usually arouses hostility; as anyone well knows who has tried to introduce "desirable changes" into the worship of an English village church. Hence the two outstanding and opposing dangers, of ritualism and of formalism, which dog the history of ceremonial religion; both arising from the same source—a failure to look through and beyond worship to its end.

Ritualism represents the constant tendency of the human creature to attach absolute value to his own activities, whether personal or corporate: to assume that the precise way in which things are done is of supreme importance, and that the traditional formula has an inherent authority extending to its smallest details, from which it is blasphemy to depart.[1] For ritual always acts as a conservative force. It is the very home of tradition ; one of the chief means by which the historical character of worship is preserved and carried forward, and permanence given to the devotional discoveries of men. But this irreplaceable function carries with it its own perils of exaggeration and over-emphasis, leading straight to the absurdities of the ritualist and the "folly of the sacristy". The right form of the vestment, the right number and placing of lights, the correct performance of manual acts or genuflections—or even by inversion, the determined rejection of these things—may then assume such importance that attention is transferred from the meaning of worship to the means, from the total adoring action of the creature to the detail through which it is expressed ; and Martha takes the place of Mary as the pattern of the worshipping soul.[2] Ritual worship only retains sanity and spirituality where there is a clear and constant realization that it is a form taken by the creature's homage and love. "It is not for the purpose of pleasing ourselves. It is the offering of wealth in form, art, or substance to God for His Glory, since all creation belongs to Him."[3]

Moreover, the ritual sense is always hostile to novelty. It is always inclined to reverence mere length of pedigree in a rite ; and to encourage the survival of ceremonial movements which serve no useful purpose, or symbols and formulas which have ceased to express the actual beliefs of the worshippers—even those of which the original meaning

[1] This point is delightfully brought out in the story of the old priest who was accustomed to say at the first ablution in the Mass, "Quod ore mumpsimus". Rebuked for this by a fellow ecclesiastic, he merely replied, "My mumpsimus is as good as your sumpsimus!"

[2] In the second phase of the Anglo-Catholic revival the real issues were almost forgotten in angry discussions concerning clothing, gesture, and church ornaments. See W. J. Sparrow-Simpson, *History of the Anglo-Catholic Revival*, caps. IV and V.

[3] R. M. Benson, *Letters*, p. 255.

has long been lost. Thus the *Oremus* before the Offertory in the Roman Mass, which once ushered in the great common "prayer of the faithful" is still retained, though at least since the eighth century it has been, as Duchesne remarks, "barren of result":[1] and an Offertory at which nothing is offered is too frequently a feature of the Anglican rite.

At the opposite pole from the unbalanced enthusiasm of the ritualist and religious æsthete, so busy with the particular that he forgets the universal which that particular is intended to incorporate, there is the tendency of the formalist to allow the ceremony to degenerate into a mechanical substitute for genuine religious action. The exact but uninterested routine performance of the prescribed movements, attendance at services, or punctual repetition of traditional words, is then regarded as a full satisfaction of the duty of worship. The Buddhists' prayer wheel is the extreme example of this perversion. But instances can be found much nearer home; whether in those Christians who attach an almost magical efficacy to the reading of the "daily portion" or those who put their trust in the obedient recitation of "indulgenced prayers". If the extreme ritualist is an artist so interested in the acting that he loses sight of the total movement and intention of the play, the extreme formalist is a practical man, who acknowledges his religious obligations and fulfils them in the cheapest and easiest way. Such formal worship may at its worst lose all contact with reality; and justify Dr Heiler's wholesale condemnation of ritual as "a fixed formula which people recite without feeling or mood of devotion, untouched both in heart and mind".[2] In practice, of course, these aberrations are constantly found together; and most congregations contain examples of both. Every ritualist

[1] L. Duchesne, *Christian Worship, its Origin and Evolution*, p. 172.
[2] F. Heiler, *Prayer*, Eng. Trans., p. 65.

has his "bad days", on which he becomes a formalist; and on the other hand even the most bored and conventional of church-goers may have his moment of fervour, in which the over-familiar phrases of the liturgy are suddenly lit from within, revealing to him the beauty and power of that ordered and historic worship in which man expresses his humble adoration of God.

Ritual weaves speech, gesture, rhythm and agreed ceremonial into the worshipping action of man; and thus at its best can unite his physical, mental, and emotional being in a single response to the Unseen. The use of symbols and images—which is, in some form or degree, a feature of every cultus—is again forced on him by his own psychological peculiarities; the fact that all his thinking and feeling is intimately related to that world of things in which he lives. It is to the apprehension of these that his mind and senses are trained: it is by the responses they wake up in him that he becomes aware of an external world, independent of himself and imposing its conditions upon him. So, the attempt to respond to God without some acknowledgment of the order within which He has placed us, and reveals Himself to us, is hardly likely to be either a spiritual or a psychological success. It is only by recourse to our image-making faculty, or by some reference—direct or oblique—to the things that are seen, that we can ever give concrete form to our intuition of that which is unseen.

> Præstet fides supplementum
> Sensuum defectui,

says St Thomas in his great Eucharistic hymn. But though it be true indeed that faith makes good the defects of the senses, it is no less true that the senses must also play their part in making good the limitations of faith, and bringing into focus within our field of vision the far-off objects she discerns.

This reinforcement of belief by the use of symbolic objects appears in its crudest form in the fetish; but it persists in the highest forms of worship, in the tokens, symbols, and sacraments of faith. Indeed, it is arguable that every approach of the conditioned mind to the Absolute God must take place by symbolic means; though these may not be of a material kind, and may even be unrecognized by those who use them. With the growth of spirituality these mediating symbols tend to become more abstract; but this does not mean that they are left behind. The "emptiness", the "darkness", the "nothing", the "Cloud of Unknowing" of the mystic, though they be negative statements, are still symbols drawn from his sensible experience, in and through which he seeks to actualize his obscure experience of God. The difference between this and the naïve use of a visual image is really only the difference between the allusive and the direct: and, in the highest reaches of spiritual experience, either may become the vehicle of a genuine communion with the supra-sensible Reality. For, since the true Object of man's worship always lies beyond his comprehension, we are obliged to bridge the gap by means of symbolic images; chosen objects which signify mediate or suggest, but never explain, the Reality that we adore. "The secrecy of the Godhead," says Maritain, "is inviolable. Nevertheless the Divine Essence can be known by us, not as It is in Itself, but by a certain participation of Itself communicated to us by means of created things."[1]

A learned Brahmin, quoted by Professor Pratt,[2] summed up the use of the image in worship as "aiding visualization and concentration". "It is," he said, "a sensuous symbol, just as the word GOD is. Both are symbols, one tangible and visible, the other audible; and both are helpful to our

[1] J. Maritain, *Les Degrés du Savoir*, pp. 456, 457.

[2] *The Religious Consciousness*, p. 275.

finite minds, in standing for the Infinite. The man who worships before an idol in effect prays 'O God! Come and dwell in this image before me for the moment, that I may worship Thee here concretely'." A Catholic Christian might say as much as this of his crucifix, or an Orthodox of his ikon; and the witness of the vast majority of Christians should warn us against hasty condemnation of the use of the visible and tangible to arouse, maintain, and express our worship. Thus the ikon gives to the pious Orthodox a genuine sense of the Presence of God. He will pray before it, as if to Christ Himself; yet without any risk of idolatry, since he remains perfectly aware that the ikon itself is part of the world of things. It is an object which has been set apart by consecration to be a channel of the supernatural and a peculiar focus of prayer, "a conductor and transformer of the Divine current";[1] and by its very form reminds him that God cannot be represented in His Essence, but only through His revelation in man.[2] Nor can the theologian whose faith is based upon the Incarnation assume that the God who tabernacles among men necessarily disdains these humble instruments.

Whether the symbols which man uses for the purposes of worship be drawn from religious tradition or from his own rich phantasy-life, or whether he frankly accepts and gives symbolic rank to certain things which the sensible world presents to him, the principle involved is the same. Particular things and images are accepted and used, as in some way representative of that which lies beyond all things and images; as carriers of a spiritual reality. By this

[1] Robert Will, *Le Culte*, II, p. 553.

[2] Not only the veneration, but also the actual making of the ikon is regarded by the Orthodox as an act of worship. The true painter of ikons prepares himself for his work by prayer, and considers it to be in the nature of a religious vocation. The Orthodox regard with horror the commercial production of crucifixes and sacred images, and are accustomed to say that Fra Angelico is the only true maker of ikons in the history of the Western Church.

association of sensible object and idea, a new entity is created of which the reality is guaranteed by the fusion of sign and significance: even though the symbol is never truly adequate to the fact conveyed. Once the group or the individual worshipper has given this rank to any image or act—for the symbol may be, often is, a bodily action, e.g. the sign of the Cross, the kiss of peace, the prostration, the laying on of hands—it is henceforth placed in a special class, as carrying a spiritual reference. In a general, not a technical sense, it has become a " sensible means of grace "; and the first step has been taken on the road to sacramental worship. For the symbol, or significant image, is not, as its unfriendly critics suppose, a substitute for spiritual truth. It is rather the point where physical and metaphysical meet —a half-way house, where the world of things and world of spirit unite, and produce a new thing possessed of sensible and supra-sensible reality. And man, who partakes himself of this double character, finds in it the natural means of access to God.

It is true that popular devotion will always tend to confuse image and reality, give absolute rank to particular embodiments, and identify the carrying medium with that which it carries. Hence arises " idolatry "; the danger which ever waits on symbolic, as formalism waits on ritual, worship. Nevertheless the distinction between symbol and idol is an absolute one. In real symbolic worship there is a twofold spiritual activity:

> The transcendent action of God does not stop short and accumulate itself in the religious object; but tends to pass through it to reach the soul of the subject. And on the other hand the immanent action of God presses subjective devotion to overpass the phenomenal level and ascend towards the transcendental world by an act of adoration in spirit and in truth.[1]

[1] Will, *Le Culte*, Vol. II, p. 553.

In practice, ritual and symbol perpetually reinforce and enrich one another in all developed cultus. The symbolic act or object comes to the rescue, where words and ordered movements fail. The smoke of incense, the lighted taper, the solemn exhibition of the sacred sign—all this is found to say something, to add something deeply satisfying to the worship, which cannot otherwise find sensible expression. Here all the great religions, even those which most sternly repudiate everything which savours of idolatry, seem to be agreed. For the Jew, the Eternal God, though He had no image, yet " dwelt between the Cherubims " upon the mercy-seat within the veil ; and was worshipped, not only with sacrifice and the ritual use of the psalter, but with incense, lights, and sacred dance. Even the intense transcendentalism of Mohamed recognized " the consolidating effect of fixing a central spot round which through all time should gather the religious feelings of his followers " ;[1] and gave symbolic rank to the Kaaba at Mecca, as the sacred shrine of the true faith and focal point of the believer's prayers. So, too, Buddhism and Jainism, beginning as ethical and largely un-embodied faiths, have produced under pressure of human necessity an organized cultus, rich in concrete symbols, images, sacred objects, and other sensible aids to worship : and those Christian sects in which the use of visible symbols is at a minimum, and the cultus has been deliberately stripped of sensuous appeal, seem to tend instinctively to hymns rich in concrete images and emotional suggestion—thus giving to the primitive layers of the worshipping mind the sensuous food that they need, by means of the ear instead of the eye.

[1] Ameer Ali, *The Spirit of Islam*, p. 167.

CHAPTER III

SACRAMENT AND SACRIFICE

I

A SYMBOL is a significant image, which helps the worshipping soul to apprehend spiritual reality. A sacrament is a significant deed, a particular use of temporal things, which gives to them the value of eternal things and thus incorporates and conveys spiritual reality. Hence sacraments involve an incarnational philosophy; a belief that the Supernatural draws near to man in and through the natural. It is true that the distinction between the symbolic and sacramental aspects of cultus is not absolute. All sacraments do and must employ symbolic methods. Symbols and symbolic acts easily acquire a sacramental character—e.g. the use of holy water, or objects and images which have been specially blessed—since being charged with religious suggestion, devout minds find in and through them a genuine contact with the Divine. Christian tradition is justified in creating a class of "sacramentals", which are more than symbols and less than sacraments: efficacious signs, which when taken into the atmosphere of worship become means by which the successive creature lays hold on the Unchanging. Indeed, many of the common things and acts of daily existence can be given such sacramental quality, by the Godward intention of those who are accustomed to seek and find the Eternal in the temporal; and so woven into the fabric of the worshipping life.

Generally speaking, however, it is true to say that from the point of view of cultus, symbols represent and suggest, whilst sacraments work. Effective action is essential to them ; and this action is from God to man, not from man to God. The water cleanses, the bread and wine feed, the oil anoints, the imposition of consecrating hands conveys new character, the marriage act unites ; and all this in the interior and spiritual as well as in the exterior and natural sense. Such interior and spiritual action cannot be achieved by man. His part, as worshipper, consists in the preparation ; the adoring and confident reference to God, opening up a pathway for His grace. But the essence of the sacramental action consists in the " actual conveyance of spiritual meaning and power by a material process . . . not only God's meaning to the mind, but God Himself to the whole person of the worshipper ".[1]

A valid sacrament, therefore, always leaves the situation different from what it was before. By means of the natural needs and actions of men, it effects a communication of the Wholly Other, over against men ; and it is a fundamental part of worship, because it is an acknowledgment of the presence and priority of the divine, and is directed towards the sanctification of life. This is already seen in embryo, in those primitive rites of initiation and transition, those sacred meals and purifications, which Dr Marett has well named the " Sacraments of Simple Folk ". Here we first find men becoming aware of the mysterious significance of life, and their own dependence on the Unseen : and reaching out towards it through and in those very facts and compulsions of natural existence, which they feel to be the channels of a non-natural Power from beyond themselves.[2]

[1] W. Temple, *Nature, Man and God*, p. 484.

[2] Compare the following definition : " A sacrament is any spatio-temporal reality which by its occupation of space or time expresses to us God's will and purpose and enables us the better to co-operate with them." Oliver Quick, *The Christian Sacraments*, p. 104.

Thus we may say in a general sense, that sacraments convey the numinous, establish a relation between human and Divine, more precisely and more effectively than the most august of symbols; for their contact with our life is more complete. This conveyance is achieved by means of tokens; objects or actions set apart for a special office, and therefore taking rank as effective instruments. These tokens constitute a sacred currency which not only signifies but also conveys to those who take it seriously the wealth for which it stands. Like any other coinage, it may and often does become debased: yet still it is representative of the spiritual gold. Moreover, the obvious inadequacy and arbitrary character of the token over against the holy reality which comes by these humble channels to transform, refresh, and sanctify the life of men, once more reminds us of the freedom and priority of God's action; the homely plane on which human worship must be content to move. It checks presumption and keeps adoring gratitude alive.

Thus sacramentalism, emerging as a primary means of worship appropriate to the nature and situation of man, grows and deepens with our growth. It has something to give the most naïve of primitives; its possibilities have never been exhausted by the most supernaturalized of saints. For it reveals God, the Supernatural, ever at work seeking and finding us through the natural; the objects and actions of our temporal experience, as the effective means of our deepest and most transforming apprehensions of Eternity, and our most insistent invitations to worship coming to us where we are, and taking us as we are—creatures of soul and body, conditioned by time and space. Therefore the cultus which excludes sacraments does not in consequence draw nearer to God; but renounces a sovereign means by which He is self-imparted to us, and in and through which His action may be recognized and adored. It is true that sacramental methods are always open to the dangers of formalism and exteriorization, and may even slide down into a crass materialism. Yet on the other hand, it is those who have reached out through the sensible to an apprehension of the supra-sensible, who realize most fully the deep mystery and unexhausted possibilities which abide in the world of sense, and therefore its power of conveying to us that which lies beyond, and gives to it significance and worth.

It is a very short-sighted spirituality which ignores these patent facts; or tries to maintain an absolute contrast between matter and spirit, seen and unseen, nature and grace; and worship the Creator whilst disdaining the help of those things which He has made, and which are pre-supposed as the vehicles of the spiritual experiences of men. Since we are men and women and not angels, it is surely to be expected that God's prevenient action should reach us through and not in defiance of our humanity; penetrating, informing, and consecrating the life He has made for Himself, giving the invisible and eternal order through that visible and fleeting order to which our mental life is adjusted, and calling us to an intercourse consistent with our condition —in, and yet not wholly of the visible world. The ultimate aim of all expressive worship is the increase of Charity; the pure love of God, for Himself alone. This must take precedence of all other considerations; and all ways and means are to be judged by the degree in which they conduce to it. This awakening and response of the soul to God is clearly served by a living sacramentalism, with its abundance of material for the embodiment of every aspect of God's self-giving action and man's response.

Thus some form or degree of sacramentalism must enter into human worship: whether of the diffuse and generalized kind which "finds the inward in the outward", or of the more definite sort which embodies sacred mysteries and divine communications in specific acts. In it we first see clearly man's deep instinct for the supernatural, his realization of " one thing working in another thing ", spirit giving significance to sense. For the universality of sacraments is not, as is sometimes thought; a witness to the Divine Immanence. It is rather a proclamation of the Divine Transcendence; man's realization of the gap between Creator and creature—a certain tragic disharmony—and the need of a bridge, an ordained path along which the Eternal Perfect may penetrate Time and the things of Time. Here man is pressed by God immanent to prepare the matrix; but it is God transcendent Who pours into it His quickening love to cleanse, feed, and transform. In the genuine sacrament, this action and this penetration must be so complete, so entirely independent of the worshipper's uneven religious sensibility, that here men can be sure of laying hold of a spiritual reality truly present in its own right; awaiting their recognition, but in no way conditioned by it. In other words, it must be effective *ex opere operato* if it is to meet the creature's deepest need.

It is plain that such a religion as Christianity, which has for its object the worship of the Divine self-revealed in history, the Logos incarnate in time and space—which seeks and finds God self-given, in and through the littleness of the manger, and the shamefulness of the cross—is closely bound up with a sacramental interpretation of life. Christ, as Bérulle said so deeply and so boldly, is " Himself the major sacrament "; the visible sign of the nature of the Eternal God, and the medium of that Eternal God's self-giving to men. And the Church, as His Mystical Body, the organ of His continued presence, lives with a sacramental life from which the reality and power of the specific Christian sacraments proceed, and which indeed gives to them their credentials. This precision, this apparent canalizing of a grace and power which are felt by the religious soul to be boundless in generosity and unconditioned in action, and operative throughout the whole of life, repels many spiritual minds. They can easily accept a diffused sacramentalism; but reject the notion of a special and ordained channel of grace. Nevertheless the distinctness of the Holy will never be sufficiently realized by us, unless His self-giving be apprehended as coming to man the creature in a special sense by particular paths; held sacred, and kept for Himself alone. And this means sacraments. The deep conviction of the Platonist that everything is a shadow and outward sign of a deeper and more enduring reality, is indeed precious as far as it goes; and is justified in those rare moments when the lovely veil is lifted and we catch a glimpse of greater loveliness behind. But this can never be enough for Christianity; which discloses a real God to real men by means of a real life and death in space and time. And here the law of belief must be the law of worship too.

II

Worship, the response of the human creature to the Divine, is summed up in sacrifice; the action which expresses more fully than any other his deep if uncomprehended relation to God. As man begins to wake up to the Reality over against him, there comes to him as the sequel to his sense of awe and dependence the feeling that he wants to offer something—indeed, must offer something—to the unseen Power. He wants to do this long before he is able to say why he is moved by this profound impulse; and when he does produce reasons, often enough they are of a mixed, and even apparently self-interested kind. Thus the sacrifice may have as its immediately inciting cause awe, fear, anxiety, the impulse to propitiate, or the sense of need or guilt; for by all these paths, the spirit of man is persuaded to seek communion with God. But whether this declared cause be the desire to adore, to atone, or to obtain benefits

—whether the anthropologists be right in finding the essential meaning of sacrifice to be "life offered in order that life may be received"[1]—behind all and colouring all is the remote cause; the deep conviction that sacrifice is the sum of worship, the way in which man must approach God, his first lesson in creaturely love. For sacrifice is a positive act. Its essence is something given; not something given up. It is a freewill offering, a humble gesture which embodies and expresses with more or less completeness the living heart of religion; the self-giving of the creature to its God. By this self-giving action, man takes his conscious part in the response of the universe to the Source of its being; and unites the small movements of his childish soul to the eternal sacrifice of the Son.

Mere renunciation for its own sake, then, may sometimes be a salutary, but never a sacrificial act. Though often enough degraded to the purposes of fear or self-interest, or allowed to become a ceremonial substitute for the inward offering which it is intended to express, real sacrifice is still essentially a movement of generosity. Without it, worship may easily degenerate into emotional admiration; and on the other hand the "spiritual" sacrifice without concrete embodiment lacks at least one element of costliness, and is out of touch with the here-and-now realities of human life. Isaac bound on the altar, Ornan the Jebusite, offering all his substance for the sacrifice which shall consecrate his threshing floor to God,[2] reveal to us its very heart. Here we see the first stirring of that total and unconditioned response, that Charity to which the generosity of God is always inciting us; that impulse to offer "Thine own things of Thine own" which finds its fulfilment on the summits of the consecrated life. The sacrifice in itself is something very small. In the real approach to the Eternal "Lebanon is not sufficient to

[1] See E. O. James, *Origins of Sacrifice*, p. 256.
[2] 1 Chron. xxi. 18–23.

burn, nor the beasts thereof sufficient for a burnt offering ".[1] But because it unveils the deep movements of the Spirit, and offers us a sensible means of expressing them appropriate to our state, it is alike the root and crown of human worship.

It is true that the ritual sacrifice, whether votive or piacular, is always regarded as doing something of great importance for man; but only because in it, at his own cost and of his own choice, he approaches God, and does something costly as towards God. This something is done, as all the expressive acts of worship must be done, by means of admittedly inadequate tokens; which at first are thought of as suitable gifts for such a Divinity as primitive men are able to conceive, but afterwards are continued as the representative signs of that total and invisible oblation which is the essence of human worship. De la Taille surely uncovers the spiritual roots of sacrifice when he says: "Because man is not a pure spirit, he feels the need to translate this interior gift of himself into an outward rite which symbolizes it. For this reason, he presents to God the homage of some material gift ".[2] He "makes a covenant with sacrifice" as the child makes its small offering to the parent; not because he possesses anything worth giving, but because it is the best that he can do. Thus the building of the Temple was Israel's supreme act of sacrifice; and the great Christian cathedrals, to which generations gave of their best in skill, thought, and effort, are not really understood until we recognize in them a corporate expression of that same spirit—the impulse to give of our best to the Unseen.

The genuine sacrifice is, therefore, both symbolic and sacramental; a concrete here-and-now act which carries a super-sensual reference. The gross surroundings and apparent

[1] Isaiah xl. 16.
[2] De la Taille, *The Mystery of Faith*, p. 6.

E

materialism of the primitive forms should not blind us to its deeply religious character. For it represents more than itself; becoming ever richer and more significant with the deepening and purifying of man's spiritual sense, till at last in Christianity it achieves complete sublimation, and in so doing exhibits its fundamental significance. For in sacrifice something is given voluntarily and unconditionally to God, in defiance of the inveterate possessiveness and claimfulness of man; and this gesture of generosity is felt to be the best that we can do (*a*) to atone for our shortcomings in other respects, (*b*) as a means of that approach to God which is an essential element in worship, (*c*) as an earnest of devotedness. From the point of view of primitive thought, this gift could not fully be made without the death of the victim; for its life—the essence of the offering, and token of the offerer's own life—must be released and handed over to the supernatural powers. The act of sacrifice consists in the transfer of the gift we offer from the earthly to the heavenly realm; and the altar is the place where the transfer is effected. Here, then, we have an explanation of some of the more terrible aspects of sacrifice; even including those human sacrifices in which, with a dreadful logic, the awakening soul of the primitive acknowledges the absolute priority of the Unseen. For sacrifice emerges in the jungle; and indeed always carries with it a reminiscence of the jungle. But its full meaning is disclosed in the absolute oblation of the Cross. Cost is always essential to it. Thus wild animals and fruits are never used by agricultural peoples for the purposes of sacrifice. They must give something into which they have put their own life and work;[1] for within that total, visible offering which is ritual sacrifice, is always implied the total invisible offering of the self, and everything the self best loves.

[1] See F. C. Hicks, *The Fullness of Sacrifice*, p. 24. I am indebted for much in this section to suggestions received from Dr Hicks' work.

The Old Testament describes and ordains as the central acts of the cultus, three main types of sacrifice. Each answers to a particular relation between God and man, and gives expression to a profound instinct or need which appears again and again on every level in the history of human worship. There is first the burnt-offering, or total gift, accepted in its wholeness by God, and consumed by His sacred fire—oblation. Next there is the peace offering, culminating in the sacrificial meal wherein the worshipper, through this sacramental feeding on the thing which has been offered and made holy, enters into a closer fellowship with God. Here the emphasis lies on communion, and new life received through communion, as the sequel and completion of sacrifice. Last, there is the sin-offering, or sacrifice of reconciliation and atonement, the faulty creature's acknowledgment of his shortcomings and his obligations—propitiation and penitence. These three great forms of sacrifice with their ritual accompaniments, giving vivid if naïve expression to three constant and complementary impulses and needs of the religious soul, form an essential part of the religious and historic background of the New Testament writers.[1] They represent the universally accepted substance of ceremonial worship as understood by the ancient world, the ordained method of approach to God; and, within this, the substance of spiritual worship too. Thus they provided a rich symbolic language which all Jewish Christians understood; but of which we must never forget the origin, when trying to assess what our Lord and His first witnesses meant by Atonement, Redemption, Communion, Oblation, or the many needs and insights which find their fulfilment in the Eucharist, and conditioned its developed form.

For the devout Jew, to whom the ritual sacrifice was the natural and traditional way of approach to God, the

[1] See further on this point, Part II, cap. X.

distinctions and classifications of the Mosaic sacrificial code were probably more technical than real. For him Adoration, Atonement, Thanksgiving, Communion, Penitence, Need, had their part in every offering; as they have for the Christian in every Eucharist. The total unanalysed impulse of worship, with its aura of associated thoughts and feelings, found its visible focus in the altar; the "seat of God", where His purifying and transforming fire was always alight, symbol of His acceptance of the little gifts of men. In every sacrifice, whatever the declared intention, something of value was solemnly and willingly offered to God; and being offered, was taken up into the supernatural order, consecrated, and transformed. First the crude and tentative vehicle of man's address to God, and next the earnest of his filial devotedness, it became more and more the vehicle of God's approach to and communion with men. Perhaps the most significant development in human religion has been the movement of the idea of sacrifice from propitiation to love. This transformation, affecting the deepest levels of the spiritual life, has been both evoked and expressed through the experience of worship and finds its consummation in the Christian Eucharist.[1] Here then we see again the double movement at the heart of worship; man incited to offer, urged to a movement of generosity, that so a channel may be opened through which God can give. "There went up an insignificant human offering—there came down a divine largesse."[2]

The Biblical use of sacrificial language shows how completely the religious minds of the Old Dispensation assumed that this concrete giving of our best to the Eternal, whether by way of thanksgiving or of atonement, was representative of an interior movement of worship; a personal self-giving, which carried with it profound supernatural results. The

[1] See below, cap. VIII.

[2] De la Taille, *op. cit.*, p. 11.

apparent condemnation of ritual sacrifice by the prophets is found on investigation to be directed, not against sacrifice as such, but against its degradation: that caricature of sacred action which substitutes the ceremonial for the sacramental, the offering of "the blood of bulls and goats" and exact performance of a prescribed ritual for the essential offering under tokens of the heart. Their repeated denunciation of those who sought to fulfil their religious obligations, obtain benefits and buy off the anger of God by means of "meal offerings and fat beasts", is really a condemnation of the stupidity of those who mistake means for ends. Though actually intended as a corrective, this condemnation has in its expression all the uncritical violence and one-sided emphasis of the reformer, conscious only of the sacred realities which are being profaned, the substitution of outward sign for inward grace.[1] It is the same sort of hatred as that which the Iconoclasts directed against sacred images, Latimer against the Mass, or Fox against the steeple-house.

> "I hate, I despise your feasts, and I will take no delight in your solemn assemblies. Yea, though ye offer me your burnt offerings and meal offerings I will not accept them, neither will I regard the peace offerings of your fat beasts."[2]
>
> "I desire mercy and not sacrifice; and the knowledge of God more than burnt offerings."[3]

But even the most extreme of these denunciations—coming as they do from a period of national degradation—leave us in no doubt that the spirit of penitence and self-oblation, and the mystery of communion, which are dramatized in the ritual sacrifices still remain for the great prophets and psalmists of Israel the very essence of worship, and

[1] See below, cap. VIII.
[2] Amos v. 21, 22.
[3] Hosea vi. 6.

sacrificial language the natural expression of the Godward life.

Let my prayer be set forth in thy sight as the incense:
And let the lifting up of my hands be an evening sacrifice.

Behold, O Lord, how that I am thy servant: I am thy servant and the son of thine handmaid; thou hast broken my bonds in sunder.
I will offer to thee the sacrifice of thanksgiving: and will call upon the Name of the Lord.

The sacrifice of God is a troubled spirit:
A broken and contrite heart, O God, shalt thou not despise.[1]

Moreover when we come to the New Testament, it is clear that Our Lord's life and mission are conceived by Him from beginning to end in terms of sacrifice. Indeed many of the incidents of that life, as described by the Synoptists, seem to have been determined by those conceptions and can only be fully understood by us in the light of the Jewish sacrificial ideas which are so plainly present in His mind. If Moses and the Prophets have told of Him, the temple sacrifices have told of Him too. For Him and His closest followers, the mysterious significance of that ancient cultus is gathered up and exhibited in His Person: and it is by the picture-language of sacrifice that they describe His unique status best.[2] He is given at His baptism the sacrificial character of the dove, the meek offering of the poor;[3] and is recognized by the Baptist as the Lamb of God, the unsullied and prevailing sacrifice. Thus "He begins His Ministry with the gift of the Spirit in a form that suggests sacrifice—and that the sacrifice of the poor, as well as the age-long sacrifice of Israel; and with a message from the Father

[1] Ps. cxli. 2; cxvi. 14, 15; li. 17.

[2] e.g. St Paul. "Christ . . . gave Himself up for us, an offering and a sacrifice to God for an odour of a sweet smell." (Eph. v. 2, R.V.)

[3] The dove alone among the creatures ordained for sacrifice was said to stretch out its neck to the slayer without shrinking from the knife. Cf. Hicks, *op. cit.*, p. 195.

which links Him both with the supreme type of the true burnt-offering (Isaac) and with the mission and destiny of the Servant who is to suffer and die for sinners."[1] So, too, His deliberately accepted death is synchronized with the Passover; and in the three crucial events of the Passion —the Last Supper, Gethsemane, and the Cross—the deepest and most awful meanings of the sacrifice of communion, of total oblation, and of atonement, are declared. Life is offered, and being offered is transformed in God: and by and through this life given and transformed, God enters into communion with men.[2] In man and for man, by an entire self-offering, the Divine Logos redeems creation, atones for man's sinfulness, and fulfils man's supreme obligation to God.[3] Finally, in the great vision of the Apocalyptist we see the whole worship of heaven centred upon the altar of this Lamb, "slain from the foundation of the world". Even though the devotional language of the New Testament itself is not markedly sacrificial, these are the facts and conceptions which underlie it, and which have had a determining effect on the development of Christian worship. "Thou hast given us," said James Martineau the Unitarian, "as author and finisher of our faith, One who offered himself up a living and a dying sacrifice."

For Christian sacramentalism, as expressed in the great liturgies of the East and West, it is this "one true, pure and only sacrifice"—the eternal movement of charity whereby the Son is self-given to the Father, and in union with Him, His Mystical Body, the Church—which is represented, but not repeated, under the conditions of time and space, in every Eucharist: for the sacrificial aspect of the Christian liturgy is not, as is sometimes supposed, a mediæval accretion, but comes to us in its completeness from the

[1] Hicks, *op. cit.*, *loc. cit.*
[2] Hicks, *op. cit.*, p. 271.
[3] Hebrews vii. 26–28; ix. 13–15.

noblest period of the undivided Church.[1] Even in Apostolic times, the ideas of offering and of communion—the Cross and the Heavenly Food—are felt to be united in the Eucharistic action; which takes up and transfigures all that is striven for in the Temple cult.[2] This sacrificial intention is given ever greater precision, until in the fourth century it attains complete expression; and is openly linked, not with Calvary alone, but also with the ritual sacrifices of the Old Covenant. Thus in the Liturgy of St John Chrysostom, the first part of the Eucharist, or Office of Oblation, is in substance a solemn preparation of the elements, and especially of the altar bread, or Holy Lamb, by means of a ceremonial which symbolizes the events of the Passion; and when all is ready, the deacon comes to the celebrant saying: "It is time to sacrifice to the Lord!" Again, in the prayer of the Cherubic Hymn, Christ is set forth as Priest and Victim, offerer and offered, receiving and Himself received; and after the censing of the Elements the celebrant prays:

> Grant us to obtain grace in Thy sight, that our sacrifice may be acceptable unto Thee; and that the good spirit of Thy grace may rest upon us, and upon these Holy Gifts, now offered up unto Thee!

In the Liturgy of St Basil, the sacrificial references are still more precise:

> Accept us who draw near to Thy Holy Altar, according to the plenitude of Thy mercy, that we may be worthy to offer unto Thee this reasonable and unbloody sacrifice for our own sins and for the errors of Thy people; which do

[1] Definite sacrificial language first appears in the *Didache*, c. 125, and seems to have been taken directly from Jewish sources; so manifesting the conviction of the early Church that a real connection did exist between the Temple offerings and the Christian Eucharist. The references of St Ignatius, early second century, to "one altar and one bishop" show that this conception had by his time become common form.

[2] 1 Cor. x. 16.

> Thou accept upon Thy holy and heavenly and supersensual Altar . . . as Thou didst accept the gifts of Abel, the sacrifices of Noah, the burnt offerings of Abraham, the priestly offices of Moses and Aaron, the peace-offerings of Samuel !

In the Roman Missal, among many prayers of the sacrificial type, two stand out with special distinctness. First the invocation of the Holy Spirit at the Offertory, or oblation of the elements : " Come ! O Sanctifier, Almighty Eternal God, and bless this sacrifice set forth in Thy Holy Name " ; and next the invitation to the people before the Canon : " Pray, my brethren, that my sacrifice and yours may be acceptable to God the Father Almighty ! " The Anglican rite, too, has carefully preserved this ancient orientation ; and in its own quiet way witnesses to the fact that the Eucharistic action is first and foremost a sacrifice of thanksgiving, offered to God in and with Christ.

> O Lord and heavenly Father, we thy humble servants entirely desire thy fatherly goodness mercifully to accept this our sacrifice of praise and thanksgiving . . . and although we be unworthy, through our manifold sins, to offer unto thee any sacrifice, yet we beseech thee to accept this our bounden duty and service.

Thus the combined witness of the Scriptures and Liturgy indicates how deeply, from early times, Christian worship has been coloured by sacrificial ideas ; how closely united in the thought and practice of the Church are the twin realities of communion and oblation, the systole and diastole of love. Nor indeed could it be otherwise. That humiliation of the Word which is the essential truth of Incarnation would hardly be complete enough to meet the need of His creatures, unless He were conformed to the mysterious law of sacrifice. Nor would the responsive worship of man be complete, unless there were included in it some sacrificial act or implication. Hence for the Christian all sacrifice is gathered up, and sanctified, upon Calvary; and placed at the centre of the Godward life. Here Divine Love in its fulness is revealed to man in and through the total self-oblation of Man; the willing death of the Victim giving eternal life to the world.[1]

Christian worship, then, can never be divorced from sacrifice; even though it may seem to move far from the crude methods by which our spiritual ancestors tried to give visible expression to this invisible oblation of the heart, or repudiates (perhaps with an unnecessary violence) all outward signs of this inward act of grace. Indeed, it is remarkable that those reformers who repudiate most vigorously the sacrificial aspect of the Eucharist are most insistent on the importance of the sacrificial principle for Christian worship, and its fulfilment in prayer and thanksgiving.

> When I declare the Word of God I offer sacrifice; when thou hearest the Word of God with all thy heart, thou dost offer sacrifice. When we pray, and when we give in charity to our neighbour, we offer sacrifice. So, too, when I receive this Sacrament, I offer sacrifice—that is to say, I accomplish the will and service of God, I confess Him, and I give Him thanks. This is not a sacrifice for sin, but a sacrifice of thanksgiving and praise.[2]

As man delves deeper and deeper into the mysterious truth of his relation to God, so bit by bit it seems that the meaning of sacrifice is disclosed to him: and the death or setting aside of the apparent life is realized as the very condition of communion with the divine life. Thus gradually through the religious acts to which he is impelled—but only fully at last in Christianity—he discovers the costly paradox of life surrendered that life may be achieved.

[1] For further development of this subject see below, cap. VII and VIII.

[2] Martin Luther, *Sermon for Maundy Thursday*. Quoted by Will, *Le Culte*, Vol. I, p. 113.

And when the interior life of prayer is reached—that life on which, in the last resort, the reality of the cultus must depend—those three great motives of sacrifice which the ancient rituals express: the deep sense of sin and penitence, the need and longing for communion, the impulse to that total self-giving which is the preparation of sanctity—are all found operative in the most profound experiences of the soul. A speechless self-offering, a total oblation of personality, is described to us by the mystics as the apex of contemplative prayer. "As a whole burnt offering He accepted them," says the writer of the Book of Wisdom of the saints; and no other image could so perfectly express that self-loss of the creature in its Home and Father, which is the consummation of worship. For the essence of the burnt offering was not destruction, but transformation: God, by His sacred fire, taking, accepting, transmuting that which was offered, that so it might enter His very life.

> "Thou ghostly friend in God," says the author of *The Cloud of Unknowing*, "look that, leaving all curious seeking in thy natural wits, thou do wholly worship thy Lord God with thy substance, offering up unto Him plainly and wholly thine only self, all that thou art and such as thou art . . . and say thus: 'That I am and how that I am, as in nature and in grace, all I have it of Thee Lord, and Thou it art. And all I offer it unto Thee, principally to the praising of Thee, for the help of all mine even-Christians and of me'." ([1])

All the methods and disciplines of the cultus—ritual and symbol, sacrament and sacrifice, evoking and expressing the Godward life of the creature—here find their meaning and end.

[1] *The Epistle of Privy Counsel*, cap. III.

CHAPTER IV

THE CHARACTERS OF CHRISTIAN WORSHIP

I

THE character of worship is always decided by the worshipper's conception of God and his relation to God: that is to say, whatever its ritual expression may be, it always has a theological basis. Though the cultus may not tally at every point with the creed, since it often carries along many traditional and even primitive elements which have long ceased to bear their original meaning, in general the relation between the two is close; and only the believer, acting from within that cultus and conforming to its ritual pattern, can truly appreciate the meaning or the spiritual value of those devotional words and acts by means of which his worship is expressed. All this is eminently true of Christianity. In the bewildering variety, and even the apparent contradictions, of its many practices, from the extreme of liturgic ceremonialism to the extreme of silent or informal prayer, and from a close dependence on sacramental acts to their entire rejection, Christian worship is yet always conditioned by Christian belief; and especially belief about the Nature and Action of God, as summed up in the great dogmas of the Trinity and the Incarnation. Though the awestruck movement of the soul over against the surrounding mystery, and intimate devotion to the historic Person of Christ, in Whom that mystery draws near to men, both enter into it, its emphasis does not, or should not, be on either of these completing opposites of our spiritual experience. Its true secret is hidden between them, and is at one and the same time a personal communion and a metaphysical thirst.

Perhaps we come as near to that secret as human language permits, if we define Christian worship as the total adoring response of man to the one Eternal God self-revealed in time. This adoring response is full of contrast and variety; and has a span which stretches from the wordless commerce of the contemplative soul with "that which hath no image" to the most naïve expressions of popular belief. Profoundly historical, it accepts, carries along, and transforms to its own purpose the devotional language and methods of antiquity: and no one will understand it who does not keep this fact in mind. Yet on the other hand it possesses an inherent freshness and power of adaptation, which again and again accepts new embodiments for its worship of unchanging Truth. Its possibilities, indeed, are too rich to be fully explored by any one worshipper or any one group of worshippers; for it is at once thoroughly personal and thoroughly corporate in character, and in its expression can use many contrasting devotional methods—spontaneous and liturgical, symbolic and spiritual, sacrificial and contemplative—and embody these in the most ornate or the most austere of ritual forms. But careful study will discover a certain character which conditions and gives inward unity and significance to all these different, and even superficially conflicting, expressions of the Christian spirit of worship: and this character is neither ethical nor mystical, institutional nor personal, but doctrinal.

Genuine Christian worship, whatever its special emphasis may be, always requires as its foundation belief in one Holy and Eternal God, the Being of Beings, the "Maker, Lover, and Keeper"[1] of all life; utterly transcendent to His creation, and yet fully present with and in it, besetting,

[1] Julian of Norwich, *Revelations of Divine Love*, cap. V.

sustaining, moulding—above all loving—all that is made. Its object is a Reality "higher than our highest yet more inward than our most inward part",[1] uniting within His mysterious Nature the cosmic and the personal, the extremes of tenderness and power. This majestic vision it shares to some extent with other great theistic religions—e.g. Judaism and Islam—and here the devotional expressions of many of its greatest masters of theocentric worship, such as St Augustine, do not go beyond the language of the Hebrew Psalter, the Neoplatonic mystics, and the Sūfi saints. But the peculiar note of Christianity is struck when, within this awed yet delighted recognition of the Eternal Godhead, we place as the focus of devotion one single revelation in time and space of His essential character—"the effulgence of his glory and the very image of his substance"[2]—made in the person of Jesus Christ; and complete this by acknowledging the presence and power of His holy personal and eternal Spirit—His absolute Will and Love—at work within the world of Time. For this means that we discover and adore the Supernatural, in its independence and completeness, truly immanent in the natural; proceeding from the deeps of Absolute Being, yet charged with the self-giving ardour of Absolute Love.

Christian worship in its wholeness must include or imply such equal, loving, and costly responses to this threefold Reality as we find for example in the writings of St Paul:[3] awestruck adoration of the self-existent Eternal, "the only Wise God", total self-offering to Him in Christ, and an active and grateful recognition of the Holy Spirit of God, in His creative guiding and purifying action upon the Church and the soul. It involves, then, an adoring acknowledgment first of God's cosmic splendour and otherness, next of His

[1] St Augustine, *Confessions*, Bk. III, cap. 6.
[2] Hebrews i. 3 (R.V.)
[3] Romans xi. 33–36; 1 Corinthians ii. 6–16; and many other places.

redemptive and transfiguring action revealed in history, and last of His immanent guidance of life. The full Eucharistic canon—now only found in the liturgy of the Orthodox Church and its derivatives[1]—passing from the *Sanctus* to the commemoration of Christ's life and passion, and thence to an invocation of the Spirit, gives liturgical expression to this, the norm of Christian worship; and it is this constant association of the Eternal and temporal, the transcendent and the incarnate, majesty and generous love, which gives that worship its unique character.

> Who can tell Thy lofty and eternal magnificence, O Word of God: and who may comprehend Thy voluntary self-emptying for us? . . . Who is sufficient to adore and celebrate the whole of Thy ministry of salvation? [2]

The emotional colour of Christian devotion tends to soften this contrast. Yet the deepest possibilities of that devotion are only fully realized when the self-giving of the Eternal in and through a humble life and a criminal's death, and the continuance of that self-giving under the most homely sensible signs—water, bread, and wine—is set over against the unspeakable mystery of the Pure Act, the Divine Will and Love: the fact that "God is God, already apart from His occupation with us . . . not even Jesus Christ and His redemption exhaust God".[3] The greatest passages in the New Testament and the earliest of our liturgical documents alike witness decisively to this profoundly theocentric character of primitive Christian worship; its awed sense of the vast Divine Action, its Apocalyptic insistence on the eternal significance of Jesus, the Lamb "slain from the foundation of the world", its constant other-worldly reference to "the deep things of God". The Eternal Father,

[1] e.g. in the Scottish Episcopal rite.

[2] Liturgy of the Syrian Jacobites. Linton, *Twenty-five Consecration Prayers*, p. 47.

[3] Von Hügel, *The Life of Prayer*, p. 9.

the Divine Word, and the Holy Spirit are indeed conceptions already present in Hebrew religion; but the supernatural realities which they convey are newly disclosed "in Christ". That aspect of the unfathomable Godhead which is turned to man in love, is for the first time fully experienced in Him. He is, as Brunner puts it, "God's own Word about Himself";[1] and in and through the life which He sets going, the holy and creative Spirit of that same God Whose Reality is beyond our conceiving is disclosed to us, in His besetting action and intimate pressure on the soul. Thus Catholic faith proposes to our devotion three equal Objects which yet are One, "the glory equal, the majesty co-eternal": or rather, perhaps, three sidelong disclosures of a Reality transcending all objects and all disclosures, and in Its Nature inaccessible to men.

In practice, of course, the equality of this triune revelation of Reality is seldom observed. For many Christians, devotion to Our Lord's Person is the sum of worship; and this obscures the fact that His Humanity is only to be adored, because in it the Eternal Word of the Godhead is uttered within time. That living and realistic devotion to the Holy Spirit—the direct source and cause of all the experiences of religion—which was the inspiration of the primitive Church, and which the ancient hymns to the Spirit so grandly express, has lost its place; and our total Christian response to the rich self-disclosure of God is gravely impoverished by this. But it remains true that the full possibilities of Christian worship are only realized when it is based on the mysterious and far-reaching formula which binds together the eternal and temporal worlds, "Glory be to the Father, through the Son, in Holy Spirit."[2] This truth rules the Divine Liturgy of the Eastern Church, where "the ascription of praise to the most Holy Trinity, like a uniting thread, runs through

[1] E. Brunner, *The Mediator*, p. 238.

[2] The most ancient form of the doxology.

the whole; beginning and ending each act."[1] It is the real foundation of the mighty Christian cultus, with its many shrines and chapels grouped round the focal point where Divine love and human love meet.

That which is primary for the Christian in this cultus, at least as he moves towards fulness of worship, is the self-giving of the Absolute God—"the love which the Father has us-ward",—flowing out unceasingly to His creation, to evoke from that creation an answering movement of love. This Johannine account of the relation between God and man is the only one which makes any sense of Christian worship. Indeed, the education of the worshipping soul chiefly consists in a deepening realization of all that is implied in it; and so his own growth in wide-spreading love. For the creative Charity of God, as experienced by man, is a redemptive force. It comes into human life in Christ, His Spirit, His Church, His sacraments, and His saints, not to inform but to transform; to rescue from the downward pull which is felt throughout the natural order, to reform, energize, and at last sanctify the souls of men, making those rescued souls in their turn part of the redeeming organism through which the salvation of the world shall be achieved. Christianity recognizes that man needs something done to him which only the action of God can do, if he is ever to be capable of Eternal Life; and that this something is done to him not as any part of the economy of creation, but out of the boundless supernatural Charity of God. This is the second truth which rules its worship and it is this which gives that worship the persistent note of humble gratitude and contrite love, which is heard even in its greatest outbursts of adoring delight. "Not as one worthy but looking only to Thy goodness, I lift up my voice unto Thee!"[2]

Thus for the Christian, standing in awed and grateful

[1] N. Gogol, *Meditations on the Divine Liturgy*, p. 29.
[2] *Liturgy of St. James.*

worship before the loving-kindness of the Eternal, thanksgiving, Eucharist, must be the prevailing colour of devotion. And in that thanksgiving, that hallowing of the name of God, he dares, according to the most ancient precedent, to associate himself with that whole spiritual universe, which exists to declare the ineffable glory of the Godhead; as if he were dimly aware that in his worship man is taking his small part in a cosmic mystery too great for his mind to grasp, yet near enough for his soul to apprehend.

> Before the glorious seat of thy Majesty, O Lord, and the exalted throne of thine honour, and the awful judgment seat of thy burning love, and the absolving altar which thy commands have set up and the place where thy glory dwelleth, we thy people and the sheep of thy fold do kneel with thousands of the cherubim singing Alleluia, and many times ten thousand seraphim and archangels acclaiming thine holiness, worshipping, confessing and praising thee, at all times, O Lord of all.[1]

II

The Christian, then, looks out upon a metaphysical landscape of almost unbearable grandeur which compels him to an awestruck adoration. But within that landscape, bathed in the light of charity, he sees in its full and touching beauty the specific object of his worship. This specific object is not simply the human Figure of the Incarnate, the "historic Jesus", but the Eternal Godhead Who here utters His Word within the human arena and stoops to the human level; and Whose inmost nature that Figure reveals to men. Certainly that which stands out in Christian worship, gives it its special colour, and is commonly most attractive to the religious mind, is devotion to Christ, in His Person, life, teaching, or sacramental presence. Here, in the paradox of

[1] *Nestorian Liturgy of the Holy Apostles Adai and Mari.*

the Cross, the self-given Messiah dying to redeem humanity and living for evermore, it finds a focus for adoring love: here, too, the Infinite is seen condescending to the finite, and the Eternal for which we thirst is revealed in time. Here, as Von Hügel puts it, God "gave us the rampart of His tender strong humanity against the crushing opposition of the pure time-and-space-less Eternal and Absolute of Himself".[1] But the real splendour of Catholic devotion, its combination of spaciousness and transcendency with homely and intimate love, is missed unless there is a remembrance of that unconditioned glory which enters our conditioned world through this narrow door.

> While all things abode in tranquil silence and the night was in the midst of her swift course, thine Almighty Word, O Lord, leapt down out of thy royal throne. Alleluia![2]

It is this constant recognition of the unmanifest Eternal "in which nothing is flitting but all is at once present"[3] irradiating and exceeding its manifestation in time, which makes the early Liturgies the greatest of all embodiments of Christian worship: for devotion soon becomes petty and even cosy, turns back from self-oblation to self-consolation, where there is no acknowledgment of the august realities of faith.

> It is meet and right to praise, to hymn, to glorify thee the uncreated Father of the only-begotten Jesus Christ. We praise thee, O uncreated God, who art unsearchable, ineffable, incomprehensible by any created substance. We praise thee who art known of thy Son, the only-begotten; who through him art spoken of and interpreted and made known to created nature. We praise thee who knowest the Son and revealest to the Saints the glories

[1] *Selected Letters*, p. 93.

[2] *Sarum Breviary*. Antiphon to the Benedictus: Octave of the Nativity.

[3] St. Augustine, *Confessions*, Bk. XI, cap. 11.

that are about him: who art known of thy begotten Word, and art brought to the sight and interpreted to the understanding of the Saints. We praise thee, O unseen Father, provider of immortality. Thou art the fount of life, the fount of light, the fount of all grace and all truth, O lover of men, O lover of the poor, who reconcilest thyself to all, and drawest all to thyself through the advent of thy beloved Son.[1]

This double orientation to the natural and the supernatural, testifying at once to the unspeakable otherness of God transcendent and the intimate nearness of God incarnate, is felt in all the various expressions of genuine Christian worship. The monk or nun rising to recite the Night Office that the Church's praise of God may never cease, and the Quaker waiting in silent assurance on the Spirit given at Pentecost; the ritualist, ordering with care every detail of a complicated ceremonial that God may be glorified thereby, and the old woman content to boil her potatoes in the same sacred intention; the Catholic burning a candle before the symbolic image of the Sacred Heart or confidently seeking the same Divine Presence in the tabernacle, and the Methodist or Lutheran pouring out his devotion in hymns to the Name of Jesus; the Orthodox bowed down in speechless adoration at the culminating moment of the Divine Mysteries, and the Salvationist marching to drum and tambourine behind the banner of the Cross—all these are here at one. Their worship is conditioned by a concrete fact; the stooping down of the Absolute to disclose Himself within the narrow human radius, the historical incarnation of the Eternal Logos within time. The primary declaration of Christianity is not "This Do" but "This Happened"—indeed, is happening still, since the path of incarnation remains open, and Christ lives and acts in His Body, the Church, and gives Himself in its sacraments.

[1] *Bishop Sarapion's Prayer-Book*, ed. J. Wordsworth, p. 60.

And the primary Christian response to this stupendous proclamation is and must be *Venite adoremus*. This is the " short point " about Christian worship ; and must be given priority over all its special forms and expressions. Though it is true of this worship as a whole that " here elephants can swim, and lambs can wade ", still the deep things of God are implied even in the devotional shallows, and are always present in the Church's liturgic life. That life centres on His eternal Being, as self-disclosed to man through man in the Incarnation ; meets and adores " the Dayspring from on high " which has entered our arena to tabernacle among men. This is the theological justification of all Christocentric worship ; which is, when rightly understood, not an alternative to pure theistic devotion but a special form of it.

> " For," says Bérulle, " the name, the greatness, the virtue, the dignity, and the majesty of God, in so far as these are communicable to the creature, reside and repose in this Humanity. God joins it to Himself, quickens it in Himself, and makes it consubsistent with His Divinity. And because of this, when it is adored, God is adored in it, and when it speaks, when it moves, God is speaking and moving, and its footsteps should be kissed and its words should be heard as being the steps and the speech of God. . . . thus God the Incomprehensible makes Himself to be comprehended in this Humanity, God the Ineffable makes Himself heard in the voice of His Incarnate Word, and God the Invisible makes Himself visible in the flesh which He has united with the nature of Eternity ; and God, terrible in His resplendent grandeur, makes Himself felt in His gentleness, His kindness, His humanity."[1]

Thus Christian worship is focussed on the eternalization of a historical fact, accepted as the revealing medium of divine truth : and this means that each phase and aspect of this historical fact, this unique life—each state and act and

[1] Bérulle, *Œuvres*, pp. 216–18. Quoted by H. Bremond, *Histoire Littéraire*, Vol. III, p. 53.

word of Jesus, in the language of religion, the "mysteries of His life"—carries spiritual significance; points beyond itself, and opens for the believer a door upon Eternity. Each is a disclosure of the Logos, and therefore an invitation to worship. Hence the paradoxical union of the transcendental and the homely which is so characteristic of Christian devotion; its power of weaving the whole world of things—from the ox and ass of the Christmas crib, to the wood and iron of Calvary—into its worship. It shows its profundity in the ease and completeness with which it does this; linking the opening of the heavens, the "leaping down of the Eternal Word" with the child in the manger, and the awful phrases of the *Sanctus* with the breaking of bread. The dangers which haunt this type of devotion, its too frequent relapse into phantasy and sentimentalism, are obvious; yet it still remains true that here, the personal and intimate devotion to One who has disclosed in His own person the character of God and the meaning of sacrifice, brings a deepening adoration of that Infinite God Who thus reveals Himself to men—"by love made visible, we are caught up to the Invisible Love".[1]

From all this certain consequences follow. Since Christian belief, and Christian experience, declare the richness and variousness of the simple Divine Nature—the triune Reality of God Transcendent, God Manifest, and God Immanent—so they endorse the richness and variousness of man's response. They have a place, and should have a great place, for the absolute, the non-utilitarian, the utterly adoring temper of the soul: the alabaster vase broken, and the precious ointment poured out. No human approach to the Eternal Love can truly claim to be worship, where this essential element is suppressed, and less than our best is given. So the great service, the incense, all that is finest in music, colour, and light, are true expressions of worship. They do not exist for the sake of

[1] *Roman Missal*, Preface for Christmas Day.

the congregation, or because of their devotional appeal. They are the inadequate offerings of creaturely love, as much in place in some remote and unvisited sanctuary as in the crowded aisles of a great parish church. Moreover, as a Lutheran scholar has pointed out, such sensible expression is proper to an incarnational faith.

> Because the historic Incarnation assures us that the most mysterious of invisible facts can become sensible to the soul, man is called to continue the divine work of translating into artistic and other symbols the mystery of the transcendental. Therefore the use of art in worship is not a mere imitation of the creative work of God, nor is it only a homage rendered to Christ; by giving an embodiment to invisible realities, it continues the Incarnation of the Word.[1]

Yet over against this, all Christian attempts at a splendour and beauty which shall incarnate something of our reverent delight in the splendour and beauty of God, and witness to His penetration of time and space, must be balanced by at least an equal recognition of the bareness and humility through which His approach was made to us, and the hopeless inadequacy of created beauty, as a medium for the disclosure of the secret of the Uncreate. The bareness of the meeting-house, the poor stripped chapel, bring their own witness to the Holy; as exceeding all symbol and image, yet self revealed in and through all that men reject and despise. A worship of the Cross in all its mysterious significance is found in many sanctuaries from which the Crucifix is banned. Again, Christian worship in its fulness should include and harmonize all the various phases of our human experience. It has room for the extremes of awestruck adoration and penitent love, humble demand and inward assurance. All levels of life and action are relevant to it; for they are covered and sanctified by the principle of incarnation.

[1] Will, *Le Culte*, Vol. II, p. 498.

It can therefore weave every detail of the daily routine into the devotional life. It is thoroughly sacramental; and shows its true quality, not by an increasing abstraction and other-worldliness, but by an ever-deepening recognition of the sacredness and inexhaustible meaning of homely things. Especially a deep realism as regards human imperfection and sin, and also human suffering and struggle, is at the very heart of the Christian response to God; which if it is to tally with the Christian revelation of disinterested love as summed up in the Cross, must include the element of hardness, cost, and willing pain. It is this sacrificial suffering, this deliberate endurance of hardship for the sake of the Unseen, which gives nobility and depth to worship. The costly renunciations and total self-stripping of the consecrated life contribute something to the Church's oblation, without which her reasonable and holy sacrifice would not be complete. The "altar of the Cross" is no idle phrase; but reminds us that Christianity is a sacrificial religion, and that Christian worship is unintelligible if we eliminate the tension which is inherent in it, and the unconditioned self-offering by which it is crowned.

From all this it follows that the demand for a purely spiritual cultus is one that can never be made by Christianity; committed by its very nature to a belief in the visible as vehicle of the invisible—to history, personality, sacraments, and sensible signs, as channels of God's communion with man, and body as well as soul as part of man's offering to God. Here then, those who feel a fastidious dislike for some of the more crude and unlovely expressions of our poor human worship, are warned against a critical attitude which may easily degenerate into priggishness. As the figure of Christ stands on the frontier of two worlds, so both worlds—and indeed all levels of those worlds—must play their part in a truly incarnational worship. Neither the silent and formless communion of spirit with Spirit, nor the richest and most dramatic of rituals, lies outside the frontiers of Christian devotion, or is sufficient by itself to cover the ground. For this devotion, sharing in that tension between the Eternal and the successive which is inherent in our mysterious life, requires and uses the constant collaboration of spirit and sense—all the resources of symbol and sacrament, all the creations of the poetic faculty, and all the insights of the contemplative soul. Since it is a response evoked by the self-disclosure of the Holy, and this disclosure was made to human sense as well as to human soul, it will be the response of man in his wholeness, accepting and using the resistance and inequalities of life as material for the expression of sacrificial love. Every act which reveals God, and every movement of surrender to God is a part of it. Yet all these still leave its final secret unexpressed.

III

Since the Christian revelation is in its very nature historical—God coming the whole way to man, and discovered and adored within the arena of man's life at one point in time, in and through the Humanity of Christ—it follows that all the historical events and conditions of Christ's life form part of the vehicle of revelation. Each of them mediates God, disclosing some divine truth or aspect of divine love to us. Here lies the importance of the Christian year, with its recurrent memorials of the Birth, the Manhood, the Death and the Triumph of Jesus, as the framework of the Church's ordered devotion. By and in this ancient sequence, with its three great moments of Epiphany, Easter and Pentecost, its detailed demonstration in human terms of the mysteries of Incarnation and Redemption, the Christian soul is led out through succession to a contemplation of the eternal action of God. In Christ, and therefore in all the states and acts of Christ, history and eternity meet.

Here, in One "who lived and died and is alive for evermore" the worshipper adores the abiding God, self-revealed among men. "His resplendent figure lights up the whole liturgy."[1] Moreover, since in Christ the Christian sees God acting, each phase of His life is to be regarded as a theophany, and has a sacred significance. It is the expression of an interior state directly produced by God, a necessary part of the redemptive action of God; and so invites a particular acknowledgment in worship.[2]

> "This truth," says Bérulle, "obliges us to treat the deeds and mysteries of Jesus, not as things past and finished but as things living and present, and even eternal, from which we too must gather a fruit present and eternal."[3]

This doctrine may seem too abstract to affect the common course of Christian devotion. Yet it has great importance; for it gives an explanation, agreeable to theology, of a persistent trend in that worship both in the East and the West, which is otherwise easily discredited as the work of religious sentimentalism. We cannot enter a Catholic or an Orthodox Church, without finding ourselves confronted by a type of devotion entirely concentrated on the events and phases of the life of Jesus, especially the circumstances of His infancy and His death; which is part and parcel of historic Christian worship, and therefore even in its crudest forms demands our sympathy and respect. The ikon or image of the Virgin and her Child; in the West the Christmas crib, the "stations" of

[1] Cabrol, *Liturgical Prayer*, p. 171.

[2] So, in the Divine Liturgy of the Orthodox Church, the whole movement of the service is correlated with the successive phases of the life of Jesus. The solemn preparation of the elements behind the closed doors of the sanctuary commemorates His humble birth and hidden childhood; the Liturgy of the Catechumens, centred on the ceremonial proclamation of the Gospel, His public ministry. The Liturgy of the Faithful, with its "great entrance" of the Offering and acts of oblation, consecration, and communion shadows forth the awful mysteries of the Passion and Risen Life.

[3] Bérulle, *Œuvres*, p. 1052.

the Passion, and the Crucifix ; in the East, the glorious and triumphant figure of the Risen Christ—these attract a devotion which finds here the focus of a genuine worship, an open and visible path leading to the invisible God, yet seldom pauses to ask why this should be so. The reason, says Bérulle, is that the living Christ disclosed and still discloses to the Christian soul, by these mysteries of His earthly life, the supernatural dispositions, the grace, and the love which are always living, present, and active in eternity. As it is God Who in and through this human life utters His Word and reaches out to men ; so in each phase and moment of this human life, He shows something of His beauty and generosity.

> " Let us," says Bérulle, " take an example. The childhood of the Son of God was a transient state, the circumstances of this childhood are past, He is no longer a child ; but there is a divine something in the Mystery which endures in heaven and which works a kind of grace like itself in certain souls upon earth . . . and it is by this kind of grace, that the Mysteries of Jesus Christ, His childhood, His sufferings, and the rest, continue and live upon earth, until the end of the world."[1]

So, the homely pieties of the Christian year, directed as they are to the successive phases of the Divine redeeming action in history, point beyond themselves, and witness to those profound spiritual realities which transcend history and yet give history its significance—" the divine, holy, spotless, immortal, heavenly, life-giving, awful Mysteries of Christ ".[2] Hence their value as vehicles of God's continuing self-communication and man's response. Hence even in their most naïve expression, they must never be despised by us : for they are a necessary part of that distinct revelation of the Holy to which Christian worship is the creature's answering movement of gratitude and love. Is it not therefore surprising that emphasis upon the Christian year is

[1] *Loc. cit.*, p. 1053. [2] *Liturgy of St. John Chrysostom.*

common to all forms of Christian traditional worship; and has, especially in the East, a deep mystical significance.

> It is not merely a commemoration of the events of the Gospel or other events in the Church's life, in an artistic form. It is also an actualization of these facts, their renewal upon earth. The Christmas service does not merely commemorate the birth of Christ. In it Christ is truly born in a mystery, as at Easter He rises again. So with the transfiguration, the entry into Jerusalem, the mystery of the Last Supper, the passion, burial, and ascension of Christ. . . . The life of the Church in her liturgy, discloses to our senses the continuing mystery of the Incarnation. The Lord still lives in the Church, under that same form in which He was once manifest on earth, and which exists eternally; and it is the function of that Church to make those sacred memories living, so that we again witness and take part in them.[1]

For another reason, too, devotion to the Mysteries of the Gospel must form an integral part of the cultus; namely, their educative value. Since everyone, whatever his vocation, is obliged to reproduce the common curve of human life in its passage through time—to be born, to grow, make choices and accept responsibilities, form some human relationships, take some place in the social order, to meet hardship, difficulty and disillusion, to suffer, and at last to die—it follows that all have in this inevitable sequence of experiences something which can be transformed and directed Godwards; or can, in other words, be turned into worship. And it will be through the adoring contemplation of an actual life, so near his own, yet so entirely transcending it, that man will learn to do this best. So, in that devout commemoration of the successive Mysteries of the life of Jesus, from Christmas to Easter and to their consummation in Pentecost, on which the liturgical year of the Church is based, all the phases of human experience are lit up by the

[1] S. Boulgakoff, *L'Orthodoxie*, p. 180.

radiance of eternity and brought into relation with the inexhaustible revelation of God in the flesh: giving the Christian a model he can never equal but a standard to which he must ever seek to conform. The helplessness and humility of infancy, the long hidden period of discipline and growth, the lonely crisis and choice of the Temptation, above all the heart-shaking events of Holy Week, Easter, and the Forty Days—all these become disclosures of the Supernatural made through and in man, and therefore having a direct application to man's need and experience. Each shows the Divine self-giving from a different angle; and so asks from man a humble gratitude and a generous response.

IV

Arising from its incarnational character, and indeed closely connected with it, is the fact that Christian worship is always directed towards the sanctification of life. All worship has a creative aim, for it is a movement of the creature in the direction of Reality; and here, the creative aim is that total transfiguration of the created order in which the incarnation of the Logos finds its goal. Christian worship, then, is to be judged by the degree in which it tends to Holiness; since this is the response to the pressure of the Holy which is asked of the Church and of the soul. The Christian is required to use the whole of his existence as sacramental material; offer it and consecrate it at every point, so that it may contribute to the Glory of God. Historical Christianity, with its appointed prayers for each period of the day and night, its blessings of every meal and every activity, its solemn consecrations of birth and marriage, its rites for the restoring of the sinful and the sanctifying of sickness and death, its loving care for the departed, following the rhythm of human existence from its beginning to its apparent end and beyond, has always shown itself sharply aware of this. These various blessings and dedications, even the smallest and most homely, are true to the deepest meanings of the Catholic faith. Again and again they bring the imperfect human creature and his changing experiences into direct and conscious relation with God the Perfect, and remind him of the supernatural aim of human life.

Yet this sanctifying of the natural life draws its real significance and obligation from a deeper source. The actual and visible worship of the Christian in its total range of symbolic expression must represent and also nourish that virtual and interior worship of which all his thoughts, words, and deeds—and beyond them, the obscure movements of his spirit—are more and more to form part. Ever more conscious as his inner life matures of that "sinfulness" which confuses and slows down his Godward life, he knows that contrition and purification must play their part—and indeed a great part—in his response to God. "Glory be to Thee: have mercy upon me!" The life of worship swings between those poles. Set, as he is, between two worlds, the unseen and the seen, man's worship must be redemptive in respect of his sinful natural life, and also creative in respect of his still unachieved supernatural life, for it looks towards eternity: and this of course means sacrifice. Every time he draws near the altar of God, he brings his whole self in oblation; that it may become part of the mystical body which is the organ of God's redemptive action in the world.

> "Grant, O Lord," says a Maronite morning prayer, "that I may give thee choice gifts; three lighted and dazzling torches; my spirit, my soul, and my body. My spirit to the Father, my soul to the Son, my body to the Holy Ghost. O Father, sanctify my spirit! O Son, sanctify my soul! O Holy Ghost, sanctify my sin-soiled body!"[1]

[1] *Prayers from the Eastern Liturgies.* Compiled by D. Attwater, p. 49.

The imperfection of his offering must always keep the Christian in humility, and colour his adoration with penitence; yet the fact that he is asked for it must transfigure contrition with joy. Though God in His eternal perfection is the one object and cause of his worship, and nothing that he can do can make him fit to raise his eyes towards that splendour; yet in so far as he can, he too is required to incarnate something of this Eternal Perfection within his earthly life. He is a child of God, a shrine of the creative Spirit. He worships One Who stands over against him in holiness, yet ever works within him by the living pressures of grace. So response to those pressures, driving him towards all possible objects of devotedness and care, small and great—in other words, a ceaseless moral striving, a steadfast effort to please God—must be for him a part of worship, in so far as he is a true part of the living Church. Each choice which he makes, each exercise of his limited freedom will either glorify or not glorify God; therefore he cannot divorce faith from works, or adoration from ethics. To worship well is to live well. His whole being, physical, mental, and spiritual, is required to be subject to the transforming action of God, and it is his privilege to co-operate in this redemptive task. His prayer too must contribute to that end. Humble supplication, passive self-abandonment, and loving adoration will all play their part; for Christian worship is in itself a purifying force. Entering it, we enter a tide of the Spirit which sets Godwards; and sanctification is accomplished in the soul in proportion to the extent in which it is self-given to that movement of love. Man is pressed towards the worship of the Holy, so that bit by bit he may be transformed by the Spirit into the likeness of that which he adores, and take his ordained place in the Communion of Saints—not for his own sake, but for the Glory of God.

This idea of the sanctification of life, as the creative goal towards which Christian worship must tend, is found under different forms of expression in all types of Christianity; and enters deeply into their worship. Thus in modern Catholicism, both Roman and Anglican, sanctification is regarded as above all the work of the Church, the Body of Christ, and the chief reason of her existence; and is closely bound up with her sacramental system, the major channel of the Grace of God. The striving for personal holiness, therefore, finds its devotional embodiment in the practice of frequent communion, and adoration of Christ's Eucharistic Presence in His Church. But this is only one aspect of a total humble correspondence with the Divine self-giving, in which both moral and spiritual factors are involved.[1] Here sanctification is thought of in close connection with the deep mystery of redemptive suffering; and the focus of contemplation is the Passion and the Cross. In Orthodoxy, which has never lost the cosmic outlook of the early Church and looks towards the transfiguration of the whole created order as the fulfilment of the Christian promise, the emphasis of Christo-centric worship is placed not on the Crucifix but on the risen and triumphant Christ, subduing the world to the rule of love. Here sanctification is above all the work of the Holy Spirit, with man's co-operation; and crowns that mystery of creation of which it is a part.

Evangelical Christianity is equally clear that the "offering of a pure heart" is an essential part of the worship of God, and perfection the ordained end of that which conversion began. Here, indeed, the moral preoccupation sometimes tends to become excessive; and obscures the purely religious element which gives it significance. Concentration on the

[1] The Catholic view is well given by Karl Adam (*The Spirit of Catholicism*, revised edition, p. 213). "The sanctifying action of the Church apparently moves along two distinct lines, being sacramental and mystical on the one hand, and moral and ascetical on the other. In reality these two lines do not run parallel to each other, still less in opposite directions; they run in each other and are mutually interlaced. There is no sanctity in the Church which is not sacramental, and there is no sacramental act which is not at the same time a striving after sanctity."

Ethos takes the place which rightly belongs to adoration of the *Logos :* and man, intent upon the moral struggle, forgets the supernatural purpose which that moral struggle is meant to serve, and with it, that patient and genial tolerance of our many levelled human nature, which is a faint reflection of the compassionate love of God. This is the vice of Puritanism and of all types of perfectionist piety. The objective worship of traditional Christianity, with its constant remembrance of the Eternal Perfection of God, here provides a valuable corrective : reminding us that self-fulfilment—even in the moral sphere—is at best only a preparation for that self-loss which is the consummation of all worship.

V

Finally, Christian worship is never a solitary undertaking. Both on its visible and invisible sides, it has a thoroughly social and organic character. The worshipper, however lonely in appearance, comes before God as a member of a great family ; part of the Communion of Saints, living and dead. His own small effort of adoration is offered " in and for all ". The first words of the Lord's Prayer are always there to remind him of his corporate status and responsibility, in its double aspect. On one hand, he shares the great life and action of the Church, the Divine Society ; however he may define that difficult term, or wherever he conceives its frontiers to be drawn. He is immersed in that life, nourished by its traditions, taught, humbled, and upheld by its saints.[1]

[1] The custom of invoking those saints, found from primitive times in the Eastern and Western Church, is a special aspect of this spiritual solidarity ; an appeal as it were from the struggling individual for family support. The obvious fact that it opens a door to superstition and sentimentalism, and often confuses history and mythology need not blind us to the more important fact that it deepens family feeling, upholds the family standard, and bridges the gap between the living and the dead. To " bless God in His Saints " would therefore seem to be a reasonable part of an incarnational theism.

His personal life of worship, unable for long to maintain itself alone, has behind it two thousand years of spiritual culture, and around it the self-offerings of all devoted souls. Further, his public worship, and commonly his secret devotion too, are steeped in history and tradition ; and apart from them, cannot be understood. There are few things more remarkable in Christian history than the continuity through many vicissitudes and under many disguises of the dominant strands in Christian worship. On the other hand the whole value of this personal life of worship abides in the completeness with which it is purified from all taint of egotism, and the selflessness and simplicity with which it is added to the common store. Here the individual must lose his life to find it ; the longing for personal expression, personal experience, safety, joy, must more and more be swallowed up in Charity. For the goal alike of Christian sanctification and Christian worship is the ceaseless self-offering of the Church, in and with Christ her head, to the increase of the glory of God.

CHAPTER V

THE PRINCIPLES OF CORPORATE WORSHIP

I

IT follows from what has been said at the end of the last chapter, that the worshipping life of the Christian, whilst profoundly personal, is essentially that of a person who is also a member of a group. In this, of course, it reproduces on spiritual levels the twofold character of his natural life; disciplined and supported by the social framework, to which each of its members has a personal responsibility and makes a personal contribution, but inwardly free. The Christian as such cannot fulfil his spiritual obligations in solitude. He forms part of a social and spiritual complex with a new relation to God; an organism which is quickened and united by that Spirit of supernatural charity which sanctifies the human race from above, and is required to incarnate something of this supernatural charity in the visible world. Therefore even his most lonely contemplations are not merely a private matter; but always to be regarded in their relation to the purpose and action of God Who incites them, and to the total life of the Church. The terms in which Plato admonished the young citizen of his real situation are appropriate to many an unwilling institutionalist; merely replacing the word "Universe" by the word "Church".

> The Ruler of the universe has ordered all things with a view to the excellence and preservation of the whole, and

> each part, as far as may be, does and suffers what is proper to it. And one of these portions of the universe is thine own, unhappy man, which, infinitesimal though it be, is ever striving towards the whole ; and you do not seem to be aware that this and every other creation is in order that the life of the whole may be blessed ; and that you are created for the sake of the whole, and not the whole for the sake of you. For every physician and skilled artist does all things for the sake of the whole, directing his effort towards the common good, executing the part for the sake of the whole, and not the whole for the sake of the part. And you are annoyed, because you are ignorant how what is best in your case for the All turns out best for you also, because of the power of your common origin.[1]

The corporate life of worship has therefore an importance far exceeding the personal salvation or blessedness of the individual worshippers, or the devotional opportunity which it gives to them. It stands for the total orientation of life towards God ; expressed both through stylized liturgical action, and spontaneous common praise. Moreover the personal relation to God of the individual—his inner life—is guaranteed and kept in health by his social relation to the organism, the spiritual society, the Church. What is best for the All, as Plato says, turns out best for him too. It checks religious egotism, breaks down devotional barriers, obliges the spiritual highbrow to join in the worship of the simple and ignorant, and in general confers all the supporting and disciplinary benefits of family life. Therefore, corporate and personal worship, though in practice one commonly tends to take precedence of the other, should complete, reinforce, and check each other. Only where this happens, indeed, do we find in its perfection the normal and balanced life of full Christian devotion ; with its vast metaphysical reference, its noble historic framework, its deep tenderness,

[1] Plato, *Laws*, 903 B.

its ordered beauty, its daily and seasonal rhythm, its sacred intimacies and willing activities, its self-oblivious spirit of oblation before God and generous fellowship with men, its sanctifying power. No one soul—not even the greatest saint—can fully apprehend all that this has to reveal and demand of us, or perfectly achieve this balanced richness of response. That response must be the work of the whole Church; within which souls in their infinite variety each play a part, and give that part to the total life of the Body.

The Christian liturgy—taking this word now in its most general sense—is the artistic embodiment of this social yet personal life. Here we are not concerned with its historic origins, its doctrinal implications, or the chief forms it has assumed in the course of its development: but simply with its here-and-now existence, value, and meaning as the ordered framework of the Church's corporate worship, the classic medium by which the ceaseless adoring action of the Bride of Christ is given visible and audible expression. It is plain that the living experience of this whole Church, visible and invisible, past and present, stretched out in history and yet poised on God, must set the scene for Christian worship; not the poor little scrap of which any one soul, or any sectional group, is capable. Thus there must be a traditional worshipping act of the Church, a great liturgical life, of which the sectional worship of its various groups and branches will form a part, and to which the many-levelled action of its isolated members with all their varying moods and insights contributes; an act which includes and harmonizes all apparent differences, looking ever more and more towards that perfected heavenly life of adoration where these differences vanish in the single movement of all loving souls towards "the Abiding, the Prevenient, the Beginning and the End and Crown of light and life and love".[1]

[1] F. von Hügel, *The Reality of God*, p. 18.

This total liturgical life of the *Corpus Christi* is not merely a collection of services, offices, and sacraments. Deeply considered, it is the sacrificial life of Christ Himself; the Word indwelling His Church, gathering in His eternal priestly action the small Godward movements, sacrifices, and aspirations of "all the broken and the meek",[1] and acting through those ordered signs and sacraments by means of these His members on earth. Whether this Church be given hard and fast juridical boundaries, as in Roman Catholicism, or is seen as a group of autonomous families, as by Anglicans and Orthodox, or felt to be independent of visible expression, as by Quakers and other Independents, the principle is the same: the eternal self-offering of Christ to God in and through this mystical body. Hence the corporate worship of the Church is not simply that of an assembly of individuals who believe the same things, and therefore unite in doing the same things. It is real in its own right; an action transcending and embracing all the separate souls taking part in it. The individual as such dies to his separate selfhood—even his spiritual selfhood—on entering the Divine Society: is "buried in baptism" and reborn as a living cell of the Mystical Body of Christ. St Paul insists again and again on this transfer of status as the essential point about Christianity.[2] Therefore the response to God of this whole Body, this supernatural organism, in life and in worshipping acts, is of cardinal importance; and since this response is to take place on earth as in heaven, it must have its here-and-now embodiment—inadequate as this must always be to the supernatural situation it shows forth. Nor should we expect simplicity, clarity, uniformity, to be the marks of this action as seen from our point of view; but rather great diversity of level

[1] F. von Hügel, *Letters to a Niece*, p. 25.

[2] Cf. Ephesians i. 22, 23; ii. 19–22; Colossians ii. 10, 13; iii. 1–3, etc.

and function within that one great organism of which no man knows the limits but God alone.[1]

We come down from these thoughts, to consider the outward forms taken by this liturgic life of the Christian Society. Here the Eucharist and the Daily Office stand out from the beginning as the classic expressions of the Church's ordered worship. But we do not get a real view of the situation, unless we add to them another and very different form of expression ; the free, enthusiastic, unstylized group worship, the spontaneous response to the stirrings of the Spirit, which began in the childhood of the Church and—now for the most part separated from her liturgical action—has continued in various expressions ever since, sometimes going underground for long periods but sooner or later breaking out with disconcerting vigour and freedom. Troeltsch's well-known division of Christian institutions into the " sect-type " and " church-type ", is doubtless too absolute in the form in which he states it. But it throws some light on the meaning of these two strands in Christian corporate worship, and the constant tension between them. The conservative Church, organic, orderly, authoritative, embracing within her family life all types and levels of souls ; universal in her scope, liturgical and sacramental in her expression, and looking towards the " Beatitude of Supernature " as the crown of the graded structure of her worship.[2] The sect, the intensive, vigorous group, realistic and unconventional in expression, thorough-going in its ethical demands, again and again revolting against the formalism and authority of the institution, and seeking to recapture the enthusiasm, freedom, and personal spontaneity of the charismatic period of the Church.

Troeltsch rightly observes that the origin of this dualism

[1] 1 Corinthians xii.

[2] E. Troeltsch, *Social Teaching of the Christian Churches*, Vol. I, p. 347.

is to be found in the very constitution of primitive Christianity;[1] for we get no true picture of Christian worship in the Apostolic Age, unless we remember that the primitive meeting had two parts, destined as they developed to represent two contrasting types of worship.[2] There was first the "breaking of bread"; the solemn and increasingly liturgic celebration of the Lord's Supper, in which the Sacrifice of Christ was remembered, and His Risen Presence experienced.[3] There were next those free "spiritual exercises" which witnessed to the new life of the believer, and the presence and direct action of the Holy Spirit in the Church. These included in the Apostolic Age the "charismatic phenomena" of inspiration, ecstatic speech or "tongues" and other forms of religious enthusiasm; and also prophecy and teaching—a true and important part of the Godward action of the Church, since by it souls were instructed and enlightened and the Christian life of worship was built up.[4]

Primitive Christian worship was therefore both sacramental and prophetic: and during the early centuries the Church seems to have fluctuated between these ideals. The free and charismatic type with its accompanying difficulties and inconveniences—already manifest in the New Testament[5]—gradually sank into the background of the Christian corporate life. Nevertheless it has never died out, and reappears in every "revival" as a protest against the supposed formality and unreality of the liturgic routine; reasserting the freedom and direct action of the Spirit, the priesthood of the individual, the prophetic office of "preachers of the Word", the call to personal consecration. Wherever the institutional life stiffens and becomes standardized,

[1] *Op. cit.*, p. 333.

[2] See L. Duchesne, *Origins of Christian Worship*, p. 48. Compare Pt. II, cap. X.

[3] 1 Corinthians xi. 23-29.

[4] 1 Corinthians xiv. 4.

[5] 1 Corinthians xii and xiv.

there is a reaction towards that primitive group enthusiasm and prophetic ministry which is described in the New Testament and—even though it sometimes oversteps the bounds of good taste and common sense—is a true part of the Church's Godward life. This is of course the accepted worshipping ideal of many Protestant sects. It has lately reasserted its claims with vigour in connection with the Buchman groups; and has its noblest modern representative in the restrained but genuinely "pneumatic" worship of the Society of Friends waiting upon the Inner Light. Though its subjective temper and impatience of external authority exposes it to many dangers, and it easily assumes unbalanced and extravagant forms—as indeed St Paul already makes plain to us—there seems little doubt that it stands for a genuine and important element in the rich texture of Christian corporate devotion; for here, God's direct action by His Spirit is recognized as a ruling fact of the Church's life, indeed the inexhaustible source of that Church's wisdom and power. This experience of the Spirit's action is assumed as a universally accepted Christian truth by the writer of *Acts*; and is there at least as prominent as the sacramental and ordered worship from which it is now unfortunately isolated, and which should steady and complete it. That emphasis on the Ministry of the Word—the sermon or interpretation of the Scriptures, stirring to adoration and godliness, presenting the awful reality and demands of the Holy, and the unlimited generosity of Love—which is so prominent a feature in the religious outlook of the reformed Churches, derives from this prophetic strand in the primitive worship; and is or should be the "completing opposite" of its sacramental trend.

It is a tragedy of the Christian life that almost from the first the prophetic and sacramental tempers have tended to separate. For the Catholic and the Orthodox, as for his Roman and Greek and Jewish forbears, the sacrificial act, the oblation with its completion in communion, as the expressive vehicle of man's response to God, is the very essence of public worship. Here we see cultus, with its antique surroundings of sanctuary, altar, and priest, conservers and transmitters of the ritual tradition ; changing their form, it is true, under the pressure of history, but again and again reasserting their value and power. Here personal initiative tends to be subordinated to the greater action of the Church, regarded as the organ of grace and redemption. But for the many reforming groups and sects which sprang up inside and outside the borders of the Patristic and mediæval Church, and for the Protestant reformers and their descendants, personal experience and personal initiative are of paramount importance. Here the essence of worship is prophetic teaching and spontaneous prayer : the announcement of the Word, and the direct and realistic response of the individual to God. Hence there is a distrust and dislike of the fixed forms and symbolic acts which are required by cultus ; an almost nervous fear of all pattern and mechanism as necessarily involving insincerity.[1] Neither ideal is sufficient in itself to satisfy the full possibilities of man's corporate Godward life : and neither can long maintain itself alone. That Godward life in its wholeness needs and has room for both spontaneity and order, personality and tradition, enthusiasm and mystery, prophecy and sacrifice. The " psalms and spiritual songs " recommended by St Paul —perhaps as an alternative to wilder forms of expression— the " revelations of the Spirit ", the ordered prayer and reading which form an ancient part of the Christian devotional life, and the solemn liturgical " breaking of bread " must all contribute to that total life of adoration in which humanity realizes the freely given Presence of the Holy and makes its

[1] Cf. J. W. Graham, *The Faith of a Quaker*, p. 186 : " A Friends Meeting is, to an ordinary ritual service, very much what a hand-made article is to one made by machinery."

small response. It is therefore of great importance that representatives of these contrasting forms of worship should learn to regard each other with sympathy and respect, and even to practise that difficult degree of generosity, which is willing to be taught by those of whom we do not quite approve. This will only be possible when there is a clear understanding of the part which each plays or should play in the total Christian response to God; and of the fact that this response cannot achieve its full and balanced reality and beauty, unless both order and spontaneity, liturgy and liberty, the ministry of the Word and the ministry of the Sacraments, the work of the prophet and the work of the priest, give it of their best.

> "These two," says Thomas à Kempis, "may be called the two tables set on either side in the spiritual treasury of Holy Church. The one is the table of the holy altar, having this holy bread, that is, the precious body of Christ. The other is the table of the laws of God, containing the holy doctrine, instructing man in the right faith, and leading him into the inward secrecies that are called *Sancta Sanctorum*, where the inward secrets of Scripture be hid and contained."[1]

II

The earliest picture we possess of Christian cultus is the ideal vision of the Apocalypse;[2] and this, when we remember the period from which it comes to us, is astonishing in its liturgical richness.[3] There we already see a developed worship of the whole company of the faithful focussed

[1] *Imitation of Christ*, Bk. IV, cap. 11.

[2] Revelation iv. 2–11; v. 6–14 and vii. 9–17.

[3] I am quite unable to follow those writers who consider that this description is "coloured by the contemporary worship of Greek Gods" (cf. J. W. Graham, *op. cit.*, p. 191). This was surely the last model likely to appeal to the Apocalyptist.

upon the altar. The Object of worship is both transcendent and redemptive ; the Eternal and Omnipotent God " which was and which is and which is to come " and His Word, the Lamb that was slain on the altar of humanity, the self-given sacrament of Divine Love. The *Sanctus*, which the Church is to carry through the centuries as the essential formula of her Eucharistic prayer, is already heard as the song of the whole created order : for this worship, beheld in its intensive form in the heavenly world, expands to include the cosmos, giving " glory and honour and thanks " to that Will by which all things were, and were created. Everyone is doing something ; but all in disciplined subservience to the universal tide of adoration which sets towards " God and the Lamb ". The sensible accompaniments of an ordered cultus—music, song, incense, ritual movements and prostrations—are all there and already taken for granted. The Eucharistic and redemptive references of this sublime picture, its Christocentric characters, are clear ; but no less clear is the influence of Jewish sacrificial ideas. Stretching back to the very beginnings of man's worship, and forward to all that worship implies, it links two religious worlds.

When we consider the date of this document[1] and its inclusion in the New Testament Canon, we can hardly deny that liturgical worship—carrying over and using with no sense of impropriety the rich symbolism of the Temple, and involving the disciplined action of all participating in it—is a true part of primitive Christianity ; at least in ideal, though we may suppose that the circumstances of the early Church seldom allowed that ideal to find adequate expression. Worship is conceived as a sacrifice eternally present at the heart of reality : a Eucharist in which the unceasing *Tersanctus* of the " living creatures " before the throne of God is answered by " every creature which is in heaven and on the earth and such as are in the sea." We understand

[1] Probably about A.D. 95 ; and possibly a little earlier.

better the spirit of the early Eucharist, if we keep this scene in mind; and note its contrast with the touching simplicity of the earliest liturgies, which yet preserve a certain homely likeness to the heavenly vision by their association of the *Sanctus* and the Passion in the Eucharistic prayer. The Orthodox Church has kept in a remarkable degree this conception of the ceaseless and ecstatic worship poured out in heavenly places, as the eternal pattern for Christian worship on earth. The songs of the Cherubim and Seraphim are heard throughout her liturgy; and in her adoration she unites herself again and again with the heavenly hosts, reminding us of all that is involved in a complete response to the great command "*Sursum corda!*"[1]

With this majestic scene to set the standard, we can now look at the chief forms which the common worship of the Church has assumed in the course of her history; the liturgical type centred on the Eucharist, and the free, prophetic, or non-liturgical type, representing the spontaneous religious movements of the group.

And first we have to consider the practical conditions under which men and women can transcend the apparent isolation of the soul and unite in a common act of worship. Here there seem to be three choices. First, there is the corporate silence which covers and unites all the individual acts of devotion, all the levels of fervour and enlightenment. Quaker worship is the best-known representative of this in its pure form. Secondly, there are the worshipping acts which can be performed either by the leader alone, or the leader and trained assistants, in the name of all present, and to which these join their own worship by intention. A Low Mass without communicants, in which the congregation takes no part in the action, but recites the Rosary or other personal prayers, is a good example of this

[1] See below, Pt. II, cap. XII.

type;[1] so, too, is any service in which ceremonies and music are so elaborate as to require professional skill, and exclude the ordinary worshipper from taking an active part. Thirdly there is the ordered ritual, or liturgy; demanding religious action from sense as well as spirit, and so constructed that all present can take some part in that which is done. The choral Parish Eucharist, the Roman Catholic rite of Benediction, the Lutheran *Hochamt*, or any other truly congregational service where the general movement is understood, and hymns, chants, and actions are familiar to all, are representative examples of the third type; so, too, the great Catholic ceremonies of Candlemas, Ash Wednesday, and Holy Week, in which the whole congregation plays its part. Here, the worship is "carried out with the full and intelligent co-operation of all the faithful, each in their several spheres and grades taking their own proper part in the adoration of Almighty God".[2] All three methods, either alone or in combination with each other, have always existed and been practised within Christianity. All are alive to-day, and all have their usefulness and importance, meeting the needs of various occasions and types of soul.

(A) The place of corporate silence is well marked in the early liturgies; and appears to be intimately connected with the development of the collect, or prayer in which the priest or leader gathered up the inarticulate supplications of the faithful and presented them to God.[3]

Sometimes he indicates more or less briefly the general character of the prayer to be made, sometimes merely

[1] It is fair to say that the present liturgic revival in the Roman Catholic Church strongly discourages this method of "assisting" at Mass, and insists upon its corporate character.

[2] W. H. Frere, *Principles of Religious Ceremonial*, p. 28.

[3] The question of the origin of the liturgical collect is a controversial one. But the Roman Missal still retains as part of the Good Friday service the ancient sequence of biddings, silent prayer and collect, to which reference is here made. See below, p. 109

> invites to it. Then silence falls. The faithful take up the attitude of prayer: standing, with lifted arms and outstretched hands. On certain days they kneel, or prostrate themselves with their faces to the ground. Thus they remain for a time praying in silence. Then the voice of the leader is heard gathering up in a few words the prayers which have issued from all hearts; and the congregation unites itself with his action by replying Amen.[1]

Though the Roman Liturgy no longer recognizes in fact the place of such corporate silence, or marks a pause after the ancient invitation to prayer in the Mass, in the Liturgy of St John Chrysostom this element is retained. The silent intercessory action of the priest within the sanctuary is intended to be accompanied by that of the whole congregation, bound together in this concerted movement of supplication and love.

> In wordless prayer, joining in the secret prayer of their pastor, all the people pray for all men and for all good things . . . and when at length the deep wordless prayer of all for all is ended and the choir chants "For all men and women!" then the priest exclaims aloud "And grant unto us with one heart and one mouth to glorify and magnify thy glorious and majestic Name!"[2]

It is obvious that such an ordered use of corporate silence, with all its advantages of freedom, sincerity, and inwardness, must enrich and deepen the worshipping life of the Church; and should never have been allowed to fall into desuetude. Here the secret response of each soul to the one Spirit forms as it were a separate thread in the woven garment of the Bride. But this united act of wordless prayer could never by itself suffice to express that Church's full life of adoration;

[1] Duchesne, *Christian Worship*, p. 107.

[2] Gogol, *Meditations on the Divine Liturgy*, p. 75.

first because it is only appropriate to the spiritually mature,[1] and secondly because—though it lifts the mind and heart to God—it leaves too much of our human nature behind. Here, too, the important reflex effect of symbolic action or expressive voice is neglected ; and thus the individual soul loses the education which it should receive by and through the common vocal worship of the Church.

(B) The second great type of corporate worship escapes some of these disadvantages. Here action and speech are delegated to a person or group ; the congregation uniting itself by intention to that which is done. Thus a focus is provided, and a certain unity of direction is ensured ; and the liturgical action covers and unites the devotion of simple and learned. This very ancient method of prayer is still widely used in various ways in all branches of the Church. It gives to all taking part a certain ordered liberty, and also a certain liturgical support ; and allows the use of language, music, and ceremonial which are beyond the capacity of the average worshipper, though not beyond his appreciation. When the Pilgrim Etheria visited Jerusalem, she found that the psalms were sung by a trained choir ; as indeed they had been in the Temple worship. Cassian tells us that in the monasteries of the Desert Fathers in the fourth century the Psalter, which formed the substance of the common prayer, was read by one voice to which all listened in deep silence and with absorbed attention ; pauses being made for meditation. Such corporate directed silence is still, with certain modifications, the method of Orthodox monasticism. Here the Divine Office is chanted by a choir of monks specially trained for this service, in the presence of the rest of the Community ; each member either following in silence the words of the Office, or joining his own prayer to it by intention. This, too, is the manner of " hearing "

[1] It should be noted that " spiritually mature " and " theologically educated " are not equivalent terms.

or assisting at Low Mass, which is chiefly practised by devout Catholics. Here the unheard and hardly seen sacrificial action of the priest proceeds on its own plane, and independently of the congregation; who are warned by a bell when the high points of the service are reached. They, by intention, unite their prayer and self-oblation to that of the whole Church with Christ its Head; each in his own manner drawing near to God, yet each subordinating his own devotional movement to the whole. So, too, the fixed prayers of the Anglican Day Office—and, still more, the extempore prayers of Free Church worship—are with few exceptions recited by the priest or ministers in the name of all.

(C) In spite of certain real advantages as to inwardness, freedom, and sincerity, which are possessed by forms of common worship that either suppress or delegate all ritual acts and leave the congregation to unhindered private prayer, it is evident that the third type of corporate service —the concerted action in which all take a real part—is a more complete act of adoration, more congenial to the Christian spirit, and also more efficacious for the common life, than the silent Meeting, the splendid ceremony in which all is done by a few professionals, the "hearing" of a semi-audible Low Mass, or docile attention to the Minister's extempore prayer. The brave attempt of the Quakers to combine the best characteristics of public and private devotion by means of their ritual silence, and the high religious value and great attraction of Low Mass for souls of a contemplative type, are only the exceptions which prove this law; and even these carry their own dangers and, save in the most carefully instructed, inevitably tend to a subjective and atomistic piety. Though we may allow that all fill a useful place in the Christian organism, and meet the special needs of various types of soul, all fall short of the ideal in which the group as a worshipping unit lifts up its heart to God, each individual contributing his share. If we have to choose between extreme cases, it is better to stand up and sing " Thine for ever, God of Love ", surrounded by other Christians of all sorts and sizes, from the Mayor and Corporation to the Brownies and Cubs, than to elude this bracing discipline and murmur the same sentiment in a nice, quiet corner of the church. The psychological reasons for this lie on the surface ; but the spiritual reasons are more important to us. The ascending life of worship to which men are invited is destined to become at last the life of charity. This is that " general dance " to which, in the old Cornish carol, Christ calls the soul of man. Thus worship in all its degrees is an education in charity, a purgation of egoism. As it draws nearer God, the Divine Light will itself effect that purification. But long before this the very circumstances of common worship can do much to mortify fastidiousness and religious self-regard.

Moreover, the Church is not a collection of prize specimens, but a flock. Though we cannot return to the family action of the primitive community, the corporate and co-operative ideal must always remain true for Christianity ; and has always controlled the Church's choice of liturgical forms. So in the Apocalyptic vision, the worship is genuinely congregational : an opportunity for the whole Body, sinking differences of understanding and feeling, to join Angels and Archangels, saints and elders, and all the creatures of the earth and sea in praising and glorifying the Holy Name. The *Sanctus* is the prayer of prayers for Christians, and the essential preliminary of Holy Communion, because it is thus world-embracing as well as world-transcending ; and enfolds all levels and kinds of worship in one adoring act. The primitive conception of liturgical worship, as Dr Frere has pointed out, was that of a concerted act of adoration in which everyone, from Bishop to neophyte, should have something to do, in word, gesture, movement, chant, or service ; though not of course necessarily the same thing. He adds that " it is not too much to say that without any doubt this is the only true ideal of Christian worship ".[1] But such joint action is impossible without an agreed pattern, a liturgy ; even though this pattern be of the simplest kind. So now we come to liturgy, as a necessity of the full concerted worship of the Christian group.

[1] *Principles of Religious Ceremonial*, pp. 24, 27.

CHAPTER VI

LITURGICAL ELEMENTS IN WORSHIP

I

THE beginnings of Christian liturgical worship have been traced to the second, if not even the first century; and this can hardly surprise us. As soon as weekly meetings of "those who followed the Way" became part of the discipline of the infant Church, some forms were needed to enable all, literate or not, to take a real part in the worship of God. Three such forms, already familiar in the Synagogue services, seem to have been used almost from the first, and still keep their ancient place in the liturgies of the Church: the litany, the versicle and response, and the psalm or hymn.[1] From these elements—together with the Scripture lections, and the prayers of the priest or leader—the whole liturgic structure has been evolved.

(*a*) The litany, or series of brief acts of prayer and praise with a fixed response, is, according to Heiler,[2] one of the most archaic forms of common worship; and is still found in many tribal rituals. It is a simple and obvious device for securing the attention and united religious action of a group without service-books or ritual knowledge; for all the congregation needs to know is the choral response by which it endorses the leader's prayer. This choral response is always brief, and may be merely Alleluia, Amen, or other mark of assent. Here is the first step towards liturgy; and this appears to be the way in which the psalms were

[1] Cf. P. Batiffol, *History of the Breviary*, cap. I.

[2] *Prayer*, p. 13.

usually recited during the first Christian centuries. The deacon or cantor read, the response of the people following each verse or pair of verses; a method borrowed from synagogue worship.[1] So St Augustine tells us that at the death of St Monica: "Evodius caught up a psalter and began to chant the psalm:

> My song shall be of mercy and judgment
> Unto thee O Lord will I sing,

and the whole household took up the response."[2]

In the Orthodox rite, where the litany still plays an important part, we find it in its richest and most varied form. Here, in the deacon's chain of supplications and the people's united response, accompanying in waves of worship the sacred actions of the priest beyond the screen, we seem to hear the very accent of the Church's ancient congregational prayer.

Deacon. Let us all say from our soul, and from our understanding let us say

℟. Kyrie Eleison!

Deacon. O Lord Almighty, the God of our fathers, we beseech thee hear and have mercy!

℟. Kyrie Eleison!

Deacon. Have mercy upon us, O God, according to thy great mercy; we beseech thee hear, and have mercy.

℟. Kyrie Eleison!

Deacon. For the precious gifts presented, let us beseech the Lord!

℟. Kyrie Eleison!

Deacon. For this holy house and all who enter it with faith, reverence and fear of God, let us beseech the Lord!

℟. Kyrie Eleison!

Deacon. For our deliverance from all affliction, wrath, peril and necessity let us beseech the Lord!

℟. Kyrie Eleison![3]

[1] See below, Pt. II, cap. X.
[2] *Confessions*, Bk. IX, cap. 12.
[3] *Liturgy of St. John Chrysostom*: Offertory Litany.

In the West, where the litany seems at first to have been used chiefly for processional prayer,[1] its range is narrower; though the *Kyrie Eleison* still stands at the beginning of the Mass to remind us of its ancient importance, and in its developed form—as we see it in the Roman Litany of the Saints, and in the litany of the Anglican Prayer Book—it attains great dignity and beauty. But this device reveals its original character and devotional quality most clearly in the short litanies which we find embedded in some of the lesser Eastern rites. So in the Nestorian evening office, a corporate prayer of extreme beauty is achieved, in which the congregational part is yet of the simplest kind.

> With request and beseeching we ask for the Angel of peace and mercy
>
> ℟. From thee O Lord.
>
> Night and day, throughout our life, we ask for continued peace for Thy Church and life without sin
>
> ℟. From thee O Lord.
>
> We ask continual love, which is the bond of perfectness, with the confirmation of the Holy Spirit
>
> ℟. From thee O Lord.
>
> We ask for forgiveness of sins and those things which help our lives and please thy Godhead
>
> ℟. From thee O Lord.
>
> We ask the mercy and compassion of the Lord continually and at all times
>
> ℟. From thee O Lord.[2]

(*b*) The litany is a true corporate devotion, so devised that even the least instructed members of the congregation can take their part. The Versicle and Response, or liturgic dialogue, requires greater knowledge and closer co-operation

[1] Cf. Duchesne, p. 164. The *Kyrie*, however, was a late comer to the West and only inserted in the Roman Mass in the fifth century.

[2] *East Syrian Daily Offices*, translated by A. J. Maclean, p. 10.

in those who use it: and also produces in them a far more intimate sense of common action. This is probably the most antique type of ordered Christian prayer, and has been traced back to the first century.[1] The *Sursum Corda*, with its responses, is an ancient, beautiful, and characteristic example; others are to be found in all the Daily Offices of the Western Church, e.g. the Suffrages at Prime and Terce, or, in the Anglican Prayer Book, before the first collect at Mattins and Evensong. The Versicle and Response seems to have been suggested by the parallel structure of the psalms, which from early times were frequently recited in this manner; either by cantor and choir, or by two groups of singers. It is a form which can be adapted to many purposes, both of praise and of supplication, and is capable of great poetical development; as in some of the Propers of the mediæval period, where the theme of the hymn or chapter of the feast is repeated with exquisite effect.

℟. The stem of Jesse hath brought forth a scion, and the scion a flower: and on that flower the gracious Spirit resteth.

℣. The Virgin Mother of God is the scion, her Son is the flower!

℟. And on that flower the gracious Spirit resteth.

℣. Glory be to the Father and to the Son and to the Holy Ghost.

℟. The gracious Spirit resteth.[2]

(*c*) The other structural units of general acceptance from which liturgical worship is built up—the hymn and the collect—are also brought into being by the necessities of the situation. The corporate expression of praise and thanksgiving, by "psalms and spiritual songs", appears to be a universal religious instinct. To "sing unto the Lord a new

[1] Cf. F. Cabrol, *Liturgical Prayer*, p. 34.

[2] *Sarum Breviary*: Nativity of the Blessed Virgin Mary, 1st Vespers.

song, sing praises lustily unto him with a good courage ",[1] is always the impulse of a living faith : since a disinterested delight in the splendour of God is the highest and purest of our religious responses, and this naturally tends to rhythmic expression. Hence those who are concerned to defend the hymn singing habits of the Evangelical Churches have both history and psychology on their side. Here worship receives, and rightly receives, all the enhancement which music and poetry can give ; and the peculiar effect of rhythmic corporate utterance, in producing corporate feeling and enhancing individual sensibility, is brought to the help of souls and the service of God. For the hymn enchants as well as informs ; and here lies both its value and its danger. Whether religious feeling be embodied in great poetry or in doggerel, its corporate expression will always have a suggestive power more closely connected with sound than with sense : and along with many of the noblest expressions of the spirit of worship, some of our most cherished and least defensible devotional images and prejudices have entered our minds through the rhythm of popular hymns.[2]

Already in the New Testament "singing and making melody unto the Lord "[3] is recognized as an important method of Christian devotion ; and there are few parts of our ordinary public worship which can more surely claim an unbroken descent from the practices of the Apostolic Church. The Hebrew Psalter, with its great range of devotional expression, covering every mood and insight of the God-desiring soul from deepest abasement to adoring delight, was of course the first, as it remains the greatest,

[1] Ps. xxxiii. 3.

[2] It would be cruel to give examples. They can be collected without difficulty from any current hymnal.

[3] Eph. v. 19. Or in the more attractive language of Col. iii. 16, " singing with grace in your hearts unto God ". Here the reference to " psalms, and hymns, and spiritual songs " suggests that already a considerable range of poetic material was used in the meetings of the infant Church.

hymn book of the Christian family. Familiar from childhood to Our Lord and the first generation of disciples, it was taken over without question from temple and synagogue worship by the primitive Church, as the inspired vehicle of its corporate praise of God. Thus it became the normal source-book of Christian vocal worship; on which indeed its unfaltering spirit of adoration and dependence has exerted an overwhelming influence.

> With thee is the well of life:
> And in thy light shall we see light.[1]
>
> O be joyful in God, all ye lands:
> Sing praises unto the honour of his Name,
> Make his praise to be glorious![2]

> So foolish was I, and ignorant:
> Even as it were a beast before thee.
> Nevertheless, I am alway by thee:
> For thou hast holden me by my right hand. . . .
> Whom have I in heaven but thee:
> And there is none upon earth that I desire in comparison of thee.[3]
>
> Who is like unto the Lord our God, that hath his dwelling so high:
> And yet humbleth himself to behold the things that are in heaven and earth![4]

These, and other great utterances of the Psalmists, recited again and again as the expression of the Church's adoring trust, have now entered so deeply into the very texture of Christian devotion that we have ceased to be aware of their range of influence. Yet it is mainly by means of the Psalms that both the historic and spiritual continuity of Christian corporate worship has been secured; and in them we have an inexhaustible storehouse of devotional material and a means of common prayer and adoration which is accepted as it stands by Christians of

[1] Ps. xxxvi. 9.
[2] Ps. lxvi. 1.
[3] Ps. lxxiii, 21, 22, 24.
[4] Ps. cxiii. 5.

every type.[1] Thus in opening the Psalter we open a door which admits us as no other can to the worship of the Universal Church; her penitence, her supplication, her invulnerable confidence, her adoring delight in the splendour of God. Here Catholic and Covenanter sing from one service book, and acknowledge themselves to be brothers under their skins. In due course the Psalter became the core of the Divine Office; and by this very circumstance has fed and coloured the worship of all the generations of the saints.

The traditional use of the Psalter, however, plainly leaves much that is most distinctive in Christian belief and worship unexpressed: especially love and devotion directed to the Person of Christ. Thus—as indeed the New Testament indicates—hymns or "private psalms" of a definitely Christian character were soon added to the Church's repertory. By the second century an original Christian poetry seems to have been current in the East; and its use in worship soon spread westwards. Hymns have ever since taken an important place in all truly congregational worship; reflecting as the centuries pass the changes of emphasis and emotional colour which mark its historical development. Though the superb liturgical hymns of the early Greek and Latin Churches have now almost ceased to be congregational in the ordinary sense, it is still possible to recapture from those which are embedded in Orthodox and Catholic service books—e.g. the ancient and beautiful

[1] Von Hügel has pointed out the powerful witness of the Psalter to the close dependence of spiritual upon historical religion. "However deeply individual these Psalms may appear to be, they reveal themselves to patient long investigation as possessing a centuries-old background of ordered public worship—of religious practices bound to particular places and to particular times . . . nor is it at all too difficult for the delicately sympathetic historical and religious sense still to trace the main outlines of this past great history in these immortal Psalms which, precisely through these particular occasions of time and space, succeed in uttering the deepest and most universal aspirations of the heart towards God." (*The Reality of God*, p. 90.)

Orthodox Vesper hymn, "O gladsome light",[1] and the *Gloria in Excelsis* of the Roman Mass, which was sung in the Eastern Church at dawn—the spirit of that worship which they were intended to express; its doctrinal temper, its theocentric emphasis, its solemn joy, its entire freedom from subjective emotion. So, too, the grave and splendid cadences of the Ambrosian Office hymns, where faith takes precedence of feeling and real poetry becomes the handmaid of real theology, tell us more about the soul of the fourth century than do many long histories of the Early Church.

> Splendor paternæ gloriæ
> de luce lucem proferens
> lux lucis et fons luminis
> dies dierum inluminans;
>
> Verusque sol inlabere
> micans nitore perpeti
> jubarque sancti Spiritus
> infunde nostris sensibus.[2]

Again, the deep religious soul of the Middle Ages still speaks in the great phrases of the *Amor Patris et Filii;* its tender Christocentric feeling—already dangerously inclined to replace thought by romantic emotion—in the "Rosy Sequence"; its sacramental mysticism in the Eucharistic hymns of St Thomas Aquinas.[3] So, too, the German pietists, the Methodist revival, the Tractarian Movement, most truly reveal their spirit and give it immortality in the best of the hymns which they have bequeathed to the Church.

Moreover, it is in hymns above all that we hear the accent of the people's worship; for the greatest religious poetry

[1] Probably dating from the second century. Translation in the *English Hymnal*, No. 269.

[2] St Ambrose. *Roman Breviary*, Monday at Lauds. Translation in the *English Hymnal*, No. 52.

[3] For translations of all these see the *English Hymnal*, Nos. 438, 238, 326, 330, 331.

has little chance of acceptance by them, unless it expresses a devotional attitude which they love and understand, and the worst of doggerel achieves a certain homely beauty when it becomes the channel of the love and confidence of simple souls. Nevertheless it is from this point of view disconcerting to observe the contrast between the austere beauty of the ancient hymns, their great metaphysical background, their stress upon the awful majesty of God, and the wonder of His self-revelation to men, and the deliberate emotional appeal or self-interested temper of modern congregational favourites. The descent is heavy from that view of the Incarnation which is represented by "Of the Father's Heart begotten",[1] to the silliest and most sentimental of the carols we so gladly take on our lips. Nor is this a descent from the worship of the learned to that of the simple. The early Latin hymns, though now incorporated in the Breviary and chiefly used by the professionally "religious", were originally theological carols composed for the use of the people; who sang these majestic verses, as St Augustine tells us, "with one heart and voice".[2] The Ambrosian *Veni Creator gentium*, now the Office hymn for Christmas Eve, was such a carol; intended to correct Arian heresy regarding the Incarnation.[3] The beautiful morning and evening hymns, *Æterne rerum conditor* and *Deus creator omnium*[4]—both attributed to St Ambrose—were meant, like those of Bishop Ken, to provide a daily devotion, easily memorized, in which the laity could unite their worship with the great liturgic action of the Church.

(*d*) Finally, there are the prayers of the priest or minister; originally intended to "collect" and present before God the

[1] *Corde natus ex parentis*; Prudentius, fourth century. *English Hymnal*, No. 613.

[2] *Confessions*, Bk. IX, cap. 7.

[3] Cf. Batiffol, *History of the Breviary*, p. 137. Translation in the *English Hymnal*, No. 14.

[4] *Roman and Sarum Breviaries:* Sunday at Lauds and Saturday at Vespers.

united, but unuttered supplications of the people, who do or should pray together in the collects as truly as in the litany or responsory prayers. This is true of all those confessions, supplications, and thanksgivings—and, in non-liturgic services, the extempore prayers—which the leader offers in the name of those present. The constantly repeated *Oremus* of the Latin service books, the elaborate biddings in the Gallican and other early rites, and the summing up of the people's litany by the priest in the liturgy of the Orthodox Church, are there to remind us of the truly corporate function of the Collect; really a device for securing the active participation of the people in the whole spiritual movement of worship, gathering up and giving detailed and explicit utterance to their secret prayer.

In the service for Good Friday in the Roman Missal, the long series of collects for the well-being of Church and State and all the necessities of men, which follow the reading of the Passion, still retain the true form of this antique method of corporate worship: and there is no part of the Roman service books which introduces us more completely into the spirit of the ancient Church. First, the bidding of the priest, calling on the prayers of the people. Then the direction of the deacon, "Bend the knee!" followed by the pause for silent prayer (now, alas, eliminated in practice), and the cry of the sub-deacon, "Rise up!" Finally, the collect, in which the supplication to which the people have been bidden is summed up and expressed. These ritual directions to kneel and rise, which now follow each other at a pace more suggestive of drill than of ordered devotion, are, says Duchesne, "the only remaining trace of that which was once the very essence of this type of worship; the silent prayer in an agreed attitude."[1] The collect or

[1] *Christian Worship*, p. 109. Cabrol (*The Mass of the Western Rites*, p. 60) sees in these prayers the last surviving example of the great Prayer of the Faithful, once an essential part of every Mass.

prayer of the leader, then, is truly congregational in the deeper if not in the obvious sense; and where rightly used, gives great beauty and precision to the liturgical action of the group. The early "collects" seem to have been brief extempore prayers, and only gradually assumed the fixed forms with which we are now familiar. Indeed, the use of a liturgical form for this purpose was at first regarded as a mark of spiritual incapacity.[1]

A certain restraint, a sense of style, is characteristic of all good liturgical action; for it exists to express the common worship of the family, not the fervour of the individual soul. Therefore the individual who prays from within the liturgy has to sacrifice something of his own will and feeling to the corporate movement; must submit to the ritual discipline, and lose his own prayer in that of the fellowship, if he is to "understand by dancing that which is being done." But on the other hand, there are great compensations. If his religious preferences and enthusiasms are checked, and subordinated to "liturgical good manners", his reserves are respected too. The Christian liturgy, as Guardini has said, is "a masterly instrument which has made it possible for us to express our inner life in all its fullness and depth, without divulging our secrets . . . we can pour out our hearts, and still feel that nothing has been dragged to light which should remain hidden."[2] There is here, of course, a marked difference of ideal between the conceptions of "free" and "ordered" worship: the extempore prayer meeting where all make their personal contribution, and there is unreserved expression of individual aspirations and needs, and the grave movement of the Divine Service, with its note of impersonal objectivity, the subordination of individual fervour to the total adoring act. The first is the social expression of that naïve prayer which is man's instinctive response to the besetting presence of God. The second is the social expres-

[1] Compare Pt. II, cap. XI. [2] *The Spirit of the Liturgy*, p. 22

sion of cultus. These completing opposites, both present in the primitive Church, are both needed if the full span and possibilities of Christian worship are to be realized; and it is one of the many tragedies of Church history that they have so often been regarded as hostile to one another.[1]

Liturgical worship shares with all ritual action the character of a work of art. Entering upon it, we leave the lower realism of daily life for the higher realism of a successive action which expresses and interprets eternal truth by the deliberate use of poetic and symbolic material. A liturgical service should therefore possess a structural unity; its general form and movement, and each of its parts, being determined by the significance of the whole.[2] By its successive presentation of all the phases of the soul's response to the Holy, its alternative use of history and oratory, drama and rhythm, its appeals to feeling, thought, and will, the individual is educated and gathered into the great movement of the Church. Here intellect as well as emotion has its part to play in stirring to activity the deeper levels of the soul; for liturgy, being in its nature a corporate and stylized acknowledgment of the most august realities of our experience, must be informed by disciplined thought—again in this exhibiting its likeness to great art. Nevertheless, since its main function is to suggest the Supernatural and lead men out to communion with the Supernatural, it is by the methods of poetry that its chief work will be done.

[1] Nevertheless it seems as though in practice the two types were better kept apart. Modern attempts to combine them in one service; e.g. by means of "biddings" in the Eucharist, or the addition of non-liturgic prayers in the daily office, make great demands on the liturgical tact of those who venture on these perilous experiments. The enrichment of Free Church services by carefully chosen liturgical forms is more easily managed; but here, too, the harmonizing of the different kinds of material is a matter needing considerable skill.

[2] This is recognized in the Eucharist and Divine Office. But the free or Evangelical service based on the Ministry of the Word should also be regarded as a devotional whole; prayer, hymn, and sermon being closely related and contributory to a total religious effect. See Will, *Le Culte*, Vol. II, p. 214.

At least three-quarters of the text of the Byzantine liturgy is poetry ; and though the proportion in the Roman and Anglican services is less, poetry still remains a chief element at least in the Daily Office, which is mainly an arrangement of psalms, canticles, and Scripture readings. Now poetry is not, and is not intended to be, realistic in the crude sense : though it is a chief means by which religious realism is achieved, since without its help mystery can hardly be expressed. We therefore entirely mistake its office and method if we seek to give literal meaning to its religious utterances ; and this mistake, which is often made, is the basis of much criticism directed against institutional worship. Setting aside its æsthetic appeal, it fulfils three chief offices ; of which the two first can be illustrated by well-known passages from the great Eucharistic hymns of St Thomas Aquinas.

(1) It is the carrying-medium of something which otherwise wholly eludes representation : the soul's deep and awestruck apprehension of the numinous.

> Adoro te devote, latens Deitas,
> Quæ sub his figuris vere latitas ;
> Tibi se cor meum totum subjicit
> Quia te contemplans totum deficit.[1]

(2) It can universalize particulars ; giving an eternal reference to those things of time in and through which God speaks to men.

> Verbum supernum prodiens
> Nec Patris linquens dexteram
> Ad opus suum exiens
> Venit ad vitæ vesperam. . . .
>
> Se nascens dedit socium
> Convescens in edulium
> Se moriens in pretium
> Se regnans dat in præmium ![2]

[1] *Roman Missal.* Thanksgiving of the Priest. Translation (poor) in *English Hymnal*, n. 331.

[2] *Roman Breviary :* Corpus Christi at Lauds. Translation in *English Hymnal*, n. 330.

(3) It is a powerful stimulant of the transcendental sense: a function in which the ancient hymns embodied in the Greek liturgy excel.

Let us, who mystically represent the Cherubim, and sing the thrice-holy hymn to the life-giving Trinity,
Now lay aside all earthly cares
That we may receive the King of Glory,
Invisibly attended by the angelic orders.
Alleluia! Alleluia! Alleluia![1]

All these characters of poetry are active in good liturgy, and indeed constitute an important part of its religious value.

Moreover, poetry both enchants and informs, addressing its rhythmic and symbolic speech to regions of the mind which are inaccessible to argument, and evoking movements of awe and love which no exhortation can obtain. It has meaning at many levels, and welds together all those who use it; overriding their personal moods, and subduing them to its grave loveliness. Thus it becomes possible for those whose spontaneous acts of worship would be of many kinds and qualities, from the most naïve to the most abstract, to make a common contribution to the worshipping action of that Church whose voice is heard in the liturgy. These facts alone are enough to account for the poetic character of genuine liturgic worship. They give us a key to its meaning, and indicate the one standard by which it can properly be judged. Perhaps we may say of liturgy at its best that which Karl Barth has said of the Church: "Situated on this side of the abyss which separates men from God, it is the place where the eternity of revelation is transformed into a temporarily concrete, directly visible, thing in this world."[2]

[1] *Liturgy of St John Chrysostom:* The Cherubic Hymn.
[2] *The Epistle to the Romans*, p. 332.

II

It seems appropriate to end this discussion of corporate Christian worship with a short account of its classic form: the Divine Office, or non-eucharistic liturgical sequence of praise. The Office is, ideally, the ordained form within which the whole Church performs from hour to hour, by night and by day, that unceasing praise of God which is the chief purpose of her existence. It is "the Work of God," as St Benedict called it; and is addressed to Him, and not to men. Hence although many strands enter into it, including those of penitence, supplication, and intercession, its prevailing note is and must be adoration not edification.

> "We believe," says St Benedict, "that the Divine Presence is everywhere; 'the eyes of the Lord are everywhere, beholding the evil and the good' (Prov. xv. 3), but we believe this to be supremely true when we are celebrating the Divine Office. Therefore we have always in mind the Prophet's saying 'Serve the Lord with fear,' and also: 'sing ye praises with understanding,' and 'In the presence of the Angels, I will sing to thee!'[1] Consider then how we should conduct ourselves in the presence of the Godhead and His Angels; and so let us sing our psalms that the mind is in accord with the voice."[2]

The Office in its developed form is an instrument of corporate worship: a device for securing concerted attention to God, and time spent in concerted adoration, subordinating the movements of the individual soul to the majestic rhythm of the Church's liturgical life. But originally it was the Biblical prayer of devout individuals, of the solitaries and the early hermits; carrying forward a method of devotion, grounded in the reading of the Scriptures and the saying of the psalms, which was no doubt the daily prayer of the

[1] Ps. cxxxvii. 1, Vulgate.
[2] Rule of St Benedict, cap. XIX.

first generation of Jewish Christians and took its general shape and much of its actual material from the synagogue worship in which they had been reared. With the development of monastic life the Office took on a corporate character, and bit by bit elements which assume choral recitation were added to it: but whether it be recited by individuals in solitude or communities in choir it remains, fundamentally, an ordered method of Biblical worship, communion with God as speaking in Scripture and praise of His Name in the psalms.

The heart of the Office, and probably the part which first achieved definite form, is the great act of worship which includes Vespers, Mattins, and Lauds, and is directly descended from the Vigils of the Primitive Church. It formed a single sequence of praise, of which the Night Office, or Mattins, was the central part; and which extended from sunset to sunrise. In the old Roman or other Western Breviaries the whole Psalter except Psalm 119 was divided between these three great services and recited in its entirety every week.[1] The day being reckoned—as it still is among the Orthodox—from sunset, the Office of every feast began with Vespers, went on to Mattins or Nocturns, which properly began at midnight, and ended with Lauds, the "morning praise of God" to be said at dawn. This ancient system of Vigils continues in the monasteries of the Eastern Church. In the sixth century it was adopted by St Benedict as the foundation of his monastic Office, the monks rising for Mattins at 2 a.m.; and with certain variations and adjustments—including the separation of Vespers, now an afternoon or evening service—it is still in use among the great religious orders of the West. It is almost entirely

[1] In the old Roman Breviary the first 108 psalms were said at Mattins and Lauds, the rest at Vespers. Psalm 119 was divided between the Lesser Hours and the *Laudate* psalms 148, 149, 150 were said daily at Lauds. But in the reformed Breviary of Pius X the Psalter is redistributed; special psalms being allotted to the ferial Lesser Hours in place of Psalm 119.

composed of Biblical material. Five or six psalms, with their antiphons, are said at Vespers, six at ferial Mattins, and six at Lauds. Each Office has its Canticle from the Old or New Testament: the Magnificat being ceremonially chanted at Vespers, and the Benedictus at Lauds. After the psalms of the Night Office, three—or in Benedictine houses four—Scripture lessons, divided by responsories, are read.[1] The metrical hymns, varying with the season, which are now sung normally in all the Offices, only won their way to recognition gradually. A few of the Ambrosian hymns were ordered by St Benedict to be sung in his monasteries; but the Office hymn as such hardly achieved liturgical status before the eleventh or twelfth century. Of the "lesser hours", Prime and Compline were originally the domestic prayers said by the monks as they rose in the morning and went to bed at night. Terce, Sext, and None—said at 9 a.m., noon, and 3 p.m.—are short acts of corporate worship appropriate to the working hours of the day. In their original form, seen in the Sarum but obscured in the modern Roman breviary, they are based on the recitation of the 119th Psalm, that great poem of the theocentric life, "infinitely varied in its expression yet incessantly one in its direction ",[2] which is begun at Prime and continued through the day. These "little offices" are of great antiquity; prayer at these hours being recommended to all the devout by the Early Fathers, and made obligatory by St Basil—and after him by St Benedict—for all religious, whether in or out of choir.

The complete Divine Office, then, consists of eight parts: sanctifying before God that recurrent cycle of night and day in which our lives are passed. It is best understood when regarded as a spiritual and artistic unity; so devised, that

[1] On Sundays and great Festivals two additional Nocturns, each of three psalms and three lessons, are said: forming together the so-called "Service of Nine Lessons".

[2] H. P. Liddon, *Clerical Life and Work*, p. 41.

the various elements of praise, prayer, and reading, and the predominantly poetic and historic material from which it is built up, contribute to one single movement of the corporate soul, and form together one single act of solemn yet exultant worship. This act of worship is designed to give enduring and impersonal expression to eternal truths; and unite the here and now earthly action of the Church with the eternal response of creation to its origin. It is her "Sacred Chant," and loses some of its quality and meaning when its choral character is suppressed: for in it, the demands of a superficial realism are set aside, in favour of those deeper realities which can only be expressed under poetic and musical forms.

The regular sequence of Hours, or sanctification of time, which is the basis of the Daily Office, is given colour and interest and variety, and brought into direct relation with the total movement of the Church's liturgical year, by the variable antiphons and hymns which adorn it; giving to the psalms and canticles a special emphasis and intention, commemorating the great events of the Christian cycle (the Proper of Time) and heroes of the Christian family (the Proper of Saints); and by the responsories attached to the lessons. Through these enrichments the Office has gradually become a stylized expression of the Church's faith and love, and a devotional commentary upon her life. They are often of extreme beauty; and some, especially those proper to Advent and Holy Week, are among the jewels of liturgical art; giving, by means of a mosaic of Scripture phrases, a dramatic unity of intention to the whole office in which they are placed. The great responsory for the First Sunday in Advent, "*Aspiciens a longe*", with its mysterious vision of the approaching Power of God, is famous.[1] Not less beautiful

[1] Given by Batiffol, *History of the Roman Breviary*, p. 87. This responsory, with its remarkable unity of effect, is built up from nine different fragments of Scripture.

are the Vesper antiphons for the Magnificat in the week before Christmas, the so-called "Great O's"[1] proclaiming the titles of the Incarnate, which are also built up from Biblical material; and the Second Responsory for Saturday in Easter week, with its reference to the newly baptized in their chrism robes:

> These are the new lambs who have cried, saying Alleluia!
>
> They came but just now to the well: they are all filled with light.
>
> Alleluia! Alleluia!
>
> ℣. They stand before the Lamb, clothed with white robes and with palms in their hands
>
> ℟. They are all filled with light: Alleluia, Alleluia!
>
> ℣. Glory be to the Father and to the Son: and to the Holy Ghost.
>
> ℟. They are all filled with light. Alleluia! Alleluia!

The whole of this majestic cycle in its due order is now recited only by the most austere religious communities, Roman Catholic, Orthodox, and Anglican. The rest make various adjustments and compromises to bring their liturgical duties into line with the supposed demands of the active life. Thus the offices of the night and even of the dawn are frequently said "by anticipation" in the evening, and vespers are pushed back into the afternoon. The secular Roman Catholic clergy fit the office as best they can into a busy day. Anglican priests, with only two daily offices of obligation, are required by their ordination vows to maintain this link with the Church's ancient worship by reciting Mattins and Evensong daily and, if incumbents, in their parish church; a duty too often performed "by intention". The contemplative orders, however, still keep up the great tradition of the *Opus Dei*, praising God by night and by day

[1] Translations in the *English Hymnal*, No. 734.

in the name of the whole Divine society and as its dedicated representatives; rising in the night to keep the ancient vigils, and saying the beautiful office of Lauds, as it should be said, at dawn.

The risks and difficulties, the constant menace of unreality, attending the obligatory use of such stylized devotion, and persistent use of traditional material, are obvious. But those who assume that it can only result in a formal and meaningless worship, might well consider the passage in which Cassian, that great master of the religious life, describes the right devotional use of the psalms; and the psalms, after all, are the substance of Christian ordered worship.

> If he is to thrive on this pasture, the monk will take to himself all the thoughts of the psalms, and begin to sing them in such a way, that he will utter them with heart-felt emotion, not as the composition of the Psalmist, but rather as his own utterance and his very own prayer. He will take them as aimed at himself, recognizing that their words were not only fulfilled in the person of the Prophet, but are daily fulfilled in his own case. . . . As we sing the psalms, we remember all that our carelessness has brought on us, or our effort has secured, or Divine Providence granted to us, or slippery and subtle forgetfulness lost to us, or human weakness brought about in us . . . thus moved from the very depths of our heart, we get at the full meaning of the psalm; not by a mere reading the text, but by the experiencing of it.[1]

[1] Cassian, *Dialogues*, IX, 18.

CHAPTER VII

THE HOLY EUCHARIST: ITS NATURE

I

WHEN we explore beneath the surface, we find that the whole liturgic life of Christendom is built on a double foundation: the Bible and the Eucharist. The uttered Word and the living Presence, the holy doctrine and the holy food, the message of salvation and the sacrifice of praise, are the gathering points of devotion wherever Christian worship retains and expresses its real character, as a loving and grateful response of the creature to the self-revelation and self-giving of God. In them, the Divine Charity speaks and acts in a way which is appropriate to that creature's state. Both types of worship are plainly needed if the whole mind of the Church—ethical and mystical, practical and other-worldly—is to be expressed; and justice is to be done to her dual nature, so profoundly historical, yet so profoundly supernatural too.

The Divine Office represents the stylized form of that Biblical and non-sacramental devotion which the infant Church took over from Judaism. Here God is praised in the ancient poetry of the psalms and canticles; and in the Scripture lessons His nature and laws, and His gracious dealings with the children of men, are brought to mind. In the common worship of the Evangelical churches, this same prophetic and Biblical temper, this sense of the primacy of the uttered Word, are given a freer and less liturgic expression. Historically considered, this line of descent carries on and continues that devotion of the synagogue which prepared the way of the Gospel.[1] It binds us to our religious past, and witnesses to the continuity of God's action and the eternal character of man's religious instincts and needs. In the Eucharist, on the other hand, we have "the only durable and permanent element which Christianity has added to the liturgy of the synagogues."[2] Here that thirst for God, and that impulse to oblation and communion, which emerge in primitive religion and inspired the temple worship of Israel, are sublimated and given their perfect fulfilment in Christ. Here, too, the entrance of the Eternal into time, and the continued cherishing action of God in Christ, are realized in their mysterious and touching beauty; and being realized, are humbly adored. Thus some general study of the principles underlying this, the characteristic act of the Christian cultus, is necessary to any balanced view of institutional worship.

Though the word liturgy can rightly be given to the whole ordered devotion of the Church, Scriptural and sacramental, it belongs in a special sense to the Eucharist; which has been from the beginning her central act of worship, obligatory on all believers. Simple in its origin, it quickly became the gathering point of all her deepest intuitions and spiritual discoveries. Living with her life, changing much yet ever remaining the same—even though suffering in periods of decadence from grave abuses—it has proved itself to possess a "seed of immortality", and a power of conveying transcendentals, which persist through the many vicissitudes of its temporal course. In spite of its genuine Biblical and historical ancestry, therefore, we risk an entire misunderstanding of the character of the Eucharist if we try to judge the worth of its developed forms by Scriptural standards alone: for it is a "Holy Mystery" in which many religious longings and insights are fulfilled. Certainly

[1] Compare Pt. II, cap. X.

[2] L. Duchesne, *The Origins of Christian Worship*, p. 49.

we understand it best if we begin where it began : namely, in the situation and practice of the infant Church, as described in the New Testament. What we find there is a simple religious rite, on the one hand clearly social, institutional, and historical in character—never the act of the ardent believer, but always that of the group—yet on the other hand recognized as the sacred means of personal communion between the individual believer and his unseen Lord.[1] Whatever enrichments later practice and reflection may have brought, obedience, remembrance, communion, and enhancement of life, stand out as features of this primitive corporate experience.[2] As the Church gradually came to realize all its implications, so the Eucharistic celebration grew in richness and significance ; gathering up the largest possible number of spiritual insights and references—both universal and personal—and harmonizing them about its unchanging heart. Into this mould the worshipping instinct of generations has poured itself ; and bit by bit there has thus been added to the Christian ritual pattern all those fundamental responses to God which are latent in the religious soul. At last, in the fully developed liturgy, the whole drama of creation and redemption—God's loving movement toward man, and man's response in Christ—is recapitulated ; and all the implications which lay hidden in its small origins, the grain of wheat which was flung into the field of the world, are brought to maturity.

Here, then, in a way which is concrete and homely and yet transcendental, the two major interpretations of the Christian Mystery—the redemptive sacrifice and the incarnation of the Word—are given sacramental expression and made operative in the experience of each soul. Here, too, the Church from the beginning has realized that Presence

[1] It is hard, for instance, not to believe that later Eucharistic experience contributes something to the story of the Supper at Emmaus.

[2] 1 Corinthians xi. 23–29 ; John vi. 53–58.

which is the source of her life and power, has expressed her adoration, thanksgiving, and penitence, has made her supplications for the living and the dead, offered her oblation, received the Food of immortality, and remembered the prevailing sacrifice from which her life began. And here, in spite of periodical relapses towards primitive conceptions, corruption, slackness, grave conflict of theory, and many bewildering divergences of practice, the Christian can still find the same essential sources of worship, refreshment, and inwardness; the same access to the inexhaustible Divine Charity, and the same invitation to oblation and communion in the offering and hallowing of bread and wine. Even were we to set aside the sacred character of its historic origin and its supernatural claim, no other rite could so well embody the homely and transcendental paradox of Christianity; the universal divine action, and the intimate divine approach to every soul; the food of daily life, and the mystery of eternal life, both given at once; the historical memorial perpetually renewed, yet finding its fulfilment in a real and enduring Presence unfettered by the categories of time and space. Here the most naïve worshipper finds an invitation to love and gratitude, and a focus for his devotion, which he can apprehend though never explain; and the contemplative finds a door which opens upon the ineffable mystery of God. Those deep levels of our being which live unchanged under the flow of outward life, and of which we sometimes become aware—those levels where we thirst for God and apprehend Him, and know our truest selves to consist in a certain kinship with Him—these levels are reached and stirred by the movement of the Eucharist. In it they find incitement and opportunity for that secret self-oblation, that adoring abandonment to the Divine transfiguring power, and that mysterious communion, in which the spiritual life of man consists. For here the timeless mysticism of the great discourses in the Fourth Gospel, and the real historicity on which the Synoptics insist, are brought together in one concrete yet mysterious action; delicately poised, it is true, between the ever-present dangers of a crude materialism on the one hand and a hazy subjectivism on the other, but introducing the worshipper into the real Presence of a heavenly Lord, Who is yet never to be thought of as subject to the category of space. Here, says Von Hügel in a justly celebrated passage, we find:

> The Infinite first condescending to the finite; so that the finite may then rise toward the Infinite; the soul's life, a hunger and a satisfaction of that hunger, through the taste of feeling rather than through the sight of reason; God giving Himself through such apparently slight vehicles, in such short moments, and under such bewilderingly humble veils; and our poor *a priori* notions and *a posteriori* analyses thus proved inadequate to the living soul and the living God.[1]

We are reminded here of a truth which should control all our thought about Eucharistic worship; namely, that Christian devotion to Christ is always devotion to the Transcendent God self-revealed under human accidents. Thus here, as in the historic Incarnation, it is in the last resort the Eternal and Uncreated One, self-given by means of fugitive and created species, who is the object of the Church's adoration and to whom in awe and gratitude each communicant draws near. So the mystical and universal aspect of the Eucharist, constantly bringing back this august truth into focus, and summing up the whole mystery of faith, is of deepest importance. Where it is forgotten, sentimentalism and anthropocentricism—and worse corruptions than these—inevitably creep in.

Yet the simple access to the Divine Humanity, Who is the bridge and historical means of this self-imparting of the Eternal, is important too; and offers a path which every

[1] *The Mystical Element of Religion*, Vol. I, p. 241.

Christian soul can tread. Here Christ, the Life of the Church and of the soul, is present in a mysterious manner, giving Himself to men as Food and Shepherd, and to God as the perfect sacrifice in and with His Church. Thus in the Eucharist, which is that Church's supreme liturgic action, He is both the truly present object of our human love and worship, and ever-living means of self-oblation before God for every soul "added to the Lord": the Offerer and the Offered, the Shepherd and the Heavenly Food.

> "Nowhere," says Dr James, "is the supernatural power and significance of the Christian sacramental system more apparent than in the liturgy, since in every Mass the redemptive process is reiterated and Christ Himself is born anew 'after a heavenly and spiritual manner' to bestow His grace and the bliss of immortality on those who receive Him devoutly in faith and penitence . . . regarded from this standpoint, Christ becomes the Heir of the ages, and the ritual pattern the divine scheme for the redemption and reconciliation of the human race to God."[1]

When we compare this mainly immanental and anthropological view with the sublime spiritual realism of Von Hügel, it becomes clear that no doctrine of the Eucharist which emphasizes one aspect alone—whether that aspect be the over-ruling divine action, the mystery of the Presence, the Memorial of the Passion, or the great rhythm of worship which passes from the earthly oblation to the heavenly sacrifice and thence to the communion of the faithful with Christ—can be adequate to its richness, or explain its central position in the worship of the Church. These strands, with others, are indeed truly present in it; and each has been and is given special prominence at different periods, or by

[1] E. O. James, *Christian Myth and Ritual*, p. 325. The marked Anglo-Catholic colour of this passage should not blind Evangelical Christians to the deep truths which it contains; nor should the reference to primitive cultus, rightly understood, be offensive to the most strict of traditionalists.

different branches of the Christian family. But it is only where all are recognized as true elements in a concrete single act of worship which transcends, embraces, and unites them, that the full power and meaning of the Eucharist is experienced.

It is significant that no one name has ever been found capable of expressing all the aspects of the Eucharistic action. That of Holy Communion, with which we in England are most familiar, describes one moment and character of the service to the virtual exclusion of the rest; and so tends to disturb its rightful balance. The New Testament names of "Lord's Supper" and "Breaking of Bread" cover the historical Memorial and the social character of the sacrament. Those of Eucharist, and Offering,[1] which quickly established themselves in the early Church, bring into the foreground the essential elements of worship and oblation; and stress the truth that this is the chief ritual act of the whole Christian family, gathering up and offering the homage of creation in Christ. Holy Sacrifice, and New Sacrifice—titles much used by St Cyprian and by the early Latin Fathers—are valuable witnesses to the antiquity of the sacrificial aspect, which the *Didache* also assumes. All these names possess historical and theological credentials which are at least as good as any title which narrows down the significance of the action to communion alone, and ignores the fact that the Synoptic story of the Institution bears the plain marks of worship and sacrifice. For the Orthodox Church, the official title is the Divine Liturgy, for Western Catholicism, the Mass: and these words, which in themselves have little meaning, can at least be charged with all the significance which those who use them desire. They leave room for that great conception of the Eucharist as embodying and expressing the

[1] "Eucharist"=thanksgiving, though used in a general sense in the New Testament, by the time of St Ignatius (second century) is always understood to imply the celebration of the Lord's Supper: and in the *Didache* (c. 125) has almost the status of a proper name.

Church's total religious action, showing forth the mystery of her being and making "in Christ" a ceaseless oblation before God, which alone can cover and unite all levels and all aspects of her sacramental life.

II

The form which the Eucharist has assumed in the practice of different branches of the Church, the developments it has undergone, and the change in emphasis given to its various aspects will all be considered later. But some account of the structure and high points of the typical service seems necessary here, if we are to understand its significance and position as the living heart of Christian corporate worship; and interpret the widely differing developments, both in theory and practice, in such a sense that their apparent contradictions can be carried up into a higher synthesis. For it was, after all, as the servants of one Master and believers in one historic Revelation, that the first Roman Christians brought for consecration their homely offerings of bread and wine, that St Catherine of Genoa in the fifteenth century went every day for thirty-five years, in defiance of contemporary custom, to "receive the heart's true food",[1] and the founders of Methodism in the eighteenth century drew fervour and courage from this same unusual practice. So, too, the Scottish Covenanters "breaking bread" upon the open hill-side, and Henry Martyn "spreading a fair linen cloth" with hardly more ceremony to "hold communion" in the veranda at Dinapore,[2] have something in common with the Orthodox worshipper prostrating himself before the closed doors of the iconostasis when the Holy Mysteries are accomplished within, and the presiding ecclesiastic at a modern Eucharistic Congress who passes in a motor-car through the

[1] Von Hügel, *The Mystical Element of Religion*, I, p. 115.

[2] C. E. Padwick, *Henry Martyn*, p. 183.

kneeling ranks of the faithful, exhibiting the sacred Host in its monstrance for the adoration of the crowd. According to our temperament and institutional outlook, one or other of these methods of worship may repel us. Yet each can claim descent from the sacred scene in the Upper Room, and each can impart grace and power, and release and express worshipping love. Perhaps too all are needed if those extremes of mystery and simplicity, of awestruck abasement and child-like confidence, which are included in the span of the Church's Eucharistic worship, are to be harmonized and expressed.

Some account of the essential features of the Eucharistic action is all the more necessary, because elaborations on the one hand and unfortunate suppressions on the other, have obscured the noble outlines of the original rite, especially in the West : and seriously disturbed its devotional balance. The Roman Mass as it exists to-day, says Abbot Cabrol frankly, is a " composite mosaic ", and therefore inevitably appears to those unacquainted with its history " rather incoherent ". " Rites have been added to rites ; others have been—rather unfortunately—suppressed ; and where this is the case gaps, or what have been styled ' gaping holes ', appear."[1] This is the considered verdict of Roman Catholic scholarship. On the other hand, the Reformed Churches, in their eagerness to get rid of obvious accretions and opportunities for superstition, have pruned with excessive vigour : and by suppressing the whole sacrificial reference of the Eucharist, have destroyed the true balance of its closely related aspects and so the character of the whole. For though the great moment on which the whole action converges, with its successive movements of contrition,

[1] F. Cabrol, *The Mass of the Western Rites*, p. vii. Perhaps the worst of these " gaping holes " appear at the points once occupied by the Gradual psalm, the Prayer of the Faithful and the Offertory procession. The Roman Catholic Movement for liturgical reform is now seeking to restore the first and last of these.

supplication, docile attention and awestruck worship, is for sacramental Christians of all types the hallowing and the distribution of the sacred Bread and Wine: still, were this all, we should indeed have a service of Communion but hardly a Eucharist. Moreover, it is certain that any interpretation which places the chief emphasis on the benefits received by the communicants does not do justice to the rich significance of the Christian liturgy; and is a dangerous encouragement of religious individualism. For this service and "bounden duty" as the English prayer of oblation names it, is orientated to the glory of God, not to the advantage of man.[1] It includes or should include in one harmonious movement all the essential phases of the Christian response to God: and in such manner, that the total action has a significance far exceeding that of the words which are used. The successive acts of oblation, consecration, fraction, and communion both incite and express the deepest realities of human worship: and no conflict in doctrinal explanation can touch this central fact.

It is true that the heart of the service, its "Christian and original element", consists only of three essential phases: the offering of the Eucharistic prayer, the breaking of the bread, the distribution of communion.[2] But as, more and more, the significance of these actions and the need of safeguarding their sacred character was realized, so a devotional preparation, and a supporting ritual pattern, came bit by bit into existence. In the early Church the usual prelude to the actual celebration consisted in the common Sunday worship and instruction of the whole fellowship, with its catechumens and "hearers": the catena of psalms, prayers, and Bible

[1] Compare Dr. F. Gavin in *Liturgy and Worship*, pp. 112–113. "The early Christians . . . were infinitely more concerned about God than about themselves, far more preoccupied about doing His Will, than given to speculating how much they received, in the Eucharist. . . . Communion, in short, was not *the* moment of the early Eucharist: it was a corollary, an inevitable consequence of God's Will for man."

[2] Duchesne, *op. cit.*, p. 49.

readings which the first Jewish Christians, trained in the Synagogue, accepted as a matter of course, as the material of corporate devotion.[1] This gradually developed into the Liturgy of the Catechumens, which still forms the first part of the Eucharistic service in all Eastern and Western liturgies, and culminates in the reading of the Gospel. The second part of the service, from the Offertory to the Dismissal, is the true Liturgy of the Faithful, or Eucharist.[2]

The Liturgy of the Catechumens began in the West with introit-psalm, now reduced to a fragment, and in the East with a litany. This was introduced in the fourth century into the Western rite; where it is now represented by the ninefold Kyrie, and in the Anglican service is attached to the Ten Commandments. The Collect or "first prayer" of the celebrant was followed by the Scripture lessons; which were originally three, from the Prophecies, Epistles, and Gospels, and were separated by the chanting of psalms. The reading of the Gospel, always surrounded by special ceremonies, was the climax of the service; which is clearly based on Jewish models, and almost certainly represents the most ancient common prayer of the Church. The extreme conservatism of Eastern Christianity has preserved its form and character—its alternation of congregational litany, Scripture reading, and psalms—much better than have the Churches of the West. In the solemn bringing-in of the Book of the Gospels, or "Little Entrance", with marks of ceremonial reverence only inferior to those afterwards accorded to the Oblation, she still reminds us that the Ministry of

[1] *Infra*, Pt. II, caps. X and XI.

[2] *Infra*, Pt. II, cap. XI. In normal Catholic and Orthodox practice, the two parts are now of course never separated; though the Byzantine rite retains the ancient dismissal of the Catechumens by the deacon after the Gospel: "As many as are Catechumens, go out!" The Anglican "ante-communion" service, and the Sunday service of the Lutheran Church on days when there is no communion, are practically identical in form with the Liturgy of the Catechumens.

the Word is also a revelation of the Holy; and therefore as much a part of the Church's method and duty as the Ministry of the Sacraments. The Gospel Book, in fact, was from early times "regarded as representing Our Lord Himself" and the ceremonies surrounding its use are of great antiquity.[1]

This two-step pattern of the Liturgy has much more than a merely historical or liturgical significance: for here the Christian consciousness marks its enduring conviction that the sacred record no less than the sacred rite is a disclosure within time of the Eternal, and that the movement of worship which culminates in the reverent hearing of the Word, is a true response to the revelation of God. Within the stiff frame of the liturgic pattern, that revelation still keeps its magical and dewy freshness; and perhaps the most poignant of the many contrasts of the Eucharist, is the contrast between the ceremonial reverence, the incense and the lights with which the Book of the Gospels is surrounded, and the living world to which that Book admits us again and again: Galilee, the lakeside, the healing Presence, the stories that convey the mystery of the Kingdom, and the solitude of the Garden and the Cross. Yet "Jesus in the Sacrament is the same as Jesus in the Gospel": the mystical presence and the historical presence are two aspects of one theophany. Therefore meditation on the human life of Christ Incarnate is the proper preparation for communion with His sacramental life. The Gospel, and the Sermon or Homily which expands or interprets it, complete the essential parts of the Liturgy of Catechumens. The *Gloria in Excelsis* and Creed, found in most Western rites, are enrichments and no part of the original structure of the service.

In its typical form, the Eucharistic service proper, or Liturgy of the Faithful, has three "high points" of special significance; all claiming Apostolic origin, and certainly of great antiquity. There is first the Offertory, or solemn

[1] See E. Bishop, *Liturgica Historica*, p. 21.

oblation of the bread and wine ; usually followed in Eastern liturgies by the Kiss of Peace.[1] Next, the great Eucharistic prayer of adoration and sacrifice, within which the gifts are consecrated ; and last, the communion of the celebrant and the faithful.[2]

In the West, the Offertory—which is properly an act, not a prayer—is now generally represented by the collecting of alms from the congregation,[3] the singing or saying of the "offertory sentences" which replace the ancient congregational psalm, and in the Roman Mass by the priest's recital of a series of beautiful mediæval prayers, for the acceptance before God of the Eucharistic elements prepared for sacrifice. In the East, the solemn bringing into the Sanctuary of the prepared gifts or "Great Entrance" still reminds us of the signal importance of this action : which was once the realistic offering by the congregation, and bringing to the altar, of the bread and wine to be used in the Eucharistic sacrifice—a sacrifice in which, by this significant act, they became direct participants.[4] So in the Liturgy of St Clement

[1] Matt. v. 23, 24. But in the Roman rite the Kiss of Peace is placed immediately before the Communion.

[2] These all appear in the description given by Justin Martyr, *c.* A.D. 150. Both this writer and Clement of Rome (*c.* A.D. 98) state that the manner of celebration of the Eucharist was arranged by Our Lord and the Apostles. The point to notice here is not the historical probability of this tradition, but the reverence which would in consequence attach to the structure of the service.

[3] But not always. An effort has been made in some Anglican churches and also by the Roman Catholic movement for liturgical reform, to restore the ceremonial bringing-in of the offering of Bread and Wine. This bringing-in of the elements is also one of the most solemn moments of the Scottish rite. As to the collection usually made at this point, we must remember that according to the teaching of the synagogue the giving of alms was the equivalent of sacrifice. It therefore represents the people's oblation.

[4] The well-known fresco in the crypt of St Clemente at Rome, in which we see the faithful bringing to the celebrant large circular loaves for consecration, shows the Offertory as it still presumably existed in the ninth or tenth century ; and reminds us of its homely and practical aspect. In France the custom of offering a brioche tied with ribbon at the Confirmation or First Communion of a child seems to represent the survival of the primitive oblation in kind. This brioche is distributed to the congregation at a subsequent Mass as "blessed bread".

after the catechumens have gone out, the deacon cries " Let us stand upright, to present our offerings with fear and trembling to the Lord."

The Offertory, though almost certainly originating in the practical necessities of the situation, quickly became in fact the Christian equivalent of the first essential phase in all sacrificial worship: the bringing and offering of a gift to God, which shall be a token of the worshipper's self-oblation. It is or should be the solemn concerted act of the whole Church by its appointed representatives; expressing the very character of her Godward life, the bringing to the altar, the giving to God, of the common stuff of everyday existence that it may be divinized—" thine own things of thine own ". It is the first phase in that great action which mounts towards the awful moment when the " immortal and life-giving Mysteries " touch the lips of sinful man. And further, all this signifies on the one hand the self-offering of man as he is, that he may be hallowed, and become in some sense a living Eucharist and medium of the divine self-imparting; and on the other hand the relation in which, for Christian intuition, the whole created order stands towards the Being of God. It is perhaps as already self-identified with that created order by the mystery of the Incarnation, and giving Himself in, with and for it, that Christ is held by the Orthodox to come to the altar in the Great Entrance, with the prepared oblation, or " Holy Lamb ".[1]

The great Eucharistic Prayer, which forms the heart of the service, consists in its classical form of three inter-related parts, which directly refer to the triune Nature of God. (*a*) There is first the so-called Preface, or Thanksgiving; with its invitation to adoring worship in the *Sursum Corda*, its recital of the glories of God in creation as incitements of man's praise and thankfulness, " the earth and all that therein is, the sea, the fountains, the rivers, the lakes,

[1] *Supra*, p. 56 and *infra*, p. 153 and Pt. II, cap. XII.

and all things that are in them,"[1] and its conclusion in the *Sanctus*, lifting the heart and mind of the assembled worshippers to the " unwalled world " of eternity and selfless delight in the splendour of God. The most superb and joyous outbursts of adoration in the early liturgies are found in this opening phase of the Eucharistic prayer ; so shorn of its glories in all existing Western rites, which hurry on from the heavenly world and its radiant population to the situation and needs of men. The *Sanctus*, however, adopted in early times from the worship of the Synagogue, and baptized into Christ by the writer of the Apocalypse, remains as an essential feature in all liturgies. It has been a determining influence in the development of Eucharistic devotion, especially in the East ; all the surrounding circumstances of Isaiah's vision providing images to remind the worshipper of the awful character of the mystery in which he is to take part.[2] Thus the coal of fire which the seraph brought from the altar to the lips of the prophet soon becomes an image of the sacramental species. So in the Liturgy of St James the priest says, before making his own Communion :

> " The Lord shall bless us and make us to receive with the pure tongs of our fingers the burning coal and to place it in the mouths of the faithful, for the purifying and renewing of their souls and bodies now and for ever. O taste and see the Lord is good ! "[3]

And in the Orthodox rite, there is said to the communicant after administration the very words of the seraph :

> " Lo ! this hath touched thy lips, and shall take away thy transgressions and purge thy sins ! "

(*b*) The second phase of the Eucharistic prayer moves from the praise of God's transcendence to that of His incarnate

[1] Anaphora of St Mark. Linton, *Twenty-five Consecration Prayers*, p. 88.

[2] Isaiah vi. 1–9. Many examples in Linton, *Twenty-five Consecration Prayers*.

[3] Neale and Littledale, *Liturgies of SS. Mark, James, etc.*, p. 59.

revelation. It consists of the *Anamnesis*, or memorial of the life and death of the only Begotten " Who, having descended from heaven and having been made flesh of the Holy Ghost and Mary the Virgin and Mother of God, lived in fellowship with men and accomplished all things for the salvation of our race."[1] It always includes references to the Last Supper and the Passion, the recital of the Words of Institution—which effect, according to Western belief, the consecration of the elements—and the offering of the Oblation of the Body and Blood of Christ. " The acceptance of the sacrifice by God," says De la Taille, " and its oblation by man, and the commemoration of the Supper and of the Passion of Christ, are all realized at the same instant."[2] They are to be considered in supernatural regard as a single and indivisible act ; serially presented, because of our human limitations, by means of successive liturgic actions and words.

(*c*) In all ancient liturgies, and still in the Orthodox and other Eastern rites, the Eucharistic prayer ends with a solemn invocation of the Holy Spirit on the worshippers and their oblation ; the *Epiclesis*. This prayer that God by His Spirit will intervene in the Mystery and lift the whole action to the supernatural sphere, is regarded by the Eastern Church as effecting the consecration of the elements. At the moment of its utterance, all bow down in awestruck silence, since " the most dreadful, wonderful mystery of the whole liturgy now takes place."[3] In the developed Eucharistic prayers of the fourth and fifth centuries it is given great splendour of expression, and definitely associated with the coming of the sacramental Presence.

> May there come upon us and upon this oblation the grace of the Holy Spirit : may He dwell and rest upon this Bread and upon this Cup, and may He bless and

[1] *Liturgy of St James*. Linton, *op. cit.*, p. 41.
[2] *The Mystery of Faith*, p. 23.
[3] N. Gogol, *Meditations on the Divine Liturgy*, p. 69.

consecrate and seal them in the name of the Father and of the Son and of the Holy Spirit. By the power of Thy Name, may this Bread become the Holy Body of our Lord Jesus Christ, and this Cup the Precious Blood of our Lord Jesus Christ.[1]

The *Epiclesis* is perhaps derived from the Jewish custom of hallowing places, things, and persons by the invocation of the Divine Name. It is doubtful whether the Western Church ever considered it to be more than a prayer for the sanctifying presence of the Spirit; or gave to it the peculiar significance, as the actual formula of consecration, to which it has attained in the East.[2] Nevertheless its appropriateness and Christian character as part of the Eucharistic action is obvious; and it is a serious defect of the Roman Mass and the rites derived from it that here the direct invocation of the Holy Spirit, and with it the ancient Trinitarian pattern of the Eucharistic prayer, has been lost.[3]

For the early Church, the whole of this great prayer was a single act of worship; within which and through which God in His threefold Being was recognized and adored, the oblation of bread and wine was made at once as a memorial and as a prevailing sacrifice, the supplications of the Church were presented, and the power of the Creative Spirit was invoked on offerers and offering. There was no attempt to identify the consecration with any one formula or moment; whether the recital of the Words of Institution, or the *Epiclesis*. All was summed up and completed by the Lord's Prayer; now said in the Roman Mass by priest alone,

[1] *Liturgy of Theodore of Mopsuestia* (West Syrian). Linton, *op. cit.*, p. 76.

[2] The origin, place, and importance of the *Epiclesis* in the Western Eucharist is one of the most controversial of liturgical questions, and cannot be discussed here.

[3] Some modern liturgies—e.g. the Scottish episcopal rite and the 1928 revision of the Book of Common Prayer—have restored the *Epiclesis*. It appears also in the permissive order for Holy Communion authorized by the Presbyterian Church of Scotland (*Prayers for Divine Service*, 1929).

but in the Eastern and Anglican rites by all present. Here, in the most sacred of all Christian formulas, all the motives and meanings of the Eucharistic act—adoration, oblation, self-giving to the Divine purpose and the humble dependence of the creature on the generosity of God—are welded into one.

Since the Eucharist is not only a sacrifice but a feast, and not only an act of worship but an act of fellowship, the distribution of Holy Communion to the faithful is its proper completion and crown. Here the essentially corporate character of Christian worship is strongly emphasized; for the common reception of the sacramental gifts is in the deepest sense a communion of each with the other, and so with the universal Church, as well as of each with the present Lord: "Seeing that we who are many are one loaf, one body, for we all partake from the one loaf."[1]

[1] 1 Corinthians x. 17. (R.V. margin.)

CHAPTER VIII

THE HOLY EUCHARIST: ITS SIGNIFICANCE

WE go on from this short account of the essential characters and liturgic structure of the Eucharist to ask what this, the greatest of all Christian acts of worship, with its unchanging centre, and many kinds and degrees of outward expression, has meant and means for Christian devotion. Where does, and where should, its true emphasis lie? Which of the many strands that are united in it should be given priority, as expressing its true intention? Is it to be thought of as primarily a theocentric act of sacrificial worship, a Christo-centric act of communion, a historical memorial, a source of spiritual energy, or a sacrament of fellowship?

The answer is that no view can be adequate which neglects any of these meanings. For though some of them may seem to lie outside the intention of the simple worship of the Apostolic Church, this appearance is seen to be deceptive, when we realize all that is implied in the Eucharistic allusions which occur in the Apocalypse.[1] And, beyond this, the span of religious reference has been so widened and the supernatural significance so deepened by the ever-growing experience of the living Church and the insights and meditations of the saints, that it now embraces and harmonizes the most simple and most abstract spiritual experiences possible to

[1] E.g., in cap. I, the description of the Living Presence in the midst of the Seven Churches.

men; placing them within that universal act of worship which the world, visible and invisible, offers to its Creator and Lord.

Nevertheless, we shall better understand the deep significance of the Eucharist as a whole, if we consider separately some of the chief strands which are included in it. If we take the aspects which are brought together or implied in a typical Consecration Prayer with its completion in communion, we shall find that they are six; and it will perhaps be simplest to take as a basis these six in the form in which they are usually developed in the great Western and Eastern Liturgies.[1]

(1) Adoration and thanksgiving; the setting within which the whole action is to be developed, and which is given supreme expression in the Preface and *Sanctus*.

(2) The historical element, or memorial of the Passion; also an essential part of the Canon in all rites.

These two characters, one turned towards God Transcendent and the other towards His incarnate revelation and saving action, condition all the rest.

(3) The heart of the action: the oblation and hallowing of the bread and wine given by the worshippers, and offered upon the altar, that in union with the eternal self-offering of Christ, they may be accepted by God, and become to us the sacrament of His Body and Blood.

(4) The supplications of the Church, made in and with this "prevailing sacrifice".

(5) The mystery of the Divine Presence; and

(6) The Food of Eternal Life.

So the individual worshipper who gives himself without reserve to the total movement of the Eucharist finds himself

[1] I owe the first suggestion for this analysis of the essential elements of the Liturgy to Dr. Y. Brilioth's valuable *Eucharistic Faith and Practice*. My arrangement, however, differs from his; since it starts from a different conception of the significance of the rite.

caught into, and made part of, a spiritual drama in which the deepest impulses and needs of his spiritual life are represented and satisfied; a drama that brings together, and exhibits in their fulness under sacramental tokens, the life-giving love of God for man and the life-surrendered love of man for God. For first his small thanksgiving is joined to the "unsilenced praises" in which the whole created order responds to God; and next he is impelled to offer his whole life a living sacrifice, and in and through this offering it is hallowed and transformed; and finally, by this twofold act of worship and of oblation, he enters that inner circle of Christian experience where he knows the presence of a heavenly Master and his soul is fed with heavenly food. Yet he does all this, not as a solitary individual, but in and with the Church; sharing the ceaseless Eucharistic action in which she offers herself in Christ to God as a living oblation—and within this her sacrifice, the life of each member, covered and presented in her Eucharist.

It is true that this action is a totality, which escapes analysis. As towards God, it depends upon one single revelation of His love. As towards man, its many aspects all derive their character and sanction from one historic source. We only begin to apprehend it at the point where all analysis must cease: for it sums up man's deepest religious insights and longings, and by means of sensible signs carries him beyond sensible signs, towards the Holy and Eternal, which here comes to meet him. Thus from beginning to end the whole action is both natural and supernatural, visible and invisible: the unchanging realities of adoration, oblation, sacrifice, supplication, and communion being made more actual and penetrating, not less, by their humble outward expression in terms of our temporal experience. All this will be better appreciated if we consider one by one these great religious actions, and their place in that supreme act of Christian worship which includes and yet transcends them all.

(1) *Thanksgiving*. This poor word, with its suggestion of dutiful gratitude for benefits received, is our usual English rendering of *Eucharist*. But it is far from suggesting that total adoring acknowledgment of God in His cosmic splendour and merciful dealings with men, that disinterested worship, that delighted Godward reference and consequent sanctifying action, which this word implied first for devout Jews, and then for those early Christians who so promptly adopted it as the best of all titles for their chief religious rite. Plainly there is a sense in which the creature's approach to God must be covered, directed, and coloured by thanksgiving; since it is all occasioned and made possible first by His gracious movement towards us, and then by the incitements of His grace. In this sense "eucharistic action" runs right through the New Testament. It is present in the feeding of the Four and the Five Thousand; it controls the opening phrase of the Lord's Prayer, and is rightly given priority in all genuine Christian worship. The true note of that worship is struck in the heavenly act of adoration which was perhaps the chief source of the great Eucharistic prayers of the early Church:

> Worthy art thou, our Lord and our God, to receive the glory and the honour and the power: for thou didst create all things, and because of thy will they were, and were created.[1]

This grateful and creaturely acknowledgment of the priority of God, the note of praise and benediction already so nobly struck in Jewish worship[2] dominates the earliest liturgies. At least in the beginning it seems indeed more prominent than the thought of sacrifice with which it was afterwards integrated. It has already been said that the primitive Eucharistic prayer, the heart of the liturgy, is a twofold act of adoration and thanksgiving which effects a

[1] Revelation iv. 11. [2] See below. Pt. II, cap. X.

consecration. First, it is a thanksgiving for the mysterious splendour of God's total creative action through His Word; the "glory that fills heaven and earth". Next, for that Word's supreme act of creative love; the "stooping down" of the Holy to the redemption of humanity, His entrance into history, His incarnation and continued self-giving for the feeding of the spirit of man. If the first of these movements, with its universal reference, is taken over almost unchanged from the liturgical blessings used in synagogue devotion, the second, announcing the fulfilment of the Jewish expectation, brings to a point the motive for man's gratitude and praise. So in the typical Canon, the song of the seraphim is balanced by that of the Jewish children—"Blessed is he that cometh in the name of the Lord"—and the grateful memorial of the Passion leads to the effective hallowing of the elements set apart for a sacramental continuance of the "entry of the Eternal into Time". Thus in the Liturgy of Bishop Sarapion, after the singing of the *Sanctus* the celebrant says:

> Full is the heaven, full also is the earth, of Thy excellent glory, Lord of Hosts; fill also this sacrifice with thy power and thy participation.[1]

If we want to realize in full the character of true Christian worship we should never forget that this lifting up of human creatures to share in the heavenly Vision of God, "so that the very dust might become happy in the contemplation of thy glory",[2] comes first in all authentic Eucharistic prayers; as the greatest of all reasons for the gratitude of men. There is nothing paddock-like or parochial, nothing individualistic or subjective, in the genuine worship of the Church. The scene is set within the great landscape of Eternity, and includes in the upward sweep of adoration the

[1] Linton, *Twenty-five Consecration Prayers*, p. 85.

[2] Anaphora of the Syrian Jacobites, attributed to Severus of Antioch. Linton, *op. cit.*, p. 50.

invisible things of Him Who is invisible; so that all our various rites and methods are lost in the blaze of that light. This great claim of the Christian to participate in the worship of the supernatural world, introduces the whole Eucharistic sequence of memorial, sacrifice, supplication, consecration and communion. Again and again the early anaphoras strike this note of awed yet ecstatic joy; music and song, "spiritual exultation and joyous dances", the seraphim "with one clear voice and one loving harmony . . . raising their voices in eternal praise"[1] enwreathed the lowly Christian altar with celestial worship. "I must rejoice without ceasing, although the world shudder at my joy!" said the mystic Ruysbroeck. Here he was more truly at one with the spiritual temper of the fourth century than of the fourteenth: for those Christian voices which we hear in the early liturgies "with lips that keep not silence, and hearts that cannot be still"[2] give thanks no less for the "lofty and eternal magnificence of the Word of God" than for His "voluntary self-emptying for us".[3]

(2) *Memorial.* The remembrance before God of the saving acts of the Passion, the "memorial of Christ's death", has been from the beginning an essential part of Eucharistic worship. Those who lay special emphasis upon this strand in the total action can claim the authority of Our Lord's words at the Last Supper, as given by St Paul and incorporated in St Luke's account.[4] These words—if authentic—carried with them a religious and sacrificial reference which may well have been present in the mind of Jesus, and which no devout Jew reflecting on the incidents of that night could fail to understand: for by their use, the repetition of the acts of the Last Supper was constituted as a

[1] Liturgy of the Syrian Jacobites, attributed to St John Chrysostom. Linton, *op. cit.*, pp. 45, 49.

[2] Liturgy of St Mark, Anaphora. (Neale and Littledale, *Liturgies of SS. Mark, James, Clement, etc.*, 2nd ed., p. 14.)

[3] Linton, *loc. cit.*, p. 47.

[4] 1 Corinthians xi. 24; Luke xxii. 19.

"memorial" or reminder, and this was an idea indigenous in Hebrew religion. In the first place some of the chief ceremonies—e.g. the Passover and Feast of Dedication—were memorial repetitions of past events and saving actions of God. In the second place, the memorial offering, or *'azkāra*, was a familiar feature of the temple worship. It was a representative or token sacrifice, calling the total sacrifice to mind. Thus at every meal-offering, a handful of flour was burnt upon the altar as a "memorial" which represented before God the whole sacrifice, the total gift; and when the loaves of Shew-bread were placed on their table "before the Lord", frankincense was put with every row, to serve as its *'azkāra*.[1] The meal-offering, with which the *'azkāra* was connected, always accompanied every burnt offering or total sacrifice, and every peace-offering with its communion meal.

All this is an integral part of the religious background of the first Eucharist; and was of course well known both to those who were present at it, and to St Paul, our earliest witness to its character. Though we need not suppose that any precise identification was intended, yet there was a sense in which, for Jewish Christians nourished on sacrificial ideas, each Eucharist was an *'azkāra*, a token of the total sacrifice of Calvary, and of the self-giving of the Church in and with its Lord. At least so long as that Church was centred on Jerusalem, such conceptions as these would inevitably be present in the minds of those who met for the "breaking of bread"; and must be reckoned with as probable sources of this primitive character of Eucharistic worship.[2]

[1] Cf. Leviticus ii. 9; v. 12; vi. 15; xxiv. 5–7.

[2] Dr. Hicks, who discusses the evidence for the connection of the Eucharistic memorial with the *'azkāra*, concludes that "all we can be sure of is that the idea of 'memorial before God' was a familiar part of the ancient sacrificial thought: and if we adopt that interpretation here, it will be just so far as we are convinced on other grounds that it is the ancient sacrifices that Our Lord has in His mind." *The Fullness of Sacrifice*, p. 212.

Moreover, this calling to mind and remembering before God of the sacrificial death of Jesus, as a central interest for Christian worship, has an importance which goes far beyond its Jewish origins. For it means the anchoring of man's faith and love on specific divine acts accomplished within history; God's revelation by and in concrete happenings in space and time, vouchsafed to creatures who are themselves conditioned by space and time. It means that the sturdy realism of the Synoptics is as important to religion, and as great an incentive to worship, as the sacramental mysticism of St John. Therefore the Eucharistic prayer of thanksgiving is incomplete without the memorial of the Passion; and in fact this remembrance of the self-offering of Jesus, "Who fulfilling Thy will and winning for Himself an Holy People, stretched forth His hands when He was suffering that by His death He might deliver those who believed in Thee",[1] was from the first an integral part of the Church's "sacrifice of praise and thanksgiving". In its developed form or "Proper of Time", it follows the course of the Christian year; commemorating within the Eucharistic action, and in close connection with the offering, each great phase in Our Lord's life, death and triumph, and balancing the timeless mystery of the divine self-giving by a reminder of the human series through which the gift was made. To this feature of the liturgy we owe those special Prefaces which are among the most beautiful creations of Christian liturgical art.[2]

It is this strong insistence on history, here at the very heart of mystery, this reference to fact as an incentive to

[1] *Apostolic Tradition of Hippolytus:* Eucharistic Prayer. Early third century.

[2] The Roman Preface for Christmas Day is famous: "It is very meet, just, right and salutary, that we should always and in all places give thanks to thee, Holy Lord, Almighty Father, Eternal God: because by the mystery of the Word Incarnate, the new light of thy brightness hath shone upon the eyes of our minds: that, knowing God made visible, thereby we may be caught up to the invisible love."

worshipping love, which differentiates the Christian Eucharist from even the highest and purest of the Pagan Mystery cults. The memorial is liturgic. It is made, like its Hebrew prototype, to the glory of God, not for the information of men; and as a due part and occasion of the Church's praise and thanksgiving. For indeed it is the cause and cost of her very existence which she commemorates in her oblation: "calling to mind the blessed Passion of the same Christ thy Son Our Lord, likewise his Resurrection from the grave and his glorious ascension into Heaven" as she offers "the holy Bread of eternal life, and the Cup of everlasting salvation."[1] Thus in all liturgies the history of redemption, God's loving operation on the stage of history, is set forth as an essential feature of the Eucharist: sometimes, and especially in the East, with elaborate and poetic beauty, sometimes with the reserve and precision characteristic of the West.

There is another reason for this which, though secondary, has yet its importance: namely, the impressive value of this memorial. Von Hügel has pointed out, as one of life's deepest mysteries, the fact that "the Universal and Abiding" does not as such "move the will".[2] What does move it, is the specific and concrete; the individual demand, opportunity and example, the compelling force of personality and the revelation of the supreme call and supreme self-donation in One Who made under earthly conditions the unconditioned response of love to love. So, in the "remembrance of His death and passion" the Christian worshipper is again and again confronted with his classic pattern; reminded of the demands of love, and the cost of holiness, in terms of human life. Hence those Evangelical Christians who have insisted on the worth of this memorial, even to the point of giving it priority over other aspects of the

[1] *Roman Missal:* Canon of the Mass.
[2] *The Mystical Element of Religion,* Vol. I, p. 3.

Eucharist, perform a useful service within the universal worship of the Church. Nor is there any need to oppose to one another the conceptions of a memorial made before God as an act of worship, and a memorial addressed to men for the deepening of their love and faith. Since every act of worship is impressive as well as expressive, and every devout remembrance of the Holy is a virtual adoration, in effect the two aspects of this single act cannot really be separated. To gaze at the Cross is to express our love, and also to evoke it. To recapitulate in thought or action the great events of "the dense and driven Passion" is to perform an act of worship which cannot fail to exercise a sanctifying influence. As St Augustine said, it "cures inflation and nourishes humility", by compelling the imperfect lover to contemplate within his own arena the beauty and the cost of Perfect Love.

(3) *Sacrifice.* It is strange, that the most painful of the discussions and conflicts which have raged round the Eucharist, have centred on the extent, and sense, in which it can be regarded as a sacrifice. For, if it cannot be so considered, Christian worship can no longer claim to be either a "fulfiller of the past" or a complete satisfaction of the religious sense; since it lacks an essential factor in man's response to God—the costly offering under tokens of his very life—and has no continuity with its own historic origins.

Clearly, the whole visible action of Jesus at the Last Supper, must be thought of as conditioned first by the Jewish religious background within which His earthly life was lived, and secondly by His own deep consciousness of His unique destiny. This action is only to be understood as the opening phase of the Passion; the phase in which He declares the purpose and meaning of His death, already indeed accomplished within the eternal purposes of God. "This is My Body which is given for you" is a phrase which no Jew could fail to understand in a sacrificial sense. It evokes at once the thoughts of the victim and the altar, the total oblation, the atonement for sin, the peace-offering that culminated in a sacramental meal. So the Last Supper must be regarded as a moment in that single action which moves to the crisis of Gethsemane and the Cross: and as setting on that action the seal of sacrifice. "The Supper-room faces the Cross, and consigns to it the Holy Lamb."[1] The offering indeed is already made and accepted. All that remains, is the carrying through of the sacrificial action to its term; but first by anticipation He distributes to His own its life-giving fruits—"the Body broken and the Blood outpoured".

> In mortem a discipulo
> Suis tradendus æmulis,
> Prius in vitæ ferculo
> Se tradidit discipulis.[2]

The Eucharist, then, is first the Church's representation before God of this perfect self-offering of Christ; that threefold oblation of the Upper Room, Gethsemane, and Calvary, in which all the deepest meanings of sacrifice are gathered and declared. Secondly, it is her own self-offering and that of each of her members, in and with Christ her head: since His sacrifice "once for all in fact externalized on Calvary, is ever real in the inward and heavenly sphere".[3] To that inward and heavenly sphere the Church by her Eucharistic worship is admitted, to join her sacrificial acts to the eternal self-offering of her Lord. These sacrificial acts, this total and loving dedication of life to the purposes of the Eternal—whether expressed in ritual action or not—form the very heart of her liturgic life. For the fullest act of worship, whether of the Church or of the soul, must be

[1] De la Taille, *The Mystery of Faith*, p. 11. Compare Pt. II, cap. XI.

[2] St Thomas Aquinas, Hymn for the Office of Lauds, Feast of Corpus Christi. Translation in the *English Hymnal*, No. 330.

[3] Oliver Quick, *The Christian Sacraments*, p. 198.

the surrender of the created life to the purposes of the continuing Incarnation: a mergence of the created will in that single stream of Charity which manifests the Divine Will. The ritual oblation which forms one strand in every Eucharist represents this living sacrifice and includes in its consecrating action many elements which are not directly or apparently religious. Thus it is true to say that the whole of Christian worship is focussed upon an altar where there is perpetually set forth the redemptive offering of pure love; and in that eternal offering, all other movements of love and sacrifice are sanctified before God.

> "The external and visible sacrifice," says Grou, "is but an image. The bread, made of many grains of wheat united in one whole, the wine made of many grapes dissolved together, these represent the faithful united to form one single body, having Jesus Christ for Head, and offering itself to God in unity of spirit . . . the mystery of the Body of Christ is accomplished when His members are offered in Him and with Him."[1]

So here, the Christian Eucharist lifts up to heavenly places that willing self-offering of the creature under sensible signs which is the essence of sacrificial worship. Yet it cannot be denied that there is another side to all this. The tendencies to substitute the outward offering for the self-oblation it should carry with it, and to emphasize the advantage sought and gained by man, rather than the offering made to God, which dog the history of sacrifice and are so vigorously denounced by the Hebrew prophets, have not spared Christian sacramentalism. The increase of these deformations during the later Middle Ages, the exaggerations of the propitiatory element in the Eucharist, and crude belief in the almost mechanical efficacy of the private or votive Mass, drove the reformers to their equally

[1] J. N. Grou, *La Science Pratique du Crucifix*, cap. XXIV.

crude and exaggerated horror of the very idea of oblation;[1] and so deprived the liturgies of the reformed Churches of that sacrificial element which, rightly understood, is the very life-blood of the Body of Christ. In some quarters, at least, these tendencies still exist; and account for the nervous anxiety of Protestant theologians as regards the "Eucharistic sacrifice".[2]

(4) *Supplication.* From every point of view it is plain that the Church's unceasing supplication to God and remembrance before Him of all her members—her "great intercession" for their needs and the needs of the world—must form an essential part of her liturgical life. Whether we consider its sacrificial or its social aspect, the confident appeal to God in and with the total self-offering of "Christ and His Christians", the lifting up of our temporal necessities into the atmosphere of Eternity, is itself an act of adoration and indeed a fundamental character of full worship. So from the beginning the intercessory prayer of the faithful, and the reading of the diptychs, with the names of those—whether living or dead—whom their fellow Christians were desired to remember before God, were important features in every Eucharist; emphasizing the corporate life and action of the household of faith. These memorials and intercessions were at first associated with the Offertory, as still in the equivalent Prayer for the Church Militant in the Anglican rite. In both the Roman and the Orthodox Liturgy, they are now placed within the Canon, in closest possible proximity to the consecration and oblation of the gifts "on behalf of all and for all": that is to say at the heart of the sacrificial action. None who have been present at an Orthodox Eucharist, and heard the long litanies of the deacon and the people accompanying the unseen action of the priest,

[1] "It stinks of oblation" was the reason given by Gardiner for the suppression of the Offertory.

[2] See further on this point, cap. XII, p. 260.

or realized the vast sweep of remembrance and petition which is covered by the memorials of the living and the dead, with their close association of the Church Invisible—" Forefathers, Patriarchs, Prophets, Apostles, Preachers . . . every righteous soul made perfect in faith "—and the here-and-now necessities of " all men and women ", can fail to recognize in this the authentic voice of Christian worship ; at once so theocentric in its orientation and so social in its sweep, so confident in its demand on the Infinite Power, and so conscious of its utter dependence.

> Do thou therefore, O Master, make effectual to us all for our good the gifts set forth, according to the need of each. Sail with those who sail upon the waters, journey with the wayfarers upon their way, heal the sick, thou Physician of our souls and bodies, by the grace and mercy, and love of men, of thine Only-begotten Son.[1]

For the Intercession of the Liturgy, though no detailed petition or individual need is too homely to be brought within its radius, is always a corporate action ; a reminder of the fact that the Communion of Saints and Communion of Sinners is one Body, and that within that Body the true interests of one are also the interests of all. There is no separation here between the Church visible and the Church invisible : it is as reasonable to seek a place in the supplications of the Saints as in those of an Intercessory Guild. So in the Roman Canon, the remembrance of the humble needs of the living in their weakness and imperfection—" Thy servants and handmaids N. and N. and all here present . . . who pay their vows to Thee, Eternal True and Living God " —is directly followed by the long roll-call of their great

[1] Compare the terse finality of the Western equivalent: " Oremus, dilectissimi nobis, Deum Patrem omnipotentem, ut cunctis mundum purget erroribus : morbos auferat : famem depellat : aperiat carceres : vincula dissolvat : peregrinantibus reditum : infirmantibus sanitatem : navigantibus portum salutis indulgeat ! " *Roman Missal :* Office for Good Friday.

fellow-servants "Thy blessed Apostles and Martyrs . . . and all Thy Saints" that the offering and the supplication may be that of "Thy whole family", here associated under various conditions of time and place in the one action of the eternal Eucharist.

(5) *The Mystery of the Presence.* The real starting point of the Christian Mystery is not the memorial of a Death but the recognition of an enduring Life. This takes precedence of all interpretations, whether Judeo-Christian or Hellenistic, of the Sacrifice of Calvary. Indeed, it is the fact of the Life which endorses the sacrificial and redemptive character of the death. In the primitive Eucharist, it would seem that the disciples experienced, in a specially vivid manner, that continuing real Presence among them of the living Lord—"working with them" as the conclusion of St Mark's Gospel says—which is accepted as an established fact by the New Testament writers, and was specially known "in the breaking of bread".[1] The stories of the post-resurrection appearances, when Jesus stood at dawn by the lake-side and said to the disciples "Come, and break your fast"[2] or, passing through closed doors, appeared in their midst, offered no difficulties to the primitive communicant: they were the sacred guarantees of an experience which might at any time be his own. The beautiful Mozarabic prayer "Adesto! adesto! bone pontifex, in medio nostri, sicut fuisti in medio discipulorum tuorum",[3] gives so perfectly the temper of this realistic expectation, that we can hardly doubt its early origin.

It is clear that this Presence, in the first instance, was not thought of as limited to the sacramental species; though it was specially to be experienced in this setting forth of His

[1] Luke xxiv. 35. Compare Pt. II, cap. XI.

[2] John xxi. 12 (R.V.).

[3] "Be present, be present, thou good High Priest, in the midst of us, as thou wast in the midst of thy disciples." Cf. Bright: *Ancient Collects*, p. 142.

sacrificial and self-imparting love. Nor is there now, in the Eucharistic doctrine and practice of the Orthodox Church, such precise identification of the sacramental Presence and the duly consecrated gifts, as is characteristic of Roman Catholic devotion to the Blessed Sacrament. Thus, the Great Entrance of the oblation into the sanctuary[1] which is one of the high points of the Byzantine rite, represents for the Orthodox worshipper both the entrance of the Logos into the world of history at the Incarnation, and—yet more vividly—the entrance of the self-given Lord into the assembled congregation of the Faithful. He is escorted with lights and incense, and welcomed in unequivocal terms by the singing of the Cherubic hymn: or, on Easter Eve, by the beautiful *troparion* "Let all mortal flesh keep silence!"

> Let all mortal flesh keep silence, and stand with fear and trembling,
> And ponder within itself no earthly thing;
> For the King of Kings and the Lord of Lords cometh to be slain,
> And to give Himself to be the Food of the Faithful.
> And before Him come also the Angelic Hosts with all dominion and power,
> The many-eyed Cherubim and the six-winged Seraphim
> Covering their faces and crying aloud the song,
> Alleluia![2]

Here under homely and familiar tokens the perfect type of self-giving Love, the Incarnate Charity already present, enters the sanctuary; that there by a renewal of His self-oblation He may give to men an increase of life and love. The usual theological explanation of this apparently paradoxical identification of the real Presence with the entrance of the unconsecrated gifts, is that it is "by way of anticipation"; and is to be regarded as symbolic rather than sacramental. The Bread and Wine, having been offered as an oblation and set apart for sacrifice, have now the sacred

[1] *Supra*, p. 132, and *infra*, Pt. II, cap. XII.

[2] *Liturgy of St. John Chrysostom:* Great Saturday. For the rhymed version see *English Hymnal*, No. 318.

characters of an *ikon*. But this rather clumsy theory does not seem to take into account the whole temper of this part of the service; the intensity of its spiritual realism; the fact that the congregation is gathered up to share an eternal experience, the ceaseless self-offering in heavenly places of Christ in and with His Church. "We have been in heaven!" said the envoys of St Vladimir when they returned from Constantinople to Russia after their first experience of the Byzantine Eucharist. It is from this point of view that we should understand the heightened tone of awe and joy which follows the Great Entrance, and the remembrance which is now made of the entrance of the Risen Lord into the Upper Room.[1] From this time onwards Christ is present: it is He, Priest no less than Victim, Who celebrates His mysterious supper within the screen. Originally after the gifts were placed upon the Holy Table all present gave each other the Kiss of Peace; one saying: "Christ is among us!" the other replying: "He is, and He will be!"—a ceremony which is now confined to the sacred ministers.

Here we seem to have, enshrined in liturgy, the memory of a more ancient, simple, unlocalized experience of the Presence Who "lived and died and is alive for evermore",[2] than that which finally established itself in the doctrinal system of the Western Church. As the earliest liturgies seem little concerned to define the precise moment of consecration or the precise character of the change which then takes place: so, too, they avoid any exact and rigid pinning-down of the Mystery of the Presence to the moments that follow the hallowing and reception of the gifts. We sometimes forget the implications of two closely related facts: (*a*) That the New Testament Canon was produced within the Church, by persons whose chief religious practice and experience was Eucharistic, and whose most sacred

[1] Gogol, *Meditations on the Divine Liturgy*, p. 60.

[2] Revelation i. 18.

belief was the continued presence with that Church of the Risen Christ; (*b*) That there was for that Apostolic Church no break between the mysterious experiences of the Forty Days and the primitive Eucharistic practice. Yet these facts must have their bearing on the colour and significance of many passages in the Gospels: e.g. the stress which is laid on the stories of miraculous feedings, the accounts of post-resurrection appearances (several times linked with the blessing and giving of food[1]), and the great discourses reported by the Fourth Evangelist. In all these, truth is seen and heard through the ears and eyes of communicants; for whom there was no sharp contrast between the experienced Presence of the seen and the unseen Christ. Here we seem to have the germ of two such apparently contrasted yet really harmonious types of Christocentric devotion as the "Evangelical experience" on the one hand, and the Catholic cultus of Christ present in the reserved Sacrament on the other hand. In each, the bridge over which the worshipping soul passes to communion with the Unseen is the Humanity of Christ, conceived as truly present and living in and with His Church.

Yet this most intimate and actual Presence is none the less the Incarnate Logos "standing beyond the present and the past", and penetrating at every point the world which is upheld by His power. If for one type this spiritual fact is realized most vividly by means of the sacramental species, for the other type, the necessary carrying-medium is provided by a conceptual image; of which the raw material is supplied in part by Christian tradition, and in part by the believing mind. But it is by accepting, not denouncing these our human limitations that each reaches out to the ever-deepening realization of communion with an imageless Reality. Moreover, the witness of non-sacramental Christians warns us, that this experience of the Presence cannot be

[1] Mark xvi. 14; Luke xxiv. 30–35; John xxi. 12.

exclusively identified either with the Eucharistic or other particular devotional concomitant; but partakes of the limitless freedom of Christ. It has often visited solitary individual Christians and non-churchmen in their need. It was well known to the early Quaker assemblies, and a chief source of their confidence and strength.

> "The Lord of heaven and earth", says Francis Howgill, "we found to be at hand; and as we waited upon Him in pure silence, our minds out of all things, His heavenly Presence appeared in our assemblies, when there was no language or speech from any creature."[1]

It is hard to make a sharp distinction between such an experience of the Presence, and that which all full Eucharistic worship implies. Nor perhaps should we desire so to do. For here the free action of the Divine Charity, transcending all means and all limitations in His movement towards men, guarantees those sacred and mysterious contacts which are mediated to us by the appointed channels of sacramental grace.

(6) *The Heavenly Food.* It is not necessary at this point to develop the fact and importance of ritual meals as an element in primitive worship; nor even, to come nearer home, to discuss the connection between the Last Supper and the Jewish Kiddush.[2] It is at least probable that the Kiddush provided the ritual pattern for the first Eucharist, as the Temple sacrifices suggested its special language. But here it is essential to remember that whilst the Kiddush was by declaration a symbolic meal, the communion which forms the climax of the Eucharist was from the first a sacramental meal: giving to those who took part in it a share in that Life which was self-offered for the world. It did in reality that which it set forth under signs. Far

[1] Testimony of Francis Howgill (1618–1669). Given in *Christian Life, Faith and Thought*, p. 27.

[2] See below, Pt. II, cap. X.

more important for the inner history of Christian worship than any discussion of its ritual origins, is the emphasis which Our Lord seems to have laid both in action and in teaching upon the symbolism of food; and upon the soul's hunger and thirst, its need of nourishment and utter dependence on God—Christ—Spirit, for any spiritual life it may have. Not only the great Johannine discourse on the Living Bread—where the influence of later sacramental experience can hardly be missed—but those solemn, quasi-sacramental feedings of the multitude, with their suggestions of a ceremonial blessing of the bread, which all the Synoptics report as an outstanding feature of the Ministry, prepare the way for the more solemn, more sacramental giving of the Bread of Eternal Life. The mystery of Eucharistic communion does not stand alone; but comes on the crest of a great wave. The feeding of the Four Thousand, and of the Five Thousand, by means of the little stock of common food which was offered, accepted, and "eucharisticized", and thus made to suffice and more than suffice for the hungry crowds—and the deliberate emphasis on something of deep significance there done[1]—all this prepares the way for it, and is part of the same economy. All point towards the offering and the hallowing of the natural, that it may become the carrying medium of that divine food which is "broken but not divided, scattered but never spent": and actually gives to men that which the Pagan mysteries offered—a satisfaction of their hunger and thirst for God.

That this strand in the Eucharist had from the beginning a deep but not exclusive importance, can be seen from the Catacomb paintings, where the giving of the manna in the wilderness, and the miraculous feedings of the multitude, stand side by side as its ante-types; witnessing to the immemorial divine generosity, now at last fully declared. Here the small offerings of man are answered by the "divine

[1] Mark viii. 19–21.

largesse"—the "hidden Manna" given under earthly tokens to nourish his emerging supernatural life.[1] All the early liturgies witness to the sacred awe with which Holy Communion was approached and the deep spiritual significance which attached to it.

> I have eaten thy sacred Body; let not the fire seize me!
> I have looked upon it: let mine eyes see thy mercies.
> I have not been a stranger to thy mysteries: let me not be separated from thee![2]

The essential relationship of the soul to God is here dramatically presented by means of a sacramental mystery, which gives access to the very sources of our life and truly effects that which it declares. The ancient sacrificial meals were held to give all who shared in them a certain communion with the divine nature, by means of a spirit-infused nourishment. In the Christian sacrifice, the Logos enters the time-series and is self-given under fugitive species to the creature, that by this feeding on Reality the creature may be transformed: receiving by infusion the gift of charity to strengthen, purify, and at last supernaturalize his own imperfect love, and thus bring a little nearer that transfiguration of the world in Christ which is the creative goal of Christian worship.

> The eyes of all wait on Thee, O Lord, and Thou givest them their meat in due season. ℣. Thou openest thine hand and fillest all things living with plenteousness. Alleluia. ℣. My Flesh is meat indeed and My Blood is drink indeed: he that eateth My flesh and drinketh My Blood, dwelleth in Me and I in him. Alleluia.[3]

The Communion of the people is, therefore, the proper climax of all Eucharistic worship; essential, indeed, if the

[1] Revelation ii. 17.

[2] Post Communion of the Maronite rite. (Attwater, *Prayers from the Eastern Liturgies*, p. 44.)

[3] *Roman Missal*: Gradual for the feast of Corpus Christi.

balance and full significance of the service is to be preserved. Yet no element in the total action has been in fact so difficult to maintain. Every great revival of Christian worship, Catholic and Orthodox, Anglican and Nonconformist, has protested against the neglect of this sovereign means of grace, and struggled to restore Holy Communion to something approaching its proper place in the Church's life.[1] Indeed, at the present day, practising members of the Roman Catholic and Anglican Churches receive communion far more frequently than in the " ages of faith ". Yet in the early days of the Church, nothing less than a general communion was even contemplated as the conclusion of the Eucharist. In it the profoundly social character of Christianity is once more endorsed; for the communion in Holy Things towards which each has made a humble offering, is a " bond of fellowship " both between each Christian and his Lord, and between all members of the Body, who here share at one altar one spiritual food. Thus, Communion is an essential part of full Christian worship, because in it the Perfect is not only adored, but approached and received under sensible signs. It is therefore a sovereign means to that created perfection to which God calls the spirit of man, but which man by himself can never achieve. It dethrones egotism, the inveterate enemy of the spirit of worship; and awakens awestruck gratitude and humble love by a method which the simplest can appreciate, but which the greatest saint will never understand.

This analysis does not pretend even to an external completeness. In particular, it leaves almost unexamined the social aspect of the Eucharist; which many modern

[1] E.g. the best of the Anglican reformers had as an avowed aim the restoring of the communion of the people as part of every Eucharist; and so had the leaders of the Counter-Reformation. The giving of frequent communion was urged by the Council of Trent. At a later period the early Methodists and the Tractarians alike emphasized the importance of frequent communion of the laity; in this anticipating the present policy of the Roman Catholic Church. See below, caps. XIV and XV.

writers have emphasized, perhaps to excess. It is no doubt true that the primitive sacrament was developed in closest connection with a common meal, and that the name of Holy Communion covered the fellowship between Christians, as well as more sacred intercourse of those Christians with their Lord. The often quoted phrase from the Eucharistic prayer of Bishop Sarapion, "as this bread, scattered on the tops of the mountains, was gathered together to become one loaf, so also gather Thy holy Church", represents a real and thoroughly Apostolic aspect of the idea of communion, which was plainly present in the mind of the early Church. The thought is traceable in most of the early liturgies except the Roman;[1] but gradually faded out as Christian worship became stylized and lost its communal character, and the general communion of all the faithful ceased to be an essential feature of the rite. Yet that character of the Eucharistic mystery which enables it to bind many strands of worship and many types of worshipper in one, should never be forgotten by us. In it the extremes of theistic and Christocentric, historical and mystical devotion are united; and here, in loving remembrance of the humanity of Jesus, truly present to the devout communicant, Catholic and Evangelical piety meet.

> "Thou hast", says Grou, "comprehended in Thy Eucharist all Thy loving kindnesses, that we no less than those to whom Thou didst give their firstfruits may share them. How easy it is to remember that Thou wast made man for our salvation, when Thou dost perpetually renew that sublime mystery upon our altars; that Thou didst rest within the body of a Virgin, when we have the happiness of receiving Thee into our own; that Thou wast born in a stable, when Thou dost deign to be born in our hearts; that Thou didst live on earth for thirty years an obscure and hidden life, when Thou dost come and hide Thyself in the obscurity of our souls, and hide

[1] Cf. Brilioth, *op. cit.*, p. 30.

them with Thyself in God; that Thou didst converse with men, teaching the ignorant and converting the sinful, that Thou didst feed the hungry crowds with miraculous food, enlighten the blind, cure the sick, raise the dead, when Thou dost still accomplish in us all these marvels of loving kindness; deigning to enter into the solitude of our hearts, there to converse lovingly with us, dissipate our darkness, purify and sanctify our souls, and feed them with that bread of life which Thy love never ceases to multiply."[1]

Of those aspects which have been considered, the experience of the Presence and the reception of the Heavenly Food—which together constitute the primitive Christian mystery—represent the loving movement of God towards His creatures. The historical memorial commemorates the way in which that act of Divine Charity was accomplished; the Incarnation and its cost. In his grateful adoration and his oblation, man makes his small acknowledgment of the prevenient self-giving of the Holy; and unites his response on one hand with the worship of the whole created order, on the other with that perfect sacrifice of Calvary where the divine and human love meet. All these strands are so plaited together, so give strength and quality to each other, that any attempt to separate them or eliminate any one of them maims the supernatural beauty of the whole. For throughout the whole action the seen and unseen, the sensible and the spiritual, the historical and the eternal, interpenetrate. The Oblation is ours and yet it is His. In the words of the *Sanctus* we unite our adoration, our abasement, and our self-offering with the young Isaiah standing awestruck in the Temple, and with the angels who stand for ever in the Uncreated Light. In the act of communion, as St Augustine so forcibly reminded his flock, we who are part of Christ's Mystical Body, receive our share

[1] J. N. Grou, *La Science Pratique du Crucifix*, cap. XX.

in the Body's life. "If then you are the Body of Christ, and His members, then that which is on the altar is the mystery of yourselves. Receive the mystery of yourselves!"[1]

[1] St Augustine. Sermon 57. Migne, *Patrologia Latina*, Vol. XXXVIII.

CHAPTER IX

THE PRINCIPLES OF PERSONAL WORSHIP

I

THE "praying Church" is built of praying souls; and all that has been said of the fundamentally social character of Christian worship, as expressed in the common liturgic action of the Church, and of the status of the individual soul as an organic part of this corporate life, must not be allowed to obscure this complementary truth. Christianity proclaims, more clearly than any other religion, the value and particular vocation of the individual, his unique and direct relation to God. Its greatest triumphs have been the individual achievements of the saints: that is, persons whose lives of worship have made them tools of God. Already in the teaching and practice of Christ, the central importance of personal, indeed of solitary prayer, the free, loving, disciplined, and single-minded waiting of the soul on God, is emphasized:[1] and each great form of Christianity, Catholic and Orthodox, Evangelical and Quaker, has in its own manner and according to its particular genius, been concerned to safeguard this truth, and maintain a rightful balance between the corporate and individual life of worship. Certainly the total life of the Body is a real, indeed a personal life, transcending and enfolding that of its separate members and essential to their growth. But the quality of this total life must depend on the extent in which each unit is open towards God, and responsive to His secret action. Thus the corporate worship in which this life is offered to God must

[1] E.g. Matt. vi. 6; vii. 7; Mark i. 35, etc.

be for each member a vital interest, which kills a mere self-interested spirituality. None the less, and indeed because of this greater life, the production and maintenance in each unit of that realistic relation with God which makes of the human soul an instrument of adoration must be a concern of the whole: for it directly serves the Church's supreme object, the increase of the Glory of God. The Church "unites only in order to sanctify, and she sanctifies only the better to adore,"[1] and no enthusiasm for corporate action must be allowed to blur this truth.

Each Christian life of prayer, then, however deeply hidden or apparently solitary in form, will affect the life of the whole Body. By the very fact of its entrance into the sphere of worship, its action is added to that total sacrifice of praise and thanksgiving in which the life of the Invisible Church consists. As every creature from mayfly to elephant, each with its different rhythm and time-span, forms part of the single rich response of Nature to the creative action of God; so each distinct life of prayer, with its particular rhythm, time-span, and capacity makes its essential contribution to that total response which is the essence of worship. Hurried advocates of corporate religion have sometimes tended to regard such hidden and personal lives of prayer as exclusive, other-worldly, lacking in social value and open to the charge of spiritual selfishness. But this superficial view does not bear examination. In obeying the first and great commandment, the life of personal worship obeys the second, too. Its influence radiates, its devoted self-offering avails for the whole. Indeed the living quality of the great liturgic life of the community, its witness to the Holy, depends in the last resort on the sacrificial lives of its members; and it is only from within such intensive lives that intercessory power—the

[1] Quoted by A. G. Hebert in *Liturgy and Society*, p. 132, from the *Liturgische Zeitschrift*, Nov., 1932.

application to particulars of the Eternal Love—seems to arise. Hence it is that all the great masters of worship insist on the importance of the secret personal life of adoration as "the first essential for a Christian"; the only condition under which he can hope to become a channel of the Divine Charity, and co-operate in the sanctification of life. For it is the self-oblivious gaze, the patient and disciplined attention to God, which deepens understanding, nourishes humility and love; and, by the gentle processes of growth, gradually brings the creature into that perfect dedication to His purpose which is the essence of the worshipping life.

> "Set apart", says Bossuet, to one of his penitents, "a certain amount of time morning and evening, whether the mind be filled with God or not, doing so with no other object than the adoration which is the duty of His creature. Adore Him with all the capacity you have, yet without anxiety as to the degree of your success or of your love, as to whether you are concentrated on God or on yourself, whether your time is profitable or wasted. . . . There is no question here of stages of prayer. We are concerned only with adoring God without any motive save that we are in duty bound to do so, without any desire save to offer adoration, or if we fail in this to accept failure with patience and humility. . . . The value of our prayer depends on the degree to which we die to self in offering it. There is no place for calculations or precautions. Strive to adore, and let that suffice."[1]

If, then, on the one hand the Christian must always worship as a member of the Supernatural Society, mindful of its great interests and subordinated to its life, on the other hand he must also worship as the secret child of God; humbly aware of a direct and most sacred relationship with Him, and utterly abandoned to His Will. All

[1] Quoted by E. K. Sanders, *Jacques Bénigne Bossuet*, p. 319, from an unpublished letter in the Bâle Library.

that he does partakes of this double character. It is part of " a chain variously intertwisted with, variously affecting, and affected by, numerous other chains and other lives " ; but it also involves " another, a far deeper, a most darling and inspiring relation . . . each single act, each single moment joined directly to GOD—Himself not a chain, but one great Simultaneity ".[1] Each of these aspects of the life of worship—the successive and the absolute—safeguards and completes the other ; and a full and balanced Christianity needs and gives place for both. So a living corporate worship will only be found where this double movement is present ; where there is a nucleus of praying souls, maintaining direct essential contact with the Transcendent, whilst not forgetful of their social vocation as servants of the living God, and this realistic correspondence of the individual soul, its adherence to the Holy, is encouraged, stabilized, and fed. The periods of Christian decadence have always been periods when this costly interior life of personal devotion has been dim. Revival has always come through persons for whom adoring and realistic attention to God and total self-giving to God's purpose have been the first interests of life. These persons it is true have become fully effective only when associated in groups : but the ultimate source of power has been the dedication of the individual heart. The Benedictines, the Franciscans, and the Friends of God ; and within more recent times the Quakers, the Methodists, and the Tractarians, all witness to this. Indeed Christian history is lit throughout its course by these " flames of living love ". These facts cannot astonish us, when we consider that it is by worship alone that we have access to the Holy and the Real : and, that where His prevenient revelation truly breaks in upon a soul, an unconditioned personal devotion bringing all levels of life into subjection to His Will is the inevitable response. As the sacrificial passion

[1] F. von Hügel, *Selected Letters*, p. 287.

of the artist for a realized Beauty, and the communion with Beauty which his self-giving achieves, open a channel by which the Absolute Beauty enters succession and is revealed to other men; so the personal passion in which the soul responds to God and which lights the lamp of worship, opens a channel whereby the Eternal enters Time and there reveals Holiness and Truth.

Understood in the deepest sense personal worship is man's return-movement of charity to the inciting Charity of God;[1] and therefore organic to his spiritual life. As it develops, it will be exercised in two directions; vertically in adoration, and horizontally in intercession, as the ancient sacrifice was at once an act of oblation and impetration, a gift made to the Unseen and a petition made on behalf of the seen. Thus it is intimately concerned with both aspects of our double-relatedness, the eternal and the successive. In both, not one alone, it reaches out towards the Holy, as the final and sufficing object of worship and love; first in surrender to His pure Being, and secondly in loving co-operation with His creative activity. This loving co-operation is the essence of intercession; which is, when rightly understood, an act of worship directed to the Glory of God. Within the Eternal Charity all spirits are united. We each have our place in that order, and self-giving to its saving purposes is the substance of our worshipping life. The true intercessor offers the oblation of his imperfect love, that it may become a channel of the Absolute Love. Here he prays from the Cross. According to the degree of his self-offering is the power of his prayer; and a part of his self-offering will be an entire willingness to work and

[1] By Charity is meant, here and throughout, that love of God by which He is loved for Himself alone, and all creatures in and for Him; and which is man's response to the Divine self-giving love (1 John iv. 10, 16, 19). Cf. *The Cloud of Unknowing*, cap. XXIV, "Charity meaneth nought else but love of God for himself above all creatures, and of men for God even as thyself."

suffer in the dark, asking for no assurance of result. All that he does and endures, is done and endured as the adoring tool and servant of the Creative Love; and in the last result, his intercessory action is part of the movement of Its Will. "Even the prayer of demand", as Bremond has said, "is not truly prayer except in so far as it is also adoration."[1] It is those who best practise the loving adoration who will best practise the loving expansion; since dwelling in Charity they dwell in God, and become effective channels of His generosity. At their full development the two movements are merged in that one, all-inclusive act of self-giving and obedient love, which Christians find revealed in the life of Jesus and supremely expressed in the Cross: the arms stretched out to embrace the world, and the eyes lifted up towards the Eternal God.

There is nothing in man's mixed experience which cannot be brought within the radius of this willing and all-inclusive response to the demand of Reality. Thus the subtle experiences of his own inner life, witnessing more clearly with every advance in self-knowledge to the penetrating charity and mysterious action of God, holding up the footsteps of His creature, restoring the soul, challenging the mind, ever delicately working within life, must evoke an answering movement of gratitude and awe: and in the demands of the world without, its call upon his pity and service, he will again hear the voice of Charity inviting his devotedness by means of its creatures' needs. Some ascetic effort, too, must enter into any individual worship worthy of the name; expressing the soul's deliberate choice of God, and loving renunciation of all that hinders total self-giving to God—the act of will which throws the human spirit with its preferences and desires at His feet. Even disciplines which in themselves are childish, acquire in this context a

[1] Henri Bremond, *La Philosophie de la Prière*, p. 15.

certain nobility;[1] and humbling failures occasioned by the greatness of the aim and fragility of the creature become, when rightly accepted, a true part of that creature's self-oblation.

For the life of personal worship—that is to say the increasingly adoring relation to the Holy—is grounded in two qualities: humility and charity. Humility is or should be what man feels about himself over against God. Charity is or should be what that same creature feels about God standing over against himself, and ever more and more penetrating and possessing his life, till at last that life shall become "so far transformed and perfected in the Fire of Love, that not only is it united with this Fire, but has become one living flame within it".[2] These characters are inseparable; they rise and fall together in the soul, and are the only valid index of the worth of its worship. Their presence means that this worship has introduced it into the world of supernatural realities; however dimly, crudely, or uncertainly these realities may be conceived. Humility in its beginning arises from negative contrast; man's sense of his own faults and imperfection, his nothingness over against God. But at its height it is caused by positive contrast: the supreme love, worth, and beauty of God in Himself, His perfection striking upon the soul. Charity in its beginning is the creature's response to the divine attraction; and in its fulfilment rises to that unconditioned act of Pure Love which is the very substance of the supernatural life.

Thus the personal life of worship involves on the human side an utter self-abandonment of the creature to God, as the Existent of all existents and doer of all that is done—a total

[1] Yet on the other hand the dignity of the aim should surely exercise a controlling influence on the means employed; and forbid the repellent imbecilities in which fervour has sometimes taken a certain pride. Those familiar with this literature will easily find their own "awful examples".

[2] St John of the Cross: *The Living Flame of Love*, Prologue.

Godward reference of will and act and desire, purging egotism and quickening charity—and on the divine side, the ever-increasing action of the Creative Love, breaking in, possessing, and moulding the soul. Each worshipping movement of that soul, whether expressed under the formula of devotion or of service—each "act of the will wrought in charity" as St John of the Cross says—increases its capacity for God; and so contributes to that total transfiguration of life, that redemption of the world, which is the Christian goal. Nor is this ideal intended only to apply to "advanced souls" or persons of mystical capacity. It is, on the contrary, the essence of the Christian spiritual life as plainly taught in the New Testament.[1]

The living core of individual worship, then, is a loving dedication of the will; but a dedication which is itself the result of, and the response to, God's prevenient act and pressure. Thus we come to realize our true position, as units in a vast spiritual economy; each with a degree of freedom, and each with its own part to play, but all vivified and sustained by the Charity which is God. "Our prayer", says Von Hügel, "will certainly gain in depth and aliveness, if we thus continually think of God as the true inspirer of our most original-seeming thoughts and wishes, whensoever these are good and fruitful—as Him Who secretly initiates what He openly crowns."[2]

II

The touch of God upon the soul, which is the prevenient cause of all worship, is received by us as we are: creatures of sense and spirit, at various stages of enlightenment and growth. Our response to it is and must be conditioned by

[1] E.g. especially in the Epistle to the Romans and the First Epistle of St John.

[2] *Essays and Addresses*, Series II, p. 225.

our here-and-now human situation; and by our particular education, capacities, and temperament. We use what we have, and realize what we can; and since no two souls possess an identical equipment, this is the general reason for the various kinds and degrees of prayer described by different teachers and the confusing and even contradictory directions which are often given in respect of them. Yet all these kinds and degrees of prayer, from the most formal to the most formless, are the sacramental expressions of one simple but absolute act; the humble acknowledgment of God's objective Reality as the controlling fact of life, the "naked intent directed towards Him."[1] This act, or total theocentric disposition of the self, is a habitude of charity, implanted by the Eternal Charity and arising in that "ground" of the soul, its depth and centre, where we have a certain kinship with God: "its pure and inmost substance, wherein alone, secretly and in silence, the Word dwells as its Lord".[2] All the great masters of prayer witness to the reality of this transcendental life in man. It is to the union of the created spirit with the uncreated God in this deep ground of our metaphysical being (or "apex" or "fine point of the spirit," as teachers variously call it—for these spatial metaphors all intend one spaceless reality) that the acts and dispositions of personal worship tend. It is the absolute life of correspondence with the Eternal thus evoked and nourished, which underlies and supports all expressive worship. This absolute life, in its very nature, is not accessible either to feeling or to reasoning mind; for these are directed towards correspondence with other aspects of our rich psycho-physical experience. Nevertheless the simple yet total dedication of the finite will to the Infinite Will, which is "the essential interior act of religion",[3]

[1] *The Cloud of Unknowing*, cap. VII.
[2] St John of the Cross: *The Living Flame of Love*, stanza IV.
[3] Dom John Chapman, *Spiritual Letters*, pp. 98 and 175.

arises here; and thence overflows to colour and convert to its single purpose the psycho-physical faculties of feeling, imagination, and thought. It must do this, gathering all aspects of our personality into the creature's response to God, if it is to achieve that embodiment which Christianity requires; be given drive and precision, and be protected from those dangers of vagueness and monotony—above all, the arch-danger of spiritual superiority—which always threaten any life of prayer that seeks to maintain itself on purely spiritual levels, refusing the common means of expression and therefore isolated from the common life.

On three counts this embodiment of worship seems to be necessary to the soul. On the theological side, the very principle of incarnation requires that the whole of our human nature, and not one bit alone, shall be gathered into the worshipping life; and so laid open to the transforming action of God. On the corporate side, the Catholic character of Christianity demands that souls of every sort and at every stage of growth—the most naïve and unenlightened, no less than the spiritually alert—shall have each its place within its borders; and each one find there the means of a full personal life of worship suited to its state. This will involve not only the ascents of the loving spirit in pure acts of adoration, but also the use of the reasoning mind in meditation on the Holy, and beyond this the bringing-in of much which purists relegate to the "lower nature"—the most homely of human emotions, the crudest of sensible images, the most primitive gestures of worship—as means of apprehending the Holy. Here we have the sanction, if not the origin, of that deliberate appeal to the affections and imagination which plays so large a part in Christian devotional literature, and in the development of the personal life of prayer. None of these affections and imaginations—drawn as they must be from the common stock of our emotional life—are adequate to the ineffable Object of our worship. Yet it seems part of the discipline of the Incarnation that we should be willing to worship where we are and as we can; turning natural emotion to spiritual purposes and gratefully accepting inspiration even from the crudest picture-books of faith. Those who deliberately and priggishly strip their prayer of these homely compounds of sense and spirit, instead of quietly awaiting the stripping action of God, run the risk of leaving nothing on which their sense-conditioned minds and hearts can lay hold. The vividly-imagined Christ of popular worship, the Child in the Manger, the Redeemer on the Cross—and other figures more remote from reality—wake up and nourish a total creaturely devotion in which every aspect of our humanity can play its part: and so become the means of a richer religious experience than the mass of souls can achieve by the methods of "pure" spirituality. It is true that these means carry their own dangers; and may easily encourage the sentimentalisms of the devotee, intent on an oblique emotional satisfaction, unless safeguarded by a bracing discipline of act and thought. Yet with all their risks we are bound to accept them, as a part of the conditioned world within which the human soul is moved by God and responds to His call.

Finally, it is only in the experience of the greatest contemplatives—and then at the price of a peculiar tension and suffering—that the pure intuition of absolutes, the undifferentiated surrender of the creature to the uncreated Spirit, which is the human side of union with God, can be maintained without help from other levels of our being. The response made by a creature conditioned by time and space to a timeless and spaceless Reality will have characters which constantly break the bounds both of philosophy and of logic. The normal man, in his secret no less than in his corporate intercourse with God, must therefore be willing to use thought, feeling, and imagination as long and as much as he can; must worship under images that which is beyond image, and adapt the machinery and language of human emotion to his loving communion with the Unseen.

Within its own arena, each personal life of worship will necessarily reproduce in varying proportions the great lines of the Christian response to God: that is to say, it will react in awe to the transcendent mystery of His Being, and in loving obedience to His incarnate revelation in Christ. Because of this polarity between Eternity and History, Transcendence and Incarnation, the full Christian life of prayer will have in it an element of passive adoration, and an element of intimate communion and co-operation: since in his deepest soul each man feels himself at the same time to be attracted and daunted by the Transcendent, yet companioned and solicited by the Revealed. The peculiar character of each soul's worship, its degree of sanity, fruitfulness, and peace, will be determined by the harmony which it is able to achieve between these transcendent and homely strands of the devotional life. Where the first attraction preponderates, the worship will be mainly theocentric and contemplative in type; and as it deepens under the purifying action of God, will make less and less use of feeling and image, becoming more and more a simple state of abandonment to Him. But where the second rules, and God is chiefly known and loved in Christ, worship will find its material in His historical and sacramental revelation; and its natural means of expression in the affections and imagery of human relationships, and in acts of personal love, penitence, communion, and service.

It follows from this, that those intimate, imaginative, and romantic types of prayer which abound in devotional manuals, form for those who can use them a means of response to God entirely consistent with the spirit of Christianity. They mediate His eternal Reality in a way which is appropriate to our condition, and give to each level of our psychic life its opportunity of sublimation. Those primitive reactions to experience which are still present with us, must be given their part in the creature's reaction to the Holy. Indeed, since the act of worship is God-given, its vehicles—including our naïve imaginative embodiments of the Divine—are God-given, too; and to be humbly received as necessities of our creaturely state. Christianity is centred on the belief that in and through the natural the Supernatural Logos reaches out to us. Therefore worshipping access to the Absolute in and through the contingent is an essential character of the Christian's communion with God; and must have its place in the personal life of prayer. "Here", says Will, "the metaphysical world allies itself with the sensible world, and by its means invades believing hearts".[1]

In his humble meditations on the mysteries of Faith, his deliberate picturings of the scenes of the Incarnation and Passion, the devout Christian truly experiences the "tender mercy" of the Absolute, inviting the soul to life-giving acts of faith, hope, and love. The continued success of the *Spiritual Exercises* of St Ignatius, as a means of "procuring the Love of God", and with it the transformation of life, depends almost entirely on the way in which the soul is thus brought in its solitude into direct imaginative contact with the mysteries of the Life of Christ; and through and in this searching experience is compelled to a total capitulation to the Divine. In particular, the imaginative realization of the Passion has always held a high place in the Christian devotional life; for here, as St Bernard says: "God shows Himself incarnate in suffering humanity, that by this sensible spectacle He may touch the hearts of creatures of sense". This is why meditation on the Passion, and on the Resurrection which crowns it, is "always

[1] Will, *Le Culte*, Vol. I, p. 171.

accompanied by an increase of charity, which prepares the soul for the visit of the Word ".[1]

So, too, the Sulpician method of prayer, with its devout concentration on " Jesus before the eyes, Jesus in the hands, Jesus in the heart ",[2] is an imaginative device whereby the three chief forms of man's response to his environment can be subdued to the pattern of the Incarnate and their sanctification set in hand. Though easily discredited by a superficial psychology, such a device is more than justified as a means, appropriate to our human limitations, of developing the personal life of worship. The continuous popularity in all branches of the Church of personal devotions of this intimate type addressed to imaginative embodiments of the Invisible—the Good Shepherd, the Redeemer, the Crucified, or Risen Christ—or otherwise adapting our natural equipment of phantasy and feeling to the supernatural purposes of adoration, witnesses to a common religious need.[3] Here Catholic and Protestant, Franciscan and Methodist, though they may differ in their imaginative preferences, are in principle at one. Nor does the way in which this need is met vary much between different epochs and schools. The Christocentric rhapsodies of Richard Rolle, the hymns of St Bernard, of the Franciscan poets, or of the German pietists, the mediæval cult of the Name of Jesus, the post-reformation cult of the Sacred Heart, the Evangelical devotion to the Person of Christ and the Catholic devotion to His Eucharistic Presence, all have their origin in one single type of personal worship; which adapts to its purpose all the resources of the phantasy life, is ever apt to slide down into sentimental extravagance, and yet is justified by its spiritual results. " All these things ", says Abbot Chapman of such imaginative devotions, " are good *as means*, provided they

[1] Given by E. Gilson, *La Théologie Mystique de S. Bernard*, p. 103.

[2] J. J. Olier, *Introduction à la Vie et aux Vertus Chrétiennes.* Description in Bede Frost, *The Art of Mental Prayer*, p. 125.

[3] Compare *supra*, caps. II and IV.

are only used as means for serving God perfectly all the rest of the day. . . . An imagination of our Lord's Presence after Holy Communion (for instance) is a representation of something which is true in a sensible way: and if it is helpful, let it go on!"[1]

These sensible images and emotional apprehensions are in fact clothes put by the self upon the bare Object of its adoration; and often enough the clothes and the reality are confused by naïve worshippers, less eager to analyse than to love.[2] Sometimes, too, the clothes are bizarre or extravagant, and sin against modesty and good taste. But these are risks which must be accepted by us; for in all save those genuine contemplatives who have passed through the "night of the senses", and can "take to their love that which they cannot think",[3] one or other of these mental, emotional and imaginative concomitants will and must condition and accompany our communion with God: nor can we manage the simplest act of vocal worship without their help. Yet it would be merely uncreaturely to reject all this because we are aware of its allusive and secondary character; or ignore the wholesome advice of St Macarius, that the man of prayer should await the visitation of God "through all the doors and paths and senses of the soul"[4]

III

The individual's worship, then, is always to be thought of as a willed response to God's inciting action; a humble and costly co-operation with His grace, moving towards the complete dedication of life. Flexible in expression, but

[1] Dom John Chapman, *op. cit.*, p. 125.

[2] It is worth while to remember that among these naïve worshippers are some of the greatest of the saints; in whom the transfiguration of life witnesses to the reality of their prayer.

[3] Cf. *The Cloud of Unknowing*, cap. VI.

[4] St Macarius, *Homily XXXIII*.

N

single in aim, it takes up and adapts to its purpose with a certain ordered freedom all the faculties of the self, emotional, intellectual, and imaginative: only ceasing to use them when it must. By this organic view—which is in the long run the only possible view for Christians—we are at once delivered from many of the tiresome discussions and solemn analyses of devotional practice which have confused the life of prayer. For now that life of prayer is seen to be the sacramental expression of a more deeply hidden action, the total self-offering of creature to Creator; and the matter of this sacrament can be drawn from every aspect of our normal experience and every level of our psychic life. The depth and beauty, the tenderness and awfulness of God, require from the creature who approaches Him in worship the full employment of all those capacities and modes of perception and response with which he has been endowed.

The three great faculties at the disposal of the worshipping spirit are, of course, those of feeling, imagination, and reasoning mind. In all personal devotion below the level of contemplation one or all will and must be used. The classic "methods" of mental prayer provide for all of them; though in practice one or other will probably preponderate. Since Christian worship must never be regarded as only or chiefly the affair of contemplatives, these sensible means of response to God must be taken seriously by us. As Von Hügel said of Eucharistic devotions, whatever their theological credentials may be, they have contributed to the formation of "saints, and great saints". It is true that beyond and within all conscious and sensible worship is the supra-sensible action which this mediates: the pure act of adoration, the theocentric impulse, arising in the "ground of the soul". But so deeply hidden is that substantial movement that the Godward affections, images, and thoughts, which lie well within the field of normal consciousness, generally seem to the normal self to be the very substance of its communion with Him. When they disappear or disclose their merely symbolic and approximate character in regard to the unknowable Reality, the ensuing blankness is at first regarded as the death of worship: instead of that which it really is—the exchange of the comfortably furnished world of religious imagination for the "wilderness where lovers lose themselves".

Setting aside that intercessory work which is also an act of adoration, since it is directed towards the fulfilment of God's Will, personal worship as it passes beyond the stage of vocal prayer will generally tend to one of three modes of expression. These are first the "discursive meditation" which develops from the consideration of some scene or words of Scripture, appeals to reason no less than to feeling, and culminates in a movement of the will; next the imaginative realization of the truths of faith and silent submission to their cleansing light; last, those acts of loving devotion, "short and lively affections of the soul by which she expresses a thirsty longing after God",[1] which form the substance of affective prayer. By either or all of these, according to its disposition, the self can be trained in a constant and peaceful attention to Him and ceaseless subordination to His interests: but this is perhaps best done in those developed systems of meditation which bring all the faculties of the self into play. Thus St John Eudes teaches his disciples to divide the chief mysteries of the Gospel between the days of the week, and make of each a particular occasion of thought, worship, and love; first reconstructing by imagination the scene and the action, then applying the mind to meditation on its meaning and the heart and affections to deliberate acts of adoration, penitence, gratitude, and joy; finally the will to a renewed self-offering and particular resolution, derived from the subject-matter of

[1] Augustine Baker, *Holy Wisdom*, Sect. IV, cap. 2.

the prayer.[1] It is obvious that so complete a method, for those who can use it with sincerity, will tend to unify and give a Godward direction to the whole personality; taking within the personal life the place filled in corporate worship by the ministry of the Word. It brings the soul up against absolute standards of conduct, and subdues the will to the purposes of God; nourishing and educating the religious sense, and giving sensible expression to spiritual realities. Such meditation can purify and enhance the totality of the mental and emotional life: fulfilling the noble ideal of Samuel Rutherford—"my desire is that my Lord would give me broader and deeper thoughts, to feed myself with wondering at His love".[2]

In true meditation, considered as a form of worship, the contribution of mind, will, and emotion is fairly equal. In "affective prayer" the emphasis lies almost entirely on feeling; deliberate consideration of the subject-matter being cut out. Here the devotional technique is that of the "colloquy" or interior conversation, of which there are so many examples in the third book of *The Imitation of Christ*; or else repeated short "acts" of love, trust, self-offering, and adoration which stimulate and express devotion, and produce that "loving attention to God" which St John of the Cross held to be the essence of personal worship. At first these acts may be "forced", or deliberately produced as a means of keeping the attention alert and defeating distractions; but as this type of devotion develops, they arise spontaneously within the heart, as the expression of a dominant emotional attitude. East and West, Catholic and Evangelical, are alike in the value they attribute to this method of prayer. Thus the Benedictine Abbot Blosius advises "the servant of God" to "learn and commit to

[1] Cf. Bede Frost, *The Art of Mental Prayer*, p. 126. The chief systems of meditation can be conveniently studied in this book.

[2] *Letters of Samuel Rutherford*, p. 257.

memory certain aspirations, sweet yet burning, which he can dart forth to God, and by which, wherever he may be, and whether he be at rest or actively employed, he may constantly recollect himself in God, and join and unite himself to Him."[1] In the same period the Puritan Baxter urges his reader to "mix ejaculations with thy cogitations and soliloquies till . . . thou has pleaded thyself from a clod to a flame, from a forgetful sinner to a mindful lover."[2] And in another time and place, the beautiful Russian "Way of a Pilgrim" describes the movement of a devoted soul to perfect union with God by a ceaseless act of interior worship, expressed only in the repeated aspiration "Lord Jesus Christ, have mercy on me!"[3] The passage in which the pilgrim is taught by his spiritual guide the science of "constant interior prayer" as set forth in the *Philokalia*, shows very clearly the real character of this device for the deepening of devotional feeling and the steadying of the mind on God.

> He opened the book, found the instruction by St Simeon the New Theologian, and read: "Sit down alone and in silence. Lower your head, shut your eyes, breathe out gently and imagine yourself looking into your own heart. As you breathe out, say 'Lord Jesus Christ, have mercy on me.' Say it moving your lips gently, or simply say it in your mind. Try to put all other thoughts aside. Be calm, be patient, and repeat the process very frequently."[4]

This simple technique performs a threefold office. It acts first as a check upon distractions, next as a

[1] Blosius, *Book of Spiritual Instruction*, cap. IV. See also Augustine Baker, *Holy Wisdom*, where many examples of these aspirations are given.

[2] Richard Baxter, *The Saints Everlasting Rest*, Pt. IV, cap. 13.

[3] Compare cap. XII.

[4] *The Way of a Pilgrim*, trans. by R. M. French, p. 21. The *Philokalia*, or "The Love of Heavenly Beauty", is a great collection of mystical writings by fathers of the Eastern Church, and an important source for the Orthodox doctrine of prayer.

cumulative autosuggestion, and last as a path of emotional discharge.

"I kiss my child because I love it, and I kiss my child in order to love it," says Von Hügel. So, too, the humble practice of affective worship evokes love as well as expressing it. On this account, and in spite of its tendency to fall over into sentimentalism, it has an important part to play in the development of the Godward life, and should not lightly be discredited. For though mere emotionalism is a poor index of spiritual worth, it is none the less true that deep and rich emotion must enter into all full and living worship; since human life "exhibits the degree and kind of its nobility and fruitfulness especially in its emotions; these grow and grow in range and depth, in purity and power, in clearness and freshness, in proportion to the growth of the soul".[1] Adoration, which is worship's very heart, cannot at the same time retain fervour and lose this deep and rich emotion; even though, as it reaches its higher stages, the emotion may so change its character that ardour seems to be swallowed up in peace. Nor need the "instructed Christian" suppose that this necessity involves mere capitulation to irrational feeling or the disguised indulgence of human desires; for the noblest and simplest examples of such affective worship come to us from the greatest of the saints.

"O God, highest and sweetest!" said St Augustine. "Desiring may I find thee, and finding may I love thee!" said St Anselm. "My God and All!" said St Francis. "All love, all glory be to thee O God!" said Bishop Ken at every turn and moment of the day; sweetening each circumstance by an adoring reference to its eternal source. It is by such methods as these, that the common life is gradually transfigured and woven into the fabric of worship. "As thy Infinite Love is ever streaming in blessings on me,

[1] F. von Hügel, *The Reality of God*, p. 131.

O let my soul be ever breathing love to thee ! " says Bishop Ken once more ;[1] summing up the very method and intention of affective prayer.

IV

There comes, for many souls, a time when those feelings, images, and considerations in which their prayer has clothed itself, and which are often regarded as the real stuff of religious experience, disclose their oblique and symbolic character ; and lose in consequence their numinous quality. They can no longer be used with sincerity ; and their departure, and that of the associated emotions, leaves a painful blank behind. The pressure of God now produces at best an obscure and general knowledge, at worst a painful sense of ignorance and emptiness ; and the self's response, stripped of human images and conscious fervour, becomes difficult and dry. This is the " night of the senses " which is described by St John of the Cross and other masters of the inner life. It is not a rare or lofty mystical state ; but is experienced in some manner by all who make the transition from imaginative to recollected worship.[2] God is now apprehended darkly but directly, as a Reality wholly incomprehensible by the mind ; and is worshipped, as *The Cloud of Unknowing* says, by " a naked intent stretching towards Him ". Yet this obscure act, apparently so empty of content—this faithful listening in the darkness—is recognized by those in whom it is produced as a genuine communion with God. For that reason, in spite of the aridity and suffering which often accompany it, it is deeply

[1] *The Practice of Divine Love*, p. 85.

[2] The *locus classicus* for the study of this phase is St John of the Cross : *Ascent of Mount Carmel*, Bk. II ; *Living Flame of Love*, stanza III ; *Dark Night of the Soul*, Bk. I. See also Augustine Baker : *Holy Wisdom*, p. 421 *seq.*, and for the best modern discussion Dom Chapman, *op. cit.*, especially the tract on Contemplative Prayer printed in the Appendix.

pacifying to the soul; whose worship now becomes, more and more, a simple state of loving attention to Him.

> As we, standing in darkness, see nothing, so in contemplation that invisibly lightens the soul, no seen light we see. Christ also gives His resting darkness, and yet speaks to us in a pillar of cloud. But that which is felt is full delectable. . . . And in this truly is love perfect, when man going in the flesh cannot be glad but in God, and wills and desires nothing but God or for God.[1]

Such imageless worship is not to be thought of as necessarily "higher" or more holy than that which expresses itself in more discursive, emotional, or imaginative terms. The only test of the worth of worship is its transforming action on the creature, as bit by bit the loving will set towards the Eternal Beauty evicts self-occupation, establishes humility, and subdues the whole personality to the Divine Action.

> The one thing you should gain by quiet prayer (just remaining with God and making a number of aspirations to keep your imagination from wandering) is to feel the rest of the day that you want God's Will and nothing else.[2]

But even the most imaginative types of devotion may do this for appropriate subjects; and among these are many of the saints, whose adoring communion with Christ was either habitually or occasionally translated into distinct imaginative forms.[3] Nevertheless those who pass through the "night of the senses" leave behind many sources of illusion and opportunities of devotional self-indulgence; for the arid prayer of the will offers little food to religious sentiment and none to religious self-love. This worship consists above all

[1] Richard Rolle, *The Mending of Life*, cap. 12.

[2] Dom Chapman, *op. cit.*, p. 36.

[3] For instance, St Mechthild, St Francis, Suso, St Catherine of Siena, Angela of Foligno, Julian of Norwich, St Teresa, St Margaret Mary Alacoque.

in an act of self-stripping and abandonment, which becomes at the term of its development a total offering of the unified personality to God. Withdrawn from multiplicity that soul then achieves a greater recollection and simplification of spirit, and learns in the bare and living darkness which must now be its habitation the sovereign truth which rules all personal worship—that God Himself is the source and cause as well as the goal of His creature's prayer.

Yet even this submissive waiting on the Invisible is not free from the conditions which our human limitations impose. It too is found to need a certain technique. For, as the imagination—fully employed in the earlier stages—is no longer used in the act of worship, which has now become a mere pouring out of the soul towards God, it wanders; and constantly intrudes irrelevant images on the mind. Hence the distractions which are a common torment of those who practise this simple contemplative prayer: especially those who, deceived by the dangerous word "passivity" and forgetting the exhortation of *The Cloud of Unknowing*, "lovingly and *listily* to will to love God"[1] make no deliberate effort to steady the attention and so are at the mercy of the fore-conscious mind. Here, those short repeated "acts" of faith, love, or adoration, which once formed the substance of the prayer of affections, can still be used to support the state of prayer. But now, instead of gathering up and expressing the ardour and loving concentration of the soul, they fulfil the merely mechanical office of keeping the ground clear. They are not the prayer; but "crumbs thrown to the imagination," or even, as Dom Chapman does not hesitate to call them, "tags". Their very meaning matters little; so long as there is some association of ideas between the sound of the words and the deep action of the worshipping soul, adoring God in her ground. This

[1] A comparison with its negative "listless" best indicates what this word implies.

association prevents conflict between the imaginative and contemplative levels of the mind ; and permits that undistracted and largely uncomprehended pouring out of the will towards God, that continuous and gentle act of self-oblation, which forms the substance of interior prayer.

V

If by worship we mean the adoring response of the creature to the total demand of God, and the utmost contribution to His Glory which it is able to make—and Christians cannot mean less—it is obvious that so far as the individual is concerned, neither the spontaneous or liturgical saying of " Lord ! Lord ! " nor the practising of an equivalent devotion in contemplative silence, fulfils its requirements. The single yet composite creature must make a single yet composite response ; bringing to the altar all aspects of his nature, and not one alone. The dedicated will must bit by bit take up, transform, and unify the dedicated body and mind, welding them into a single instrument devoted to the purposes of God. This absorption and transformation of the visible and temporal is a true part of personal worship, since it is done for and towards God, and chiefly by means of the delicate and difficult oblation of each successive moment and act. Its aim is the furtherance of His Kingdom and doing of His Will, by the production of a life which shall be ever more and more an act of charity. So the individual Christian is required to adore God, adhere to Him, and co-operate with Him in the sanctification of life—that is to say, the bringing of it into conformity with the Divine Perfection—and in the interests of this great purpose to give the colour of worship to every human action and desire whether overtly religious or not.

" The ' prayer of the heart '," says Grou—and here by prayer is meant the personal life of worship—" is the

> direct effect of charity. Actual prayer is charity in action; habitual prayer is the disposition antecedent to this action . . . everything done as towards God, as being the will of God, and in the way God wills, is a prayer, and better than any actual prayer which could then be made. . . . We always pray when we are doing our duty and doing it for God. Among the actions which count as prayer, I include visits of courtesy and kindness, also necessary recreation of body and mind, so long as these be innocent and kept within the bounds of Christian conduct. None of these things is incompatible with unceasing prayer, and except those which are evil, unsuitable, or useless, none which the Holy Spirit cannot justify, find means to sanctify, and include in the Kingdom of Prayer. . . . That which I find most admirable in the religion we profess, is that it teaches us to honour God in all, worship Him in all, practise virtue in all, and finds nothing indifferent or useless to the Christian life."[1]

" As a *whole* burnt offering He accepted them ! " says the Book of Wisdom of the Friends of God.[2] Christianity has always known this to be the crown of personal worship, and honoured its achievements in her saints ; but has not always recognized the same august principle in action, in the life of every unit of the Body of Christ. Yet no other ideal of worship can in the long run meet the full demands of an incarnational faith. Indeed, the act of adoring self-abandonment which forms the heart of the " prayer of simplicity ", is only to be understood in the light of its completing opposite, the creative unity of the dedicated life : for the supposed contrast between action and contemplation is false. Contemplative action, a mixed life focussed upon the Reality of God and consistent at every point with the " Vision of the Principle ", is the true ideal of the Christian life of worship ; the surrender of spirit to Spirit achieved in the deeps of the soul overflowing into every faculty, and

[1] J. N. Grou, *The School of Jesus Christ,* 37th lesson.
[2] Wisdom iii. 6.

welding the whole personality into a single adoring response to the Eternal—sometimes by way of external action, and sometimes by way of interior sacrifice and prayer. This means in practice the surrender of personal interests, aims, and strivings to the one aim and interest of God; an ever deeper entrance into the stream of His self-giving life and more entire dependence on His pressure and incitement.

This drastic because love-impelled process of self-abandonment, often regarded by eager humanists as destructive of personality, is really in the highest degree creative. Indeed, it is the only way in which man can achieve full personality: for it means the integration of the self about its highest centre, the fine point of the spirit, and its restoration to that life of worship for which it was made. What this life is, and how different from the devotional exercises and experiences with which it is often confused, we can learn from the witness of the saints. Thus St Chantal said of her friend and spiritual father, St Francis de Sales:

> Several years ago, he told me that he had no sensible devotion in prayer; and that God worked within him without feeling, but by impressions and illuminations which were diffused in the intellectual part of his soul, the lower part having no share therein. These were chiefly perceptions and impressions of simple unity and heavenly feelings, which he did not try to fathom; for his practice was to keep himself in humility and lowliness before God, with the trustful reverence of a child. . . . For several years before his death, he was given little leisure for prayer, as business overwhelmed him; and one day when I asked him whether he had any time for prayer, he said 'No, but I do what is the same.' [1]

A comparison of this quotation with that from Père Grou will reveal an identity of doctrine variously expressed. It suggests how little the Christian life of personal devotion

[1] *Selected Letters of St Chantal*, p. 131.

is concerned with conscious spiritual contacts or achievements; how entirely its emphasis lies on loving subordination to God, a quiet acceptance of "the sacrament of the present moment" as a major means of grace, whatever its form. Here the personal response of the individual life follows the great rhythm of the Church's liturgical life. It too is Eucharistic. The total oblation of Christ towards God in His human nature, and the self-giving of God in and through that accepted sacrifice to be the Food of Eternal Life for His whole creation, which is the theme of the Christian ritual-pattern, must be actualized, openly or secretly, in the experience of each Christian soul. Its essence is an action; a taking of the stuff of every-day temporal experience and making it holy by oblation to God, so that it may be accepted, changed, and become the life-giving stuff of eternal experience—and this, not in the interest of the individual, but in order to further the creative purpose of God, open a channel for His spirit, and so contribute to the redemption and transfiguration of life. Each separate life of worship, whatever its outward expression, in so far as it is truly cleansed of egoism and bent upon God, is part of this one eternal Eucharistic action of the Logos incarnate in the world: and this fact strips the Christian life of prayer of all petty subjectivism, all tendency to mere religious self-culture, and confers upon it the dignity of the Real.

So, a free self-offering without conditions to the transforming energy of God—the oblation of the natural life with all its gifts, possessions, and capacities, "for all men and women"—must be the first movement of this organic life of worship. It is at once an adoration, an intercession, and a sacrifice. And this approach to the altar and the Cross, accompanied as it must be by a growing sense of sinfulness and nothingness, an ever-increasing dependence on the divine mercy and help, is met, answered, completed by the action of God: transforming, carrying up into the divine action, and making a vehicle of the divine self-giving, each soul thus abandoned to Him. "My life shall be a real life, being wholly full of Thee." This is the ordained consummation of Christian personal worship: the mystery of creation, fulfilled in the secret ground of every soul.

PART II

CHAPTER X

JEWISH WORSHIP

I

SEEN from the historical standpoint, Christianity in its origin was a Jewish sect ; and its Founder and His first disciples were believing and practising Jews. It still bears many marks of this ancestry ; and nowhere more prominently than in its liturgical life. Jesus was born among God-fearing people ; whose whole temper of life was theocentric, who looked for the redemption of Israel by an act of God, and who practised their religion in its most exacting form, going up to Jerusalem to observe the great feasts in the national sanctuary, and carrying out its many ceremonial demands.[1] The claims of that religion are pre-supposed, and taken seriously—even where critically—on every page of the Synoptics. For Jesus, the Temple was His Father's house, and its profanation by " buyers and sellers " was a sin against God. He accepted and loved it as the centre of His people's religious life ; taught in it, and denounced, not the nature of the worship which was offered, but the imperfect dispositions of those who dared to come unprepared to sacrifice, or prided themselves on their own piety.[2] The petitions of the prayer which He taught His closest followers are with one exception drawn from Jewish sources. When asked what man should do to inherit Eternal Life, He replied in the words of the Torah ; [3] and declared that He came to

[1] Luke ii. 22, 41. [2] Matthew v. 23, 24 ; Luke xviii. 9–14.
[3] Deut. vi. 5 ; Luke x. 27.

fulfil, not destroy, its teachings.[1] He showed a close familiarity with the Prophets and the Psalter. His most sacred ordinance was instituted at a Jewish ritual meal; of which the chief features were accepted and transformed to His purposes. He died with the daily evening prayer of every Jewish home upon His lips.

It is clear from the New Testament that the first generation of Jewish Christians continued, like their Founder, to take their share in the national worship alongside their own distinctive practices: and since the devotional routine of the Temple and Synagogue was the only kind of public worship known and used by them, it inevitably provided the matrix within which Christian institutional worship afterwards developed. The Jewish ritual use of water, oil, bread, and wine, familiar to the Apostolic Church, exerted a direct influence on the form which was taken by the Christian sacraments. The Jewish Psalter became the first hymn-book of the Church, and still remains the backbone of its ordered daily worship: the reading and expounding of the Old Testament, stressing the historical character of the Christian revelation, was from the beginning a vital part of the ministry of the Word. Thus Christian worship, though from one point of view it was indeed a "new song", from another accepts and completes the devotion of the synagogue, and shows forth in its fulness the spiritual mystery towards which the sacrifices of the Temple looked. Here as elsewhere the revelation of God, breaking in upon history, accepts and clothes itself in historical forms. Therefore some knowledge and sympathetic understanding of Jewish worship, its awed recognition of the One God, and the deep and tender piety of its saints, is essential to any real understanding of Christian worship.

The Jewish soul, as disclosed to us in its records, was from the beginning peculiarly sensitive towards God. It is

[1] Matt. v. 17.

this indeed, and this only, which distinguishes Israel from other Semitic tribes. Israel was aware of the awful presence and yet the mysterious attraction of the Holy, and His demand upon men; however crudely and imperfectly that Holy and His relation with His creatures might be—and, in the earliest periods represented by the Old Testament certainly were—conceived. In origin indeed this conception was that of all primitive Semite religion: a fact which even the vigorous re-editing of the Pentateuch in post-exilic times has not obscured. The tribal God was glorious in battle and inexorable in His demands. His presence was associated with sacred places and fiery theophanies.[1] His interests were those of His own people. His service did not exclude magical practices, and did include an elaborate system of taboos. His judgments were arbitrary. Once at least, His call to an unflinching obedience was interpreted in terms of human sacrifice; which, nevertheless, became the occasion of a sublime expression of devotion and trust which has left its mark on the three great forms of theism.[2] Yet this strange history is, from first to last, the history of a people dominated by that thirst for God, that certitude of God and that sense of obligation to God, which form the raw material of all worship.

[1] The connection of Fire with the Divine Presence runs right through the Old Testament: e.g. the Burning Bush, the Pillar of Fire, the flame and smoke of Sinai, on which God descended in His Glory "like devouring fire" (Exodus xxiv. 17; see also Ex. xix. 18 and Deut. ix. 15 and xviii. 16), the sacrifices of Elijah on Mount Carmel, the visions of Ezechiel and Daniel. The references have been collected by Miss Willink in her impressive study, *The Holy and the Living God*, pp. 52 *seq.* For Semitic thought, fire and light were essential attributes of the divine self-disclosure: and this conception has had a marked influence on Jewish ritual worship, and through it upon the language of Christian liturgic and personal devotion. In the Orthodox rite the Blessed Sacrament is constantly compared with the burning coal which touched the lips of Isaiah, and similar references are frequent among the mystics of the West. Thus the Divine Voice which said to St Catherine of Siena "I am Fire, the Acceptor of sacrifices" expressed a central conviction of Hebrew worship: nor could Pascal find any other name for the experience which revealed to him the "God of Abraham, God of Isaac, and God of Jacob."

[2] Genesis xxii. 1–19. See below, p. 201.

Even its most barbarous legends and doubtful activities are already profoundly theocentric. The light of the Eternal shines through them, and the poetry of devotion is heard in them. We seem to be in the presence of a true disclosure of the Holy, and man's struggle to apprehend, convey, and respond to it by such acts and such imagery as he has at his command.

This self-revealing action of the Eternal, and Israel's halting response, as described in the Old Testament and illustrated by archæology, seems to us long drawn out. Yet it may well be an undivided moment in the thought of God; and, in the deepest responsive movements of the national soul, there is from the first an intuition of an appointed end. Bit by bit, the devotional landscape was prepared; until there at last appeared in it one Figure, gathering in His person all its values, sacrificial, ethical, and supernatural, and exhibiting their meaning. In spite of the many inequalities and harsh details of that landscape, and the persisting memorials of the perversity and selfishness of men, their capacity for going wrong, which bestrew it, we recognize here the true preparation of Christian worship; in this great tradition of adoration, sacrifice, and humble confidence, built up through many centuries and in much suffering as elements in the real covenant between man and God.

No primitive traits can spoil the impression of first-hand and intense religious experience which is felt in the stories of Abraham, Jacob, and Moses. It is already the Wholly Other, the Living One whose name might not be uttered and whose splendour could not be endured, who is discerned under tribal disguises, and becomes the object of devoted trust and awestruck worship: and as that worship emerges from the primitive stage, it reveals itself as possessing the essential characters of a lofty theism. Indeed, among all the religions of antiquity Israel's alone is based upon that confident dependence on the Unseen which is the essence of the theocentric life; and directed towards the sanctification of conduct and its total submission to the rule of God. With the call and experience of the ancient prophets, Samuel and Elijah, the sense of the Divine action breaking in on the world of men, and evoking their awestruck recognition—the close contact of the historical and the supernatural—becomes more intense. As the religious consciousness of the nation or that of its spiritual leaders clarifies, a realization of all that monotheism must involve in man's relation to the one God of heaven and earth, develops to become the core of the *Shema* "Hear O Israel, the Lord our God, the Lord, is One!"[1] In the teaching of the prophets of the Reform of Josiah, and of the Exile, we find God recognized and adored under two complementary aspects: as the Numen, the Eternal One, the utterly Transcendent who sitteth on the Cherubim and whose Name might not be uttered, and as the giver of the Moral Law. Again, in such a scene as the Call of Isaiah, the transcendent and personal aspects are brought together, in a religious experience of surpassing significance and beauty.[2]

> I saw the Lord sitting upon a throne, high and lifted up, and His train filled the temple . . . then said I, Woe is me! for I am undone; because I am a man of unclean lips, and I dwell in the midst of a people of unclean lips: for mine eyes have seen the King, the Lord of hosts.

Here, God is revealed to His prophet as the Wholly Other, the Object of man's awestruck adoration, and also as the Wholly Good, setting a standard of holiness and convicting man of sin: and a step forward is taken in that total sanctification and redemption of experience, which is the manward aim of worship. Before Him the seraphim veil their faces; yet He asks for the willing and open-eyed co-operation of imperfect men. His nature is indeed

[1] Deut. vi. 4. [2] Isaiah vi. 1–8. Probably 740 B.C.

disclosed in those theophanies which show something of His ineffable glory, glints of a world of living splendour beyond the conception of man: but also, in the demand for purity, mercy, truth, and devotedness which He makes upon His human creatures. In both, in different ways, He requires their unlimited self-offering: an inward dedication of personality, expressed by outward signs. Therefore the Torah, the Law, is itself a disclosure of the supernatural, God's will for men. It is not a creature in the ordinary sense, but a revelation of the Eternal, a reflection of the Divine Mind, final and immutable: and the rigid obedience it demands and secures—whether in the sphere of ritual or of morals—is not mere submission to a code, but an act of adoration.[1] Love of the Torah is the very essence of Jewish piety. In the whole temper, e.g. of the 119th Psalm, we see this adoring aspiration to God, this loving and unquestioning acknowledgment of His priority, linked with acceptance of the Law as the expression of His will for men.

> Thy statutes have been my songs
> In the house of my pilgrimage.
> I have thought upon thy Name, O Lord, in the night season
> And have kept thy law. . . .
> O let thy loving mercies come unto me, that I may live,
> For thy law is my delight. . . .
> What love have I unto thy law:
> All the day long is my study in it.[2]

With this double vision of God, then, there goes a double tradition of worship: Sacrifice and Ethic, institutional

[1] The Jew, as Dr. Israel Abrahams insisted, "has an ingrained belief in the organic union of ritual with religion". He "does not appreciate the difference between the abiding principles of religion and the rules of ritual and conduct by which it is sought to realize them in daily life." Hence there is for him no contrast between "moral and apocalyptic religion". (*Pharisaism and the Gospels*, Vol. I, p. vii.)

[2] Ps. cxix. 54, 55, 77, 97. This great poem of the Godward life has been well named the "rosary of the Torah". Cf. J. P. Peters, *The Psalms as Liturgies*, p. 439.

religion and prophetic religion, ritual purity as a sacrament of moral purity, and the ritual gift as a sacrament of self-oblation. Israel's response to God was purest and deepest where these two aspects of man's single self-offering to the Eternal were harmonized: the prophets' realistic vision of God in action, their deep inwardness and sense of His moral and spiritual demand, reanimating, correcting, and spiritualizing the temple worship, and the devotion of the altar expressing the devotion of the heart. It is true that these two aspects of worship were often set in opposition. In periods of corruption, such as that preceding the reformation of Josiah, the prophets spoke like " pessimistic protestants ";[1] so sick of the many perversions of the cultus, and its divorce from reality, the orgies of popular religion at " high places " and the degradation of ritual sacrifice to a mere buying-off of God, that they became blind to its religious quality and were prepared to abandon it altogether. Yet it was, after all, the temple worship which gave form and stability to the national response to God; carried through the cultus within which the prophets arose, and preserved those spiritual values to which again and again they recalled the attention of men. So many of their greatest pages are concerned with the condemnation of formalism and correction of abuse, that we forget the true splendour of the institution so jealously watched and so constantly recalled to its ideals. It is not in their unbridled denunciations of ritual and constant opposition of the inward to the outward, but in the lofty and balanced theism of Deuteronomy, with its steady insistence on the unconditioned love of God, or those post-exilic Psalms which reproduce the liturgic spirit of the second temple[2] that we find the true line of growth; which

[1] E. O. James, *The Old Testament in the Light of Anthropology*, p. 117.

[2] E.g. lxxxiv, cxviii, cxxxiv, cxxxv. It is to be remembered that the building of this temple was itself an act of worship: a symbol of the God-ward ardour of the national soul.

stretches all the way from primitive religion to Christian worship, and has made the religious history of Israel crucial for the spiritual history of man.

We can trace that history without a break back to the tribal God, the holy fire, the ritual dance, the sacred stone and the human sacrifice: all of which have left their marks on the Old Testament. But humbly mining beneath the historic series, we also discover in it the steady unfolding of the divine disclosure and the human response. We see Ritual, carrying forward from the past that which was valuable in the past—the increasing sense of God's greatness yet nearness, His holiness and His presence; Sacrifice, summing up the craving of man to express his awe, adoration, and dependence, to atone for his inveterate sinfulness, and to enter into communion with that living, self-revealing One. We see in the ideal picture of Aaron the High Priest, who goes into the sacred "tent of meeting" bearing upon his forehead the golden tablet inscribed "Holy to Jehovah!" and on his shoulder-straps the names of the twelve tribes whom he represented before God,[1] a first hint of the ministry of mediation. We see the prophets with their vigorous realism and uncompromising moral demands breaking in upon the institutional order; correcting its tendency to crystallize and substitute the outward for the inward, and constantly pointing out the ethical implications of true worship; and the poetry of the Psalter weaving all these strands together, and turning them into prayer.

If we want to understand the ethos of Jewish worship, we must learn to see together crude slaughter and spiritual beauty, ritual sacrifice and inward oblation; to realize that the forbidding framework is the skeleton of a living body, and that in practice ceremonial rules and the offering of the free spirit can and still do live comfortably side by

[1] Exodus xxviii. 29, 36.

side.[1] Through the whole development of the cultus, from the animistic proceedings of the Patriarchs to the Jewish girl whose "Be it unto me according to Thy Word" in its totality of self-offering crowned the old era and began the new, there runs, as in no other, a growing conviction of God's priority and living presence; the unspeakable mystery of His hidden Being, yet His active concern with the life of man. The Shekinah, the immanent Divine Presence or Glory tabernacled among men, broods over it; the controlling reality of every situation.[2] It is this which makes the Old Testament the greatest of all epics of the theocentric life, and the greatest of all textbooks of worship.

For us, it gains rather than loses by the fact that its earliest documents have been drastically edited, from the point of view of post-exilic monotheism, by men who were saturated in the spirit of the book of Deuteronomy; with its constant association of national and personal worship, its spirit of adoring confidence, its emphasis on Holiness, Obedience, and Love. For these men, looking back on the long uneven course of the national history, saw it in spiritual regard. They discerned in that history the Finger of God, and the growing revelation of His holiness. Thus the inclusion of such a story as the offering of Isaac in the final revision of the Pentateuch, made long after human sacrifice had ceased, shows what the most spiritual minds of the nation felt about the significance of sacrifice. Indeed, for those more spiritual minds—especially in later days of exile and distress—the *aqeda* or "binding" of Isaac, and his willing acquiescence in the utmost demand of God, came to possess something of the devotional value which the Crucifix has for Christian

[1] Anyone who tried to grasp the character of, e.g. Roman Catholic worship by careful study of the ritual directions to the priest in the Missal, or the highly Levitical Lenten ordinances, but never went to Mass, would fall far short of the truth.

[2] Compare Luke i. 35. Note that blue, which is for Christian art the special colour of the Blessed Virgin, was and is for Jewish thought the colour of the Shekinah.

piety: being regarded both as a redemptive act, and as the perfect pattern of all oblation.[1] And so with many other stories of the national past. In the developed religion of Israel, the Bible was taken as a whole, primitive and developed religious ideas being accepted side by side—as they still are in conservative forms of Christianity—and spiritual nourishment drawn without any sense of incongruity from the tales of the Patriarchs and the lofty poetry of the post-exilic psalms. In and through each, Israel discerned and worshipped the immanent Presence of the One God moulding history to His Will.

II

From the point of view of its influence on Christian worship, it is not the primitive origin of the Temple and Synagogue cultus which chiefly matters to us: but its development in the period immediately before the birth of Christ, and the religious temper which it nourished and expressed. What, in fact, was the institutional worship of those Jews who began Christian institutional worship? What standard did their sacred books set up, and what suggestions did their sacred poetry make? And what was the devotional value of their liturgical life? Jesus was born of pious country people of the strictest orthodoxy—the "quiet in the land" who sought the deliverance of Israel by spiritual rather than political paths—and His religious background and education was that of the devout people of His day. It was dominated by Jerusalem and the Temple worship, and was nourished by a deep and instructed reverence for the Scriptures, and by the devotional routine of the local synagogue. Further, it was surrounded by a number of small ritual observances; which can easily be dismissed as formal or superstitious, but were really directed—like the small external pieties of the "good Catholic"—to the sanctifying

[1] I. Abrahams, *Pharisaism and the Gospels*, II, p. 162.

of all the common events of everyday life, by a constant and humble remembrance of the claims of the Eternal God and His Law.

The Temple sacrifices, which have so deeply affected Christian symbolism, must not be thought of as mere ritual survivals; continued for the advantage of a priestly caste, and without real spiritual content. Those denunciations of the prophets by which we are apt to judge them, were mostly uttered in the corrupt period immediately preceding the reformation of Josiah and the "discovery" of Deuteronomy; and moreover, by men whose own deep religious experience was closely bound up with Temple worship.[1] They may be compared with the violent condemnations of the shortcomings of the Papacy, the corruption of the Catholic priesthood, traffic in Masses and general degradation of the cultus, which were uttered by St Catherine of Siena and other reforming saints of the late Middle Ages. Those psalms in which mere ritual worship, divorced from self-oblation, is most fiercely denounced, were themselves used in the Temple liturgies.[2] Certainly the conservatism which is inherent in all cultus carried forward in these liturgies many crude and primitive elements; and doubtless the sacrifices were often understood in a crude and primitive way. The universal needs of popular religion were met, and met generously: as indeed they still are by certain forms of traditional Christianity. Yet at least from the time of Ezechiel onwards, sacrificial worship was understood by the devout in a truly sacramental sense; and became ever more and more an acknowledgment of the holiness of God and sinfulness of man, and a means of approach to Him.

[1] E.g. Hosea and the First Isaiah.

[2] E.g. Ps. xl. 6–8 and Ps. l. 7–15. If those scholars are correct who regard the "Selah" which precedes this last passage as marking the point at which the victim was slain and the "sacrifice cry" was raised, then a vigorous reminder of the realities of worship is here brought into direct relation with the sacrificial act.

For the Third Isaiah, God's most gracious promise to those who loved His name, was that they might be brought to Mount Zion and "made joyful in his house of prayer, and their sacrifices accepted upon its altar."[1] The offering "for sin and atonement"—that is to say, the humble acknowledgment of man's falling short of God's demand, and his longing to meet it—now became prominent in the public worship. That deepened understanding of the vocation of Israel, and its peculiar relation to God, which was born of the Exile, involved a new realization of the national failure to fulfil Israel's obligations. The need for cleansing and sanctification, that it might again be fit for acceptance before Him, was felt by all deeply spiritual minds, and gave new emphasis to this aspect of sacrifice; colouring with a sense of penitence and unworthiness both those burnt-offerings in which the worshipper expressed his desire for oblation, and those peace-offerings which offered him a certain communion with the Holy Living God.[2] These motives were blended, and expressed, both in the animal and cereal offerings of the daily public sacrifice, and in the private sacrifices through which the individual "according to his means" brought each great event of his life into relation with God; acknowledged his sin and obligation, and offered his thanksgivings and worship.

The archaic origin of all these proceedings, and the dangers of materialism and formalism which attend them, are easily recognized. But here we see them carried forward within the national life, giving that life at every level a Godward inclination, and so made to serve the purpose of the deepest religious instincts of men. They provided the opportunities for costly giving, for expressive action, for ordered ceremonial and for emotional discharge, which all institutional religion requires. If the barbarous methods of primitive sacrifice persisted and were often understood

[1] Isaiah lvi. 7. [2] Compare *supra*, Pt. I, cap. III.

in a primitive sense, Christians who still associate sacrificial language of the most primitive type with their most solemn act of worship, and adapt the ancient ritual of the peace-offering to their approach to God in Christ,[1] should be the last to complain of this. The worship was primarily corporate. The nation was the unit: and the daily public sacrifice represented the national oblation, the surrender of its life to God through and in the symbolic victim, for praise, communion, and atonement. After the institution of the synagogue, its daily services were synchronized with the Temple offerings; so that all who took part in them, however widely scattered, were present by intention at the altar of the One God in Zion and united in a single act of adoration.

The true focus of this closely knit act of national worship was not, however, the great altar of sacrifice, with its archaic and dreadful accompaniments. It was the Holy of Holies, the "House" where God by His Shekinah was believed to dwell undiscerned; in a way so entirely supernatural, so completely transcending all our apprehensions and thoughts, that only the dark emptiness of this secret shrine could suggest it. For it is a mark of Israel's spiritual genius, that from the first the Jew placed Reality within mystery: and here, perhaps, is the source of his intense aversion from all images of the Divine. It was in a thick darkness that Moses spoke with God; and the Holy of Holies made, as it were, an enclave for mystery, in the midst of the drama and clamour of ceremonial worship. Until the Exile, its darkness hid the supreme treasure of the nation—the ark or chest which held the symbol of God's covenant with His people—and under the golden wings of its cherub guardians was the place where the divine mercy was believed to await human prayer.[2] After the rebuilding of the Temple it was still before this "Most Holy Place" that the sacrifices were

[1] Lev. vii. 11–15. [2] Exodus xxv. 17–22; Ps. xci. 1–4.

offered, and into its emptiness the High Priest carried once a year the blood of the atoning victim; that he might in Israel's name renew the memorial of the great Covenant with the unseen God, on which was based their life of worship and trust.[1] We do not understand our own devotional ancestry, unless we remember all this.

Within this worshipping society, centred upon the continuous sacrificial action on Mount Zion, the individual was trained in personal devotedness and personal response: for Judaism had at its best the twofold character of a genuine Church—it fostered a life of worship which was truly organic, and truly personal too. The demand upon the individual was constant and insistent. The Temple was a house of prayer;[2] and prayer was an essential factor in every life. As in its primitive beginnings, so in the developed cultus, the fire upon the altar of burnt-offering never went out;[3] it was regarded by the people as the sacred sign of the Presence of the Invisible God, and His gracious acceptance alike of those personal sacrifices which marked every crisis of existence, and that "offering of a pure heart" of which these were the effective signs. They went up to the Temple to "appear before Him" and "seek His face", and found there, as the Christian worshipper does under similar circumstances, a religious experience proportionate to their reverence and trust.[4]

The Temple liturgy, centred upon the public sacrifices and the great festivals of the Jewish year, was at its best a solemn and dramatic act of worship; a sacramental expression of great religious realities, in which sense and spirit co-operated and all present took their part. Each morning, at daybreak, incense was offered; the perfect symbol of selfless and confident prayer.[5] Then an unblemished lamb

[1] Lev. xvi. 14; Exodus xxiv. 4–8. Compare Heb. ix. 23–26.
[2] Isaiah lvi. 7; Luke xix. 46. [3] Lev. vi. 13.
[4] Ps. xlii. 2–4; lxxxiv. 7. [5] Ps. cxli. 2.

was sacrificed,[1] and after it the meal-offering—a cake of flour and oil—whilst psalms were sung by the choir, prayers were recited, and the people made their own supplications. The offerings were followed by a service of prayer, which included the recital of the Shema and the Commandments; and a service of praise, with the libation of wine, "the blood of the grape poured out at the foot of the altar",[2] and the singing of psalms. The same rich act of worship again took place at sunset; the lamb then being slain before the offering of the incense, which closed as it began the day. We cannot be surprised that the author of the Jewish portion of the Christian Apocalypse found here so much material for his picture of the ceaseless worship of heaven: the Lamb that was slain, the incense, the prostrations, and the repeated songs of praise.[3] On the Sabbath, the sacrifices were doubled; and on great festivals the whole service, with its opening processions of the people "going up to the House of the Lord" to the song of the gradual psalms and elaborate ritual movements of the Sons of Aaron "as a garland round about" the high priest,[4] was conducted with a ceremonial splendour, a devotional fervour, and a dramatic alternation of the extremes of abasement and joy—of "ringing cries" and speechless prostration—offering full employment to body as well as soul, voice as well as heart. This can still be recognized in the liturgical psalms, and is paralleled in the great ceremonies of the Catholic and Orthodox Church. The superb description of solemn sacrifice in *Ecclesiasticus*[5] leaves no doubt of the profoundly religious character of the Temple worship in the period immediately

[1] Exodus xii. 5; Heb. ix. 14; 1 Peter i. 19.

[2] Ecclus. l. 15.

[3] By the beginning of the Christian era the idea of the sacrificial worship in heaven, the pattern of that upon earth, was familiar to Jewish thought. See G. Buchanan Gray, *Sacrifice in the Old Testament*, pp. 148 *seq.*

[4] Ecclus. l. 12. [5] *Ibid.*, 11–19.

preceding the Gospel; or the awe and enthusiasm it evoked.

> Then shouted the sons of Aaron,
> They sounded the trumpets of beaten work,
> They made a great noise to be heard,
> For a remembrance before the Most High.
> Then all the people together hasted,
> And fell down upon the earth on their faces,
> To worship their Lord, the Almighty, God Most High.
> The singers also praised him with their voices;
> In the whole house was there made sweet melody.
> And the people besought the Lord Most High,
> In prayer before him that is merciful,
> Till the worship of the Lord should be ended;
> And so they accomplished his service.

III

The local religious service of the Synagogue, or "assembly", which gave the Jewish Church something equivalent to a parochial system and linked the religious life of every village with the central sanctuary, was the chief liturgical invention of later Judaism; an invention indeed of great importance, which witnesses to the religious genius of the nation, and was afterwards copied by Christianity and by Islam. In it, for the first time, ordered corporate worship was dissociated from sacrifice, and centred upon the reading and meditation of Scripture. The influence of the Synagogue on the development of Christian worship has probably been greater than that of any other single factor; for it is the ancestor first of the primitive "Mass of the Catechumens", or Ministry of the Word, which was the normal Sunday service of instruction and worship in the infant Church, next of the Divine Office, and last of the countless forms of free Evangelical worship based on Scripture reading, preaching, praise, and extempore prayer. Historically, the Synagogue service seems to have developed during the Exile from informal gatherings for prayer and the reading and interpretation of the Law; and then perhaps acquired the communal and non-sacerdotal character which it has never lost.[1] But its full establishment as part of the structure of Jewish institutional life cannot be traced beyond the second century B.C.[2]

It is tempting to look upon the worship of the Synagogue as representing the prophetic over against the priestly element of Judaism, and therefore as a contrast or even a corrective to the sacrificial cultus of the Temple; and even to see in this contrast a foreshadowing of that which is supposed to exist between the Christian ministry of the Word and the Sacraments, or more generally between Evangelical and Catholic ideals of worship. But this temptation should be resisted. In the full religious practice of the devout Jew of New Testament times, both Temple and Synagogue were accepted as the two aspects of one total response to God: as the moral demands of the prophets, and the ritual demands of the Law, were accepted without any sense of incongruity. They were parts of a single worshipping life, in which outward and inward, provincial and national devotion, were directed to one end—two ways of expressing one love—and there was from the beginning a close organic connection between them. The sacrificial cultus was more deeply understood and more reverently performed, because of the background of personal, disciplined, and instructed religion, the constant meditation of the Law, which the synagogues provided. The prayer and adoration of the humblest local assembly was given fresh dignity by the fact that it was deliberately synchronized, and linked in intention, with the great national acts of worship on Mount Zion: the daily offering of prayer, praise, and

[1] In the Synagogue the priest as such has no prerogative. Any member may be called to the reading or exposition of the Law.

[2] Cf. Oesterley & Box, *Religion and Worship of the Synagogue*, 2nd ed., pp. 337 *seq.*

thanksgiving being regarded as the spiritual counterpart of the ritual sacrifice.[1] In the synagogue, the readings from the Torah and the Prophets formed the heart of the service, and were surrounded by acts of adoration and thanksgiving which were at first spontaneous, and only gradually assumed a fixed form. The scrolls of the Law, its chief possession, were treated with the ceremonial reverence due to sacred things; for in and through them the Eternal speaks to man.[2]

A deep piety, a recognition of the priority of God and a daily life sanctified at every point by a remembrance of His gifts and demands, were the ideals of synagogue religion at its best. It was, essentially, a religion for the devout; and tended to the formation of a class distinguished for "good churchmanship". We may be sure that the Pharisee who went up to the Temple to pray was an ornament to his local synagogue. But though the bitter and detailed reproaches addressed by Christ to the scribes and Pharisees[3] show that the religious vices of petty rigorism, exhibitionism, spiritual pride, and hypocrisy—the besetting sins of self-conscious piety—could and did flourish within it, it is important to remember that the special graces of theism, reverence, obedience, meekness, and confidence, did too. Our Lord's indictment, then, was not and could not be directed against the ideals of the synagogue, but against those ego-centric devotees who had brought these ideals into contempt; "making a pretence with long prayers", but failing to live up to their searching demands. Here the

[1] The afternoon service of the synagogue is still called the "Evening Sacrifice", and Scripture passages referring to the Temple sacrifices are read at the daily morning prayer. Oesterley and Box, *op. cit.*, p. 371.

[2] This still obtains. The place of honour in the Synagogue, answering to that of the Christian altar, is given to the ark in which the scrolls of the Law are kept. It is veiled, and a perpetual lamp burns before it. When the Torah is taken from the ark for the reading, each member of the congregation kisses it. *See* A. J. Appasamy, "An Indian Visitor to the Holy Land" (*Theology*, June, 1934).

[3] Matthew xxiii. 13–36; Luke xi. 39–52.

prophetic demand for inwardness and moral purity was always in the foreground: the "offering of a pure heart" was the only oblation, and repentance and the giving of alms were held—at least by the later Rabbis—to be the full equivalent of sacrifice.

The references in the Synoptic gospels are our only certain sources for the form of the synagogue service in Our Lord's time;[1] but much can be deduced from later notices as to its general character. There is little doubt that the services of the primitive Church, with their alternations of Scripture reading and exposition, prayer, praise, and the antiphonal chanting of "psalms and spiritual songs", were directly modelled upon it. The basis was and is the reading of the Law; a practice of great antiquity, at least dating back to the Exile. Only a few verses were read, preceded by the versicle "Blessed art Thou O God, giver of the Torah!" and followed by exposition in the vernacular or by "teaching".[2] The Pentateuch was thus read through once in three years. The lesson from the prophets seems next to have become part of the service.[3] Before this, edifying passages were read as a sequel to the liturgical lessons from the Torah. To this nucleus the *Shema*, the great confession of the Unity of God which all practising Jews must recite at least twice daily, was soon added. Though there was as yet no fixed formula for prayer, some at least of the solemn Benedictions recited before and after the *Shema*, or the series afterwards linked together to form the devotional centre of the service,[4] were probably already in use. The most ancient of these characteristic creations of the Jewish spirit derive from the Temple liturgy. They

[1] See P. Levertoff in *Liturgy and Worship*, p. 73.

[2] Cf. Matthew iv. 23; Mark i. 21 and 39; Luke iv. 31.

[3] Luke iv. 16–22.

[4] The Shemone Esreh, or Eighteen Benedictions. Text and Analysis in Oesterley, *The Jewish Background of the Christian Liturgy*, p. 54 *seq.*, and Levertoff, *op. cit.*, pp. 71–73.

are short acts of praise or supplication; thoroughly Biblical in character, and ending on the note of thanksgiving "Blessed art thou, O Lord!" Some of these acts appear to have been used by Christ as the vehicle of His most solemn invocations,[1] and provided the formula for the consecration of the first Eucharist. They have directly influenced Christian worship; especially the earliest form taken by the Eucharistic prayer. This, with its adoring recital of the various splendours and mercies of God summed up in the words of the *Sanctus*, exhibits clear traces of its Jewish ancestry.[2]

The classic Benediction, usually introduced by the formula "Blessed art Thou, O Lord our God, King of the Universe!" gives thanks for the holiness, power, and mercy of God as shown in the wonders of creation, and His care for the children of men; and emphasises some particular aspect of His goodness and might. Only when this act of praise has been fully performed does it pass on to supplication. Further, the Benediction carries with it the idea of the hallowing or consecration of any action or thing with which the blessing is connected, by bringing it into direct relation with God. It is therefore the typical act of devotion, both public and private; and ideally, a chief means by which Jewish piety maintains the theocentric temper of its life. Thus the devout Jew hallows each action of the day by a Benediction: e.g. the blessing of God before washing of hands, or the grace before meals—"Blessed art Thou, O Lord our God, King of the Universe, who bringest forth bread from the earth!" The great Benedictions of the Synagogue service are jewels of liturgical art, expressing with precision and beauty that vivid, grateful consciousness

[1] Cf. Mark vi. 41 and xiv. 22; Luke ix. 16; xxii. 17–20; xxiv. 30.

[2] In the developed Synagogue Liturgy the first group of Benedictions was followed by the Kedushah or *Sanctus*, and Kaddish, answering to the first half of the Lord's Prayer. Oesterley, *op. cit.*, pp. 67 and 72. Compare *supra*, cap. VII.

of the action and presence of God, and that dependence on His mercy, which is the inspiration of pure Biblical worship.

> With great love hast Thou loved us, O Lord our God; with great and overflowing pity hast Thou pitied us! O our Father, our King, for our fathers' sake, who trusted in Thee, and whom Thou didst teach the statutes of life, be gracious unto us, too, and teach us. Enlighten our eyes in Thy Law, and let our hearts cleave unto Thy commandments; and unite our hearts to love and fear Thy Name, that we may never be put to confusion. For a God that worketh salvation art Thou; and us hast Thou chosen from every people and tongue, and hast brought us near unto Thy great Name (Selah) in faithfulness, to give thanks unto Thee, and to proclaim Thy unity in love. Blessed art Thou, O Lord, who choosest Thy people Israel in love![1]

IV

Christian worship is mainly indebted to the Temple ritual for those primitive symbols and references which abound in the New Testament and still continue to play an essential part in its liturgies and hymns; speaking in defiance of our religious sophistication to the deepest levels of our psychic life.[2] From it we take the sacrificial imagery under which we think of the Passion and Atonement: the Lamb, the sin-offering, the saving virtue of the Precious Blood. Since

[1] The 'Ahabah, or Second Benediction before the *Shema*. Quoted by Oesterley, *The Jewish Background of the Christian Liturgy*, p. 48.

[2] The hymn books of all communions testify to this unwelcome truth; and it is precisely here, in the union of rhythmic utterance and archaic thought, that we should expect to find primitive characters surviving and producing their maximum effect. Cf. the Office hymns "Crux fidelis" (sixth century), and "Ad Cenam Agni" (seventh century), "Viva! viva Jesu" (eighteenth century, Italian); Wesley, "Victim Divine! thy grace we claim"; Cowper, "There is a fountain filled with blood" and many others. Even the sublime Eucharistic hymns of St Thomas Aquinas are not entirely intelligible without reference to our remote religious past.

every level of our being, and not the "spiritual" alone, must be turned to God in worship if the transformation of our whole nature in Him is to be accomplished, here our religious past makes us a gift which we should not despise. To the Synagogue we owe the ordered framework of our institutional worship, its balance of adoration and instruction, thanksgiving, supplication, and responsive prayer, its historical and moral emphasis, and much of the actual material which it still employs. But beyond these, our greatest and deepest debt to Judaism is the quality of that realistic conception of God and realistic attitude to God which it bequeathed to the Church: a conception and an attitude which rise to their height in the rare devotional sayings of Jesus, but are mainly transmitted to us in the Psalms which He so often quoted and so greatly loved.

The hundred and fifty poems of the Psalter, which still remain the classics of theocentric worship, have probably exerted an influence upon the Christian devotional tradition greater than that of any other single factor. They still form, as we have seen, the substance of the Divine Office of the Roman, Orthodox, and Anglican communions;[1] giving to the souls which are thus subdued to their influence a formation, a quality of spiritual culture, which is directly related to their spirit of awestruck confidence and love. Most of the psalms, at least in their present shape, are post-Exilic; and therefore represent the corporate and personal worship of Israel in its purest form.[2] But many earlier poems, representing primitive and tribal ideals, are embedded in the first two Books,[3] side by side with some of the most exquisite expressions of Hebrew devotion. As according to the most conservative estimate, at least

[1] *Supra*, cap. VI.

[2] Cf. Oesterley and Robinson, *An Introduction to the Books of the Old Testament*, pp. 79 *seq.*

[3] For instance, Psalms ii, xviii, xx.

half of the Psalter is adapted to liturgical worship—some of the psalms forming in themselves complete liturgies[1]—and we know that the singing of hymns both during and after the sacrifice, formed part of the Temple ritual for at least three hundred years before the Exile, we have here the expression in poetry of the growth of the Jewish spirit of worship over a period of five hundred years. That growth extends from savage invocations of the God of battles—

> Lay hand upon the shield and buckler :
> And stand up to help me,[2]

and passionate prayers for vengeance on enemies[3] to the sublime spirituality of the post-Exilic psalms :

> Whom have I in heaven but thee :
> And there is none upon earth that I desire in comparison of thee.
> My flesh and my heart faileth :
> But God is the strength of my heart, and my portion for ever ![4]

The peculiar function of poetry as the carrying medium of a spiritual intuition otherwise unexpressed, is fully seen when we consider the Psalter in relation to our whole religious history. Without it, we could hardly realize the depth and breadth and height of the devotional landscape within which the historic incarnation took place, for it is the gate which admits us to the inner world of Israel's spiritual experience : the world into which Jesus was born, and in which the real preparation of the Gospel was made. Here we recognize the growing-point of the Hebrew spirit of worship ; carrying forward the gifts of the past, giving with the passing of the ages new significance to ancient words, but never faltering in its orientation towards God.

[1] E.g. lxxxiv, cvii, cxvi. See for a full treatment of this subject J. P. Peters, *The Psalms as Liturgies*.
[2] Ps. xxxv 2. [3] E.g. Ps. cix. [4] Ps. lxxiii. 24, 25.

The baffled understanding of the creature, considering the glory of the heavens and the communion of the Eternal with men,[1] the agony of penitential adoration which speaks in the *Miserere*, the awestruck yet confident sense of the inescapable Divine presence,[2] all form part of it; no less than the passionate and delighted praise of God, which ran parallel with the austere moralism of the Torah and gave its note of selfless joy to Jewish liturgical life.[3]

If, therefore, our worship is true to the totality of its Judeo-Christian inheritance, it will not be all bright and clear, thin in colour, humanistic and this-world in feeling. It will retain the ancient sense of cloud and darkness, other-worldly fire and light, which still lives in the Psalter; the awe before a sacred mystery which is with us yet never of us, the deep sense of imperfection, and above all the unconquerable trust and the adoring love for a God who has set His glory above the heavens and yet is mindful of the children of men. It will remain firmly rooted in history, and be careful to maintain its traditional links with the past. Two great poems, conceived in the true spirit of the Hebrew Psalter and centred on a delighted recognition of God's action—the Benedictus and the Magnificat—carry to their height the purest intuitions and graces of Israel's long history of worship; and turn toward the revelation by which that long history is crowned. So, too, the sacrificial movement of self-giving to God's mysterious purpose in which the Blessed Virgin accepted her destiny, and the prophetic mission of the Baptist preparing the "way of the Lord",

[1] Ps. viii and xix.

[2] Ps. cxxxix.

[3] The "Hallelujah Psalms," civ–cvi, cxi–cxviii, and cxlv–cl, were all liturgic, and were so-called from the cry which invited the people to join in them. The last six were known by heart by all, and seem to have formed part of every service. Ps. cxlv was more frequently sung than any other and it was believed that whoever recited it three times in the day would attain to eternal life. See J. Peters, *op. cit.*, p. 78.

were alike the fruits of Jewish piety, and true to the two-fold ideal of Jewish worship. In those two figures, which Christian art has placed on each side of the Christ Triumphant, the promise of that ancient worship was fulfilled.

CHAPTER XI

THE BEGINNINGS OF CHRISTIAN WORSHIP

I

CHRISTIAN worship begins with a small circle of devout Jews, who believed that in Jesus of Nazareth God had spoken, and the hope of their race had been fulfilled. Its raw material was first their common religious inheritance —the practice, teaching, and symbolism of the Temple and Synagogue, which all accepted and used—next, the special practice and teaching of their Master, and last the decisive experiences of Easter and Pentecost, with their assurance of His continuing, invisible presence "working with them". Thus the worship which we find described or implied in the New Testament is of two kinds. (*a*) That fresh, direct, filial, profoundly realistic response to God which was taught by Jesus or is derived from His Spirit, and which we recognize in the Synoptic Gospels. This is given classic expression in the Lord's Prayer, and appears in St Paul's great outbursts of thanksgiving and praise.[1] (*b*) The worship which was addressed by that "new community" for whom those Gospels were written, through and in Christ to God. This included thankful commemoration of His Passion and Resurrection, trust in His guiding Spirit, adoring recognition —both mystical and Eucharistic—of His unseen presence with the fellowship, and confident expectation of His imminent Parousia. St Paul's epistles, and after them the Book of Acts, are our earliest authorities for this specifically

[1] E.g. Romans xi. 33–36.

Church worship. There we can recognize its peculiar notes: the mixed charismatic and eucharistic character, derived from the primitive experiences of the fellowship that "continued steadfastly in the breaking of the bread and the prayers";[1] and the constant reference to the unseen but vividly realized presence of "Christ Who is our life". Full Christian devotion, since it is expressive of full Christian belief, requires and from the beginning has practised together both these responses to God: the pure theocentric filial prayer of the Gospels, and the Christocentric communion in petition and adoration with the incarnate Revealer present with His Church. We already find this union of the Transcendent and the Incarnational in the great prayer to the Father embedded in the Epistle to the Ephesians,[2] in the liturgical fragment which closes the Epistle of Jude, and in the picture of heavenly worship in the Apocalypse. It achieves great splendour of expression in the earliest Eucharistic prayers. Seen in historic regard, it results from the interpretation of Jewish theism in a Christian sense: seen in spiritual regard, it means the rich reality of God disclosed to men in His Eternal Being, and in His saving action within time. No worship can be regarded as true to the primitive ideals in which both the theocentric and Christocentric elements are not thus present and harmonized. But we best understand their nature and importance when each is considered separately.

II

It is now recognized that the Synoptic Gospels are Church documents; composed for the use of an organized and missionary community, which already possessed its own theological outlook and rudimentary liturgical life. Yet

[1] Acts ii. 42. [2] Eph. iii. 14–19.

through them we receive an impression of the prayer of Jesus and His teaching on worship which in its freshness, beauty, unrigoristic fervour and spiritual realism, is in strong contrast with much that is told us of the temper of the Apostolic Church. So powerful indeed is this impression, that each successive revival of inward religion has there found fresh inspiration; and a standard by which to judge and often to condemn the institutional worship of its time.

It is true that the Evangelists maintain great reserve when speaking of the devotional practice of Our Lord and His closest followers. We can only infer its character from His few reported acts and sayings. Yet even from these scattered references, we receive the impression of a loving filial delight in God, in Himself and for Himself, which is unique in vividness and depth. A passionate longing to glorify Him upon earth, in all ways and at all costs, is the inspiring cause of every outward action of Christ's life. This spirit of trustful, unlimited, and worshipping love is the real spirit of the Gospel. The incarnate Logos turns back towards the Eternal with adoring and obedient joy, and so marks the path by which creation shall return to its source. When we consider the rhythm of the public life of Jesus; the long retreat, the crucial choice and total dedication with which it opens, the regular recourse to solitary prayer on the mountain, and return from it to arduous labour in the world, the close mingling of supernatural and natural action, the constant theocentric reference—and with this the demand on His real followers for a perfection of generosity which shall match the generosity of God, a heroism which shall fulfil itself through failure, suffering, and death—we see that the whole of this life was a single act of worship. It is thus the fountain-head of the adoring life of the Church; which, if it be true to His leadership, must be wholly bent on the greater glory of

God, and wholly convinced of His transcendent attraction, His intimate care, and His ultimate triumph.

A constant loving contemplation of the Father's realized perfection and timeless glory, and a constant effort to actualize that glory within the frame of human experience, bringing visible life at every point—even the most homely—into direct relation with the invisible God, is the substance of this life of worship. The Apocalyptic expectation of Our Lord and His immediate followers is part of it, for it is both mystical and practical; focussed on the Eternal, yet committed to the redemption of the temporal through love and for love, and a courageous acceptance of the pain and renunciation which this vocation involves. Right through His life—the thread that links its various phases, from Bethlehem to the Cross—the secret, loving, and utterly obedient conversation of Jesus with the Father goes on. The note of confident adoration in the High Priestly prayer, its theocentric emphasis, is surely a true revelation of the attitude of His soul. We see the gradual development of a movement towards entire self-immolation, as the only perfect means of abandonment to the Will of God, and a self-giving to the rescue of men, which is expressed in the sacrificial language of Jewish devotion and finds its outward expression in the triple oblation of the Eucharist, Gethsemane, and the Cross. "I glorified thee upon earth—I accomplished the work thou gavest me to do", is His own estimate of His mission as it draws to its close. In the last resort all is done to and for God alone. In all its parts, His life is a life-giving act of sacrificial worship; an unconditioned oblation which redeems, by inclusion in its perfect self-offering, all the faulty responses of men.

Seen from the earthly side, the Cross is the culminating point of this sacrificial sequence; but seen in spiritual regard, as the effective cause of the Church's supernatural life, its true significance is found in the eternal self-offering in heavenly places of One who was "named of God a high priest after the order of Melchizedek".[1] Hence the great importance for Christian worship, especially in its Eucharistic aspect, of the interpretations which the writers of the Epistle to the Hebrews and the Apocalypse place upon the self-offering of Christ, as a true sacrifice poised not on the death of the Victim, but on the release of full life effected by that death.

When we turn from His life to His teaching, we find that the central demand of Jesus on His real followers is for such a loving filial and confident devotion, and such uncompromising fulfilment of its requirements even to the point of the most costly self-denials, as conditioned His whole career. He lays stress on the secrecy, the personal and sacred character of the soul's direct communion with the Father, on the austere nature of the call and the hardness of perfect response, the essential quality of single-mindedness in all that is done for, or offered to God:[2] and applies to every soul the law of sacrifice—the surrender of life that life may be received.[3] Though He refuses to be limited by tradition, and demolishes mere rigorism by an ironic smile and an appeal to reality, He accepts the current methods of worship, the traditional responses to God which men have found and used, fulfilling them with new realism and fervour. He lights up the poetry of the psalms and great sayings of the prophets, and reveals their eternal significance. The Temple is to be reverenced as the House of God.[4] The disciplined practice of sacrifice, almsgiving, fasting, and prayer is not discredited. It is retained; but lifted to a

[1] Hebrews v. 1–10. Compare Hicks, *The Fullness of Sacrifice*, Pt. II, p. 240: "The Priestly work proper begins, therefore, after the Death. The sacrifice indeed begins before the work of the Priest. But the Cross is not itself the sacrifice. It stands in its place—and that an essential place—in the whole course of the sacrificial action, but is not either its beginning or its end."

[2] Luke xiv. 15–24.

[3] Matt. xvi. 25.

[4] Luke xix. 45.

new and costly level of sincerity.[1] Only two demands are made on those who approach God in worship, but these demands are absolute. They must be clothed with charity and humility. The unforgiving, the hard, the greedy, the vain, and the self-satisfied are warned that they can make no contact with Reality; however precise and arduous their institutional practice may be. Thus ritual is accepted, and ritualism is condemned. A very humble and love-inspired devotion, flexible and realistic, practised within the traditional ritual-pattern and not in defiance of it, and carried through into costly action,[2] seems to be the ideal of worship taught by Jesus. He neither desires prophetic realism to destroy liturgic form, nor liturgic form to quench prophetic realism. All—the secret communion and the public cultus—is to be filled with the same delighted and devoted love of God; which gives sacramental significance to the whole of life, offers its last coin to His treasury, leaves all comfort without reluctance for His service, finds and tends Him in the poor, sick, and oppressed, and exhibits its full compelling attraction when lifted up upon the altar of the Cross.

Jesus therefore taught worship by disclosing in His own person the true place of the soul of man in that current of eternal love which sets out from God and returns to God; and the cost and splendour of that destiny. But the long meditation and practice of devoted men and women were needed before all the implications of this destiny could be realized and expressed. The total adoring life of the whole Body, the Communion of Saints, is already present in His unconditioned response to the Father, His offering of Pure Love; and the history of Christian worship consists in its explication.

[1] Matthew v. 23–24; vi. 2–18.
[2] Luke xviii. 18–30; xxi. 1–4.

III

The true character, elements, and balance of the life of worship were summed up by Jesus in the sevenfold formula of the Lord's Prayer; and this at once became, and has ever remained, the classic standard of devotion for Christians of every type. It is, indeed, a complete direction for the Godward life of the soul. It lights up the human situation, with its limited but real opportunities and responsibilities; its duty of adoration, and position of filial dependence. Each of the seven clauses implies a distinct relation with God, a strand in the total life of worship. Beginning on the summits of our experience, with the most sublime invocation of Reality possible to man, they end with the creaturely confession of our utter dependence, and need of rescue and guidance. Taken together, they exhibit the richness and suppleness, the spiritual realism, of the Christian life of worship; stretching from the most awestruck delight in God's splendour, to the most simple and homely demands on His care, and justifying all the various approaches of spirit to Spirit which lie between these extremes. Here all the mixed experience of man is seen in the Eternal Light; and disclosed as material of his worship.

The plan and proportion of the prayer at once gives a standard to which, unfortunately, Christian devotion has seldom been true. It is constructed on a definite pattern. There is first an invocation, declaring the relation of the praying soul to God; and this is followed by three petitionary clauses asking that His Glory may be perfected within that created order, in and for which man approaches Him in worship. After them come three dependent clauses focussed on the creaturely need, fragility, and childlike status of men. This is, in the mind of Jesus, the right order and balance of those interests which are brought to God's presence in prayer. It sets in proportion the eternal and temporal realities of our situation. First it is turned toward God and His glory, as the chief interest and object of the praying soul; then towards man and his needs. Judged by this test, real worship as Our Lord taught it begins by an act of simple contemplation: the lifting up of the eye of the soul towards the Being of God, the confident claim to kinship with God, and an act of filial devotion born of that claim. The soul opens its eyes upon Reality and discovers itself to be a child of the Eternal Perfect; and the essence of its worship is to be a total devotion to His interests, hallowing His name and co-operating in the action of His creative Will. The supernatural world is here disclosed as the ruling factor in man's experience; and the steadfast action of the Will of God, already present directing, moulding, and creating us, as the only object of his prayer. All is covered by the three dispositions of Adoration, Oblation, and Abandonment: and all is addressed to the Absolute God, who is yet declared to be the Father of all life. Thus, asked how men should pray, Jesus lifts them at once to the summit of the worshipping life, selfless adoration—the lauding and magnifying of the Holy Reality of God—and sets the mystery of His Being before them as the object of loving delight. All else is to be subordinated to this Fact of facts: the prevenient God in His unchanging splendour, standing so decisively over against us, yet in closest and most cherishing contact with our fluctuating life.

So shalt thou bring with thee
A burning earnestness of Love,
A fiery flame of devotion, leaping and ascending into the very goodness of God Himself;
A loving longing of the soul to be with God in His Eternity;
A turning from all things of self into the freedom of the Will of God,
With all the forces of the soul gathered into the unity of the Spirit;
Thanking and glorifying God, and loving and serving Him, in everlasting reverence.[1]

[1] Ruysbroeck, *The Twelve Béguines*, cap. VII.

Here Ruysbroeck has surely caught the very spirit of the Lord's Prayer. First the Christian is to make his awestruck contribution to the *Sanctus* of the universe ; and only after that is to consider all that this hallowing of the Name of God involves.

If we continue the analysis, we see that in the mind of Jesus this hallowing of the Name is decisive for the Christian attitude to every aspect of life. First, it must involve the transfiguration of the whole created order, the unblemished rule of Love, the giving of eternal quality to the temporal world, as a chief object of his prayer. Next, the worshipper as a child of the living God has his own direct responsibility in regard to this. So worship, beginning in contemplation, is found to embrace selfless and devoted action : and if we set beside the second petition some of the ways in which Our Lord thought of the Kingdom of God, some of the things He felt that it was like, we realize that this element in worship is to be of a costly and various kind. No half-measures are possible where the Kingdom is concerned. It is the Pearl, the Treasure, for which all our possessions are too small a price ; it is the inconspicuous seed of immense vitality, which once it starts growing, will surpass all herbs of the field ; it is the leaven which, once introduced, will work in secret and change the quality of the common life. This secret but irresistible entrance of Holiness into the texture of human existence, this triumph of the Charity of God, is to be the second objective of Christian worship ; and requires from all Christians active desire and devoted co-operation, as an element in their prayer. The apocalyptic hope enters into worship, because the God Who has revealed Himself in Christianity is a God Who acts ; but it enters as a demand, not merely as a vision. Thus the Lord's Prayer looks towards a goal in which every action shall be an act of worship ; an utterance of the Name. It is touched with the creative passion of the artist, longing for beauty to appear; and willing for any labour and sacrifice, so that it may appear. And this costly intercessory prayer for the sanctification of life—which must expand with the expansion of our knowledge and love—is given further precision, and deeper significance, by the next petition; with its total subordination of the individual will to the movement and purpose of the divine Creative Will, in small things as in great—not through some future transfiguration, but here and now. Here, then, Jesus weaves the stuff of every-day existence into the tissue of worship; and gives every incident spiritual worth, as being on the one hand the medium of the hidden action of God, and on the other the possible material of self-abandonment to His purpose.

> "If", says de Caussade, "we could see the life of God within all things and how the Divine action moves them, mixes them, brings them together or sets them apart, and presses them towards the one end by contrary paths, we should recognize that everything has its reason, its limits and its relationships, within this Divine work."[1]

This realistic sense of the secret Divine action is very close to the spirit of the Lord's Prayer. It demands from the soul an active self-giving to God's present will and final purpose; strength and talents, preferences and loves, devoted to the single aim of fulfilling His creative Will. The Name, the Kingdom, and the Will are the things that matter; that their perfection may be manifest on earth as in heaven. Worship is here seen to be in essence a devotedness to God's interests, a movement, an interior disposition of love; which fulfils itself on every level of life and unites to the oblation of Gethsemane the humblest sacrifices and efforts of men.

This threefold adoring supplication, then, is given by

[1] J. P. de Caussade, *Abandon à la Providence Divine*, cap. II.

Jesus as the starting point and classic norm of all man's worship. It mounts to a spiritual summit from which the perfect triumph of God's Will, in the natural as in the transcendental order, is seen to be the only adequate aim of the praying soul, and worship and action are merged in one single movement of dedication to His purpose. Thus it links that fundamental and primary prayer which is the soul's absolute action towards God, with that secondary prayer which consists in the imbuing of man's successive actions with absolute worth by directing them to God.

The dependent clauses of the Prayer build up and complete the picture of this perfect filial adherence: taking our situation as it is, the humbling reality of the natural life with its limitations and instability and its homely needs. It is an essential part of creaturely worship to recognize this situation; to acknowledge with an entire confidence man's utter dependence on God, as the only supporter of his life, giver of his bread, and chooser of his path. Between these two expressions of our child-like state, Christ places the one clause which has no known origin in Jewish devotion; and which states, or rather assumes, the disposition of soul in which alone imperfect man can dare to adore the Perfection of God. "Forgive us our trespasses as we forgive." The demand for an unlimited mutual forbearance which is stressed in the Gospels, is here taken for granted as the precedent condition of all real communion with Him. Those who are really filial must be fraternal, too. We draw near to God as a family which is at peace with itself. The hard, the exacting, the intolerant cannot worship; for worship is a confident approach to the Infinite Charity, and here the genial humility which realizes our common fragility and need of pardon is the only passport. It is on these two poles of adoration and penitence that all Christian devotion turns; and it is these which, in the final petition of the Lord's Prayer, are given together as the essence of our relation to God—the constant trust in His unchanging Presence penetrating and over-ruling the changing experiences of life, and the constant sense of our creaturely dependence and need.

IV

The glorifying of God through the redeeming and perfecting of His human creation is the real theme of the whole Gospel. The Logos "comes down from heaven" and enters human history to redeem that history, and make it what it should be, an adoring response to God; and in His own person to bring humanity back to its perfect relationship with Reality. This thought is already present with the two evangelists in whose narrative reflection plays the largest part: St Luke and St John. The birth of Jesus "glorifies God in the Highest"; the Word is made flesh that the "Glory of the Father" may be seen. The promised Incarnation is welcomed by two great hymns of adoring gratitude—the Magnificat and Benedictus—Jewish in form, Christian in sentiment: and this double character conditions the formative period of Christian worship, as we see it in the Epistles and the Acts. For Jewish Christians, the first century was the Messianic Age. Messiah had come, though in a form hard to recognize, and had fulfilled God's promise to His people. So the victorious saints in the Apocalypse sing "The song of Moses the Servant of God *and* the Song of the Lamb."[1] The events of Easter, Ascensiontide, and Pentecost had justified His claim. He was now set on God's right hand, and His Parousia was confidently expected.[2] A strictly national exultation was therefore implicit in the worship of the Jerusalem church; and it was natural that Jewish liturgical forms, and Jewish sacrificial language should be used by it. The Christian Church which we meet

[1] Rev. xv. 3. [2] 1 Thess. iv. 16–18.

in the New Testament is not in its own eyes a "Jewish sect": it is the fellowship or assembly of those who know that the Promise of Israel is fulfilled in Jesus. Hence the authority with which the Apostolic teachers speak, and their frequent appeals to the Old Testament. Hence the double strand in their worship: "continuing steadfastly with one accord in the Temple, and breaking bread at home."[1]

It is in this situation, as described in the opening chapters of Acts, that the long history of Christian worship begins. Here it is still taken for granted that the Apostolic fellowship should continue the practice of all devout Jews; "praising God" in the Temple and synagogue, and adding to this the special devotions of their own community. To such a body, it would seem appropriate, indeed almost inevitable to apply the sacrificial language of the Old Testament to Jesus; for it accepted the whole of the ancient dispensation, as leading without a break to the Messiah who saves His people by making for them the perfect sacrifice. He is the unblemished Paschal Victim, the peace-offering, the sin-offering, the atonement.[2] These titles carried for the early Christian a realistic meaning we have long lost; as we soon recognize when we read with sympathy the Epistle to the Hebrews and the Apocalypse. At the first Eucharist, Jesus accepted and proclaimed the status of the atoning and life-giving Victim; offering His blood according to the ancient cultus as a new covenant for the remission of sin. Thus the whole of the great Temple drama pointed to Calvary: and behind it, all those premonitions of primitive religion concerning a mediator, the middle term between the movement of God to man and the movement of man to God. Equally the prophetic strain in the Hebrew Scriptures, the

[1] Acts ii. 46.

[2] Rom. v. 11; 1 Cor. v. 7; Col. i. 20; Heb. i. 3; ix; and xiii. 12; 1 Peter i. 18, 19 and iii. 18; 1 John i. 7; Rev. v. 6; etc.

conviction that a Saviour and Fulfiller would enter history and redeem the people of God, was felt by the Early Church to be fulfilled in Jesus :[1] and this fact conditioned the form taken by the primitive preaching, and the Synoptic emphasis on particular incidents of His life.[2] Thus from its beginning Christian worship was coloured by the Bible and by Biblical ideas and images ; and with no sense of incongruity made constant use of Jewish liturgical forms. The Epistle to the Hebrews and the ritual passages of the Apocalypse, documents of great significance for an understanding of the early worship, show how rich was the matrix within which that worship developed, with what mysterious splendour the triumphant figure of the Crucified was clothed, how profound was the awestruck recognition of the action of God in Christ, how intense the joy with which He was acclaimed ; and how different all this was from the "simple evangelical piety" which often lays claim to be its modern representative.

The primitive Church first appears as the synagogue of the followers of Jesus, and seems at once to have adapted to her weekly common worship the four chief elements of the ordinary synagogue service : that reading and expounding of Scripture, singing of psalms and canticles, and recital of prayers, which persists in her liturgy.[3] There was thus from the beginning a tradition of orderly prayer, praise, and thanksgiving ; offered, according to Jewish custom, by a leader, the congregation ratifying the prayer or praise offered in their name by responding Amen !, Alleluia !, or Thanks be to God.[4] But these small and humble assemblies had two other characteristics, which distinguished them from all

[1] Acts iii. 24.

[2] This subject is fully worked out by Hoskyns and Davey, *The Riddle of the New Testament.*

[3] According to Hermas (late first or early second century) the Roman Christians of his day still referred to their assembly as the Synagogue.

[4] Cf. 1 Cor. xiv. 16 ; xv. 57 ; Rev. v. 14 ; vii. 12 ; xix. 1–4.

other groups of pious Jews, and account for the note of thanksgiving, of exultant joy, in "psalms and hymns and spiritual songs" making melody to God, which is so frequently recommended or described as the proper temper of their worship. They met, in the first place, under the intense conviction of that continuing presence with them of the Spirit of Jesus which had been manifested in the events of the Forty Days. Therefore a first motive of their corporate worship was that of a common communion with Him; to be experienced, according to His promise, where "two or three were gathered together", and especially associated with the Breaking of Bread. The primitive Eucharist, always connected with a common meal, was in the first place a commemoration of the sacrificial death of Jesus. The New Testament and the earliest liturgies emphasize this. But the commemoration reached its climax in the mystical yet actual communion of the faithful with each other, and with their invisible but truly present Lord.[1] The reality of this experience in its mystery and intimacy, and its capital importance for Christian devotion, are implied throughout the New Testament; in the careful preservation of such incidents as the Supper at Emmaus, in the Johannine discourse on the Bread of Life and account of the appearances of the Risen Christ, the note of worshipping joy on which St Luke's Gospel closes, the almost matter-of-fact reference to "the Lord working with them" which occupies a similar position in that of St Mark, in many passages of the Epistles, and in the Apocalyptic promise to those who hear the Voice and open the door.[2] Ancient phrases still embedded in the liturgies point back to the time when this realistic belief was the very heart of Christian worship. "Maran-atha! the Lord is at hand." "Christ is here!" "He is and He will be!" "Lift up your

[1] 1 Cor. x. 16, 17; xi. 20–26. Compare *supra*, caps. VII and VIII.
[2] Rev. iii. 20.

hearts." "We lift them up to the Lord." "The Lord be with thee!" "And with thy spirit!" "O Lamb of God that takest away the sin of the world, give us peace!" "Come! Come! Jesus, thou good High Priest!"[1]

This conviction of the intimate presence of a living Lord, which is still the real strength and common possession of Catholic and Evangelical devotion, was the "mystery of faith" which distinguished the first Christian assemblies. There seems little doubt that it was closely associated with the Eucharist, the capital importance of which is clear from the references in Acts and Corinthians. But at first the homely ceremony of the Breaking of the Bread—which had not yet become a standardized liturgical action—seems less to have been the occasion of the Presence, than an incident in the total act of thankful remembrance and adoring communion with the Risen Master; which transcended and included this ritual expression. The discourses of Jesus given in the fourteenth and fifteenth chapters of the Fourth Gospel restore to us the heart of that belief and practice by which the first Christian groups—or at least their most devoted members—lived, and in which they met suffering and persecution with joy. It is in their light that we shall best understand the worship of the Apostolic Church.

The same Gospel also justifies by the direct promise of Jesus the second undoubted characteristic of the primitive devotion; the spontaneous, unstylized, inspirational prayer, praise, and exhortations of the prophets and ecstatics, and others to whom the Spirit gave utterance, of which St Paul gives in First Corinthians a vivid account. This charismatic worship is by no means to be set aside as the passing effect of unbalanced enthusiasm. On the contrary, it was a

[1] H. Lietzmann (*Messe und Herrenmahl*) considers that the *Sursum corda* and its equivalent phrases marked the point at which, in the primitive assemblies, the fellowship meal ended, and the Eucharistic mystery began.

genuine effect of Christian realism, of which the importance is stressed in our earliest documents; and was regarded as witnessing to the presence and action of the "quickening Spirit" promised by Jesus to His Church. Though Duchesne seems to go further than our knowledge permits in speaking of a "liturgy of the Holy Ghost", marked by prophetic utterance and speaking with tongues, and following the Eucharistic liturgy of Christ—"a true liturgy, with a Real Presence and Communion of the Paraclete"[1]—we do not get a balanced view of the worship of the Apostolic Church unless we remember that it did practise together, and held in equal honour, the sacramental and pneumatic, liturgic and prophetic responses to God in Christ. The two aspects are not to be sharply divided, but are best understood as the completing opposites of one experienced reality, and it is still true that the fullest and deepest worship accepts and uses both. In both God is acting in and on His Church; and together they witness to the central fact that He is tabernacled among men, and justify the mingled exaltation and intimacy of the Christian response.

To "worship by the Spirit of God *and* glory in Christ Jesus"[2] is therefore the Pauline ideal: for the experiences of Pentecost were for the first generation of Christians as fundamental as those of Holy Week, and were believed to be renewed in all the baptized on whom "the Spirit fell". To be "in the Spirit" was an essential character of full membership of the Church; and in the common worship, the indwelling Spirit made intercession and gave utterance.[3] It was by the Spirit that the Church was guided in all great decisions; and by His action that the Eucharistic gifts became the Body and Blood of Christ.[4] This conviction of the direct personal action of the immanent Spirit of God

[1] Cf. Duchesne, *Origins of Christian Worship*, p. 48. See also *supra*, Pt. I, cap. IV.

[2] Phil. iii. 3.

[3] Romans viii. 27, 28.

[4] So in the earliest liturgies, as still in that of the Orthodox Church.

on and in the praying Church, revealing to it the deep mysteries of Eternity,[1] controlling its decisions and supporting its labours, is seen in its noblest form in the Pauline Epistles, and in its practical consequences in many passages of Acts. It produced, at least in some places, the psycho-spiritual phenomena often associated with religious revivals : and with these, the tendency to exaggeration and to lawless individualism which dogs all inspirational worship. Yet none the less it remained in its purity, and its action on disciplined souls, the "spirit of wisdom, power, and a sound mind."

In the fourteenth chapter of First Corinthians we see St Paul struggling to keep the spontaneous and prophetic element of the common worship within the bounds of sanity and order, and apply to it the principles of spiritual common sense. The ardent but unintelligible prayer "in the Spirit" and the outpourings of those who "spoke with tongues" are not discredited ; but the ecstatic and the prophet are reminded that as members of the Church they have their duty towards the congregation as a whole, a duty which is not fulfilled by "speaking in a tongue unto God". Paul, himself an ecstatic, possessed of "spiritual gifts", knows how small a proportion these surface manifestations bear to the "deep things of God." Therefore he would rather "pray with the understanding" that his neighbour may be edified ; and warns those who "bless with the Spirit" that the Thanksgiving (possibly the Eucharistic prayer) must be intelligible, so that the "unlearned" may take his part and know when to say Amen.[2] The worship of the Church is that of a Spirit-filled Body. The whole organism is His temple ;[3] and no one unit, however enthusiastic, must act in disregard of the rest.

[1] 1 Cor. ii. 10. [2] 1 Cor. xiv. 1–19 (R.V.).
[3] 1 Cor. iii. 16 ; Eph. ii. 21, 22.

Charismatic worship, in the form in which St Paul describes it, was perhaps more characteristic of the early Hellenistic converts, who quickly moved away from Jewish models, than it was of the sober Mother-Church at Jerusalem. Nevertheless the note of delight, enthusiasm, and spontaneity, the temper of joy, the sense of the direct action of the Spirit, and total capitulation to a transforming Power which seemed to come from beyond themselves, were and are fundamental strands in the full Christian response to the saving revelation of God. "Now the Lord is the Spirit, and where the Spirit of the Lord is there is liberty!"

Christian worship enters history not as a simplification, but as a great enrichment of man's Godward life. It invites his adoring communion with a living, acting yet Transcendent God, infinite in wisdom and knowledge, unsearchable in His judgments, but revealed as incarnate Saviour and indwelling Spirit of Life. It offers him many valid means of response to this Holy Reality, not one alone. It had been from the first both liturgic and prophetic, historical and mystical, sacramental and spontaneous. It was built upon the prophets as well as the Apostles; and bathed in the atmosphere of that noble theism within which it was born, and which we recognize in St Paul's sudden outbursts of adoring delight in God.[1] Those Christians who base their worship on any of these diverse characters can claim to this extent primitive authority for their particular practice. In Catholicism, the liturgic and sacramental element has decisively triumphed. The Evangelical Churches have restored, perhaps sometimes to excess, the prophetic and Biblical strand; whilst in those frequent revivals of free worship and claims to a direct experience of the Spirit which shock the decorum of the traditionalist, we see the continued power of the charismatic strain. But a full and

[1] E.g. Rom. viii. 31–39 and xi. 33–36; 1 Cor. i. 26–31; Ephes. iii. 14–21. See also 1 Tim. i. 17.

balanced Christian cultus would find room for all these elements, and means of harmonizing and controlling them: thus achieving that synthesis of liberty and order, fervour and prudence, which represented the Pauline ideal for the infant churches in the middle years of the first century.

V

From the first there was in the Christian devotion to Christ a note of mystery, astonishment, and awe. The amazement and even fear which fell from time to time on His first followers,[1] the sense of contact with One Who was in the world yet not of it, which even the fragmentary reminiscences of the Synoptic Gospels convey to us are repeated in the experience of the early Church. His Presence, His Spirit, the mysterious communion of the faithful with their invisible Lord, Who is at once the Shepherd of their souls and the Food of Eternal Life; in all this there was something strange and tremendous, something "new", as the New Testament writers insist again and again.[2] It lay beyond the ordinary experiences of piety and the ordinary resources of speech; and we need not be surprised that inconsistencies and confusions should be present in their attempts to describe it. St Paul's "the Lord" and "the Spirit", "Christ in us" and "we in Christ", his sudden exultant declarations of union with the Divine Love, or the "high calling" which he knew ever to be beyond his grasp,[3] the great Johannine discourses on the feeding of the faithful upon that Bread of Life, which is the very Flesh and Blood of the Incarnate Word[4]—all these suggest, first from one angle and then from another, a vividly experienced but ineffable reality, a new disclosure

[1] Mark ix. 6 and x. 32.
[2] 2 Cor. v. 17; Ephes. iv. 24; Rev. ii. 17; iii. 12; v. 9.
[3] Rom. viii. 38, 39; and xi. 33–36; Phil. iii. 13, 14.
[4] John vi. 35–58.

under veils of the "deep things of God" which calls forth the utmost adoring love of the believer, while exceeding he resources of speech.

Thus mystery, hiddenness, was from the beginning inherent in Christian worship; and when that worship, deepened and illuminated by St Paul's religious genius, came out into the world, there were soon discovered in it points of contact with those mystery-cults in which the deepest religious instincts and longings of the Hellenistic world were expressed. Hence the gradually developing Christian ritual pattern—without any loss of its intrinsic character—tended to clothe itself in symbolic garments, and express its living secret by symbolic acts, which were already known and full of suggestion to its Gentile converts. These had no difficulty in understanding what was meant by re-birth, sacrifice, exorcism, and ceremonial washings; or by sacred meals in which the believer was fed by the Divine self-giving life. Thus, as Plato and Plotinus brought their contribution to the building up of Christian reflection on revealed truth, and of Christian secret prayer, so—not deliberately, but inevitably—the Church adopted from the religious world to which she was sent a language and technique by which her deepest secrets could be universalized, and given to her Gentile converts in a form which they could understand: as *the* Mystery, the unique revelation of the Divine saving Presence with men "which hath been hid from all ages and generations. . . . Christ in you, the hope of glory."[1] Here the bridge is crossed which unites Primitive and Catholic Christianity: nor does this mean, as is sometimes supposed, the paganizing of the Evangelical deposit, but rather a true "salting with Christ's salt" of the religious discoveries and longings of the Gentile world. The Hellenistic concept of the Divine Logos, in whom "the fulness of the Godhead dwelt",[2] His incarnation in time and the mysterious

[1] Col. i. 26, 27. [2] Col. ii. 9.

feeding of the worshippers on that self-given Divine Life,[1] mingled with the more precise sacrificial conceptions inherited from Judaism; and gradually transformed the emphasis on a purely national yet divine Messiah, which seems to have been characteristic of Jewish Christians of the first generation but could never have won the Gentile world.

It was primarily the religious genius of St Paul, his vivid sense of the over-plus of the Divine, the "riches of the glory" exceeding all particular embodiments, which made this transformation possible. If the Jewish convert whose mind had been formed by "the traditions of the elders" found in the Eucharist a spiritual manna, and there drank from the spiritual Rock;[2] so too for the Gentile, that same mystery fulfilled the promise of his ancient cults. In the Fourth Gospel the two strands, the Jewish and Hellenistic, the historical and eternal, personal and metaphysical, meet and are harmonized; and it is here, perhaps, that we find our best clue to the character of Christian Eucharistic worship at the close of the first century, when the primitive and unstylized experience of the Apostolic Church was losing its apocalyptic character and beginning to assume a ritual form. It is unlikely that this form was everywhere the same. Sacramental doctrine as we know it was still in a fluid state; and a comparison of the most ancient liturgies suggests that the Christian Mysteries, like all ritual embodiments of spiritual truth, had for their initiates many kinds and degrees of significance. The holy Death was shown forth, the holy Presence was realized, and the holy Food was received; but there was little desire to enclose this sacred experience within the bounds of a rigid formula, or define the precise means by which it was assured.

As the Logos became flesh through the Virgin Mary, so He descends from heaven to manifest Himself, not in a

[1] John i. 1–14 and vi. 50, 51.

[2] John vi. 48–51; 1 Cor. x. 1–4.

human body, but in the earthly substance of the bread and wine. Though spiritual, the presence of the Logos is real and effective. This reality of the divine presence is the essential fact, as regards the conception of the Eucharist as a mystery in the ancient Church.[1]

Within that ancient Church there was a gradual, but at last decisive triumph of the liturgic over the spontaneous element in the common worship. Certain Christian liturgical forms—e.g. the Lord's Prayer, which was communicated only to the baptized, and recited by them at least three times a day[2]—were probably in use almost from the beginning. Early in the second century, Justin Martyr describes an ordered service of prayer, psalms, Scripture reading and sermon, directly derived from synagogue sources and practically identical in character with the later Liturgy of the Catechumens. This preceded the celebration of the Mysteries; and all joined in it standing.[3] Nevertheless extempore and "prophetic" prayer, as the voice of the Spirit, was still preferred to any liturgical formula, especially in the Eucharist. The celebrant who was unable to present the "collected prayer" of the faithful in his own words was held in some contempt, and at least until the end of the second century even the great Eucharistic Prayer appears to have had no fixed or obligatory form.[4] The sequence of ideas and acts was established long before it was crystallized in an agreed sequence of words; for Eucharistic worship is above all an action, partly human and partly divine. The essential points of adoring praise of the Father, thankful commemoration of the saving work of the Son, and the invocation of the Holy Spirit on the worshippers and their oblation, with the offering of the elements and fraction of the Bread, were combined in the way each celebrant thought best; a practice

[1] Will, *Le Culte*, Vol. I, p. 166.
[2] *Didache*, c. A.D. 125.
[3] Justin, 1*st Apology*, I, 67.
[4] See for the earliest surviving example, *The Apostolic Tradition of Hippolytus*, (c. 217.) Translated by B. S. Easton.

indeed which was revived by the Reformers, and is still continued in the Presbyterian Church. Even the *Sanctus* and Words of Institution, which soon came to be regarded as necessary parts of the Canon, are not invariably found in the earliest liturgies: but we have no knowledge of any Eucharist in which the element of oblation does not appear.

By the time Hippolytus drew up his Church order, which we can conveniently take as the point at which the primitive period closes and the Catholic ritual-pattern begins to emerge, the main outlines of Christian liturgical worship were drawn. It was centred on the weekly Eucharist, with its two parts: the liturgy of the catechumens, or Ministry of the Word with its climax in the solemn reading of the Gospel, and the liturgy of the faithful or Breaking of the Bread, reserved to the baptized alone.[1] The Lord's Day began, in the Jewish manner, at sunset on Saturday. The Vigil, or Saturday night service of preparation, was—and in the Eastern Church still is—an important part of the weekly common worship.[2] This ancient devotion, consisting of psalms, Scripture lessons, and responsive prayers, was formed on Jewish models; and is the germ from which the existing Offices of Vespers and Mattins—originally two parts of one night service—have grown. Each Lord's Day with its solemn vigil was, in primitive times, a liturgical commemoration of the first Easter, reaching its climax in the Eucharist. Beyond this, the vigil also signified the waiting of the Church upon the return of Christ Triumphant; for there was a traditional belief that the Parousia would take place on Easter Eve.

The grave beauty of the Eucharistic prayer given by Hippolytus, or that which the Bishop "standing in the midst

[1] These, in their main features, persist almost unchanged in all the great liturgies. In that of the Orthodox Church, the direction for the withdrawal of the Catechumens, and guarding of the doors during the Mysteries, still remains. Compare *supra*, cap. VII p. 130.

[2] Thus the Western custom of beginning a feast at "First Vespers" on the evening before, reflects back to the earliest period of the Church.

of the believers " is to say at " the lighting of the lamp "[1] show that Christian liturgical worship at the opening of the third century was already developing its classic form. Definite rules for the private prayer of the individual believer are also laid down by Hippolytus. Though as yet there are no directions as to the devotions which he shall use, the seven Hours of Prayer which afterwards crystallized into the Divine Office are already made the basis of his personal and continuous remembrance of God. Each day, if literate, he must read the Bible " in passages that he finds profitable " ; and must renew the spirit of his baptism by using the sign of the Cross. He must pray on rising and on going to bed ; at midnight, because " at this hour all creation rests for a certain moment, that all creatures may praise the Lord ", and again at dawn. At the third, sixth, and ninth hours, if at home he will give himself to prayer and thanksgiving ; and if abroad must " pray to God in his heart ".[2] Thus the " praying Church " of the first centuries demanded from all her members and not from her ministers alone a personal life entirely ruled by the spirit of worship ; a sevenfold sanctification of time by the constant remembrance of God. We are left in no doubt as to the importance which she attached to the secret prayer of the faithful ; or the obligation which she laid on every soul to share in that unceasing act of adoring and penitent love which is the life of the Communion of Saints.

[1] " We give thee thanks, O God, because thou hast enlightened us by revealing the uncorruptible light. So we, having finished the length of a day, and being come to the beginning of the night, satisfied with the light of the day that thou hast created for our satisfaction ; now, since by thy grace we lack not a light for the evening, we sanctify thee and we glorify thee ! " (Easton, p. 59.) Compare the very ancient Greek Vesper hymn, *Phos hilaron*, probably of the second century. Trans. in *English Hymnal*, 269, and *Hymns A. & M.*, 18.

[2] Easton, pp. 54–56.

CHAPTER XII

CATHOLIC WORSHIP: WESTERN AND EASTERN

I

BY Catholic worship is meant the great central tradition of the Christian Church, which has continued under a stylized form, and has developed under historical pressure, the essential elements of the primitive cultus; centred upon the self-revelation of God to man by the incarnation of His Word, and the continuance of that revelation through the sacramental life of the Church. It is the worship of the Church of the Creeds and the Councils; as expressed in the Eucharist and the Divine Office, and in devotions derived from this double source and consistent with its spirit. The formation of this worship was, of course, a gradual process and many of its phases are still obscure: but by the end of the fourth century, its liturgical character was fully established, both in the East and the West. The institutional basis was the primitive double service, with its successive Ministry of the Word and the Sacrament,[1] which is continued with later modifications and enrichments in the Roman Mass and its derivatives, and in the liturgies of the Eastern Church. In and with this Eucharistic rhythm, passing from the humble listening of the learner and the welcoming of Christ in His Gospel, to oblation, intercession, adoration, consecration and communion, the Church gave and gives ritual expression to the essential movement of her whole life, and that of each of her baptized members. It is a sacrifice of

[1] Cf. Part I, cap. VII.

praise and thanksgiving, moving to its goal in communion with God. Here the central characteristics of the primitive worship live on: its Biblical quality, its Christocentric realism, its sacrificial and adoring tone.

It is true that in the course of its development and crystallization there have been some inevitable losses ; some regrettable additions and changes of emphasis. At some periods the note of sacrifice has dominated all others, and the notes of fellowship and communion have hardly been heard. The Christian liturgy lives and grows ; and, like other living and growing things, has not preserved unchanged the classic proportions of its youth. The opportunities of variation, and of spontaneous prayer under the guidance of the Spirit, which had survived from the primitive period, have long disappeared. Acts which once possessed high realistic significance—the great common prayer of the faithful, the offering of bread and wine for the oblation, the kiss of peace—are now lost or reduced to the status of tokens. The psalms of praise which the people sang at the opening of the service, at the coming of the Gospel, at the offering of the gifts and at the communion are merely represented in the West by a few verses ;[1] and their witness to the corporate character of Christian worship is entirely lost. But the general shape and rhythm of this great service was that which we still find in the Roman Mass, the Orthodox Liturgy, and the Anglican Eucharist. It is hardly possible to regard any organized Christian worship as conforming to the Catholic ritual pattern, unless its central act embodies—as for fifteen centuries all Christian public worship did embody—this twofold response to the revelation of God ; since it is the liturgical expression of the Church's Eucharistic life, her oblation, intercession, consecration, and ever-renewed communion with her Lord.

No ritual pattern can be understood by us, until we have

[1] The present Introit, Gradual, Offertory, and Communion.

penetrated below its surface and observed the spiritual realities which it embodies and seeks to express. Many absurd things have been written about traditional Christian worship by those who failed to realize this simple truth. The Christian liturgies are the ceremonial garments worn by the Bride of Christ; garments of which every detail and ornament has or had significance as an expression of her love and adoration, or a memorial of her past, but which lose all beauty and all interest when regarded apart from the life which they are intended to clothe, and the unseen realities which they are intended to suggest. So, we cannot hope to understand Catholic worship—which is, after all, the classic worship of Christendom, and within which the vast majority of the baptized still learn to respond to the love of God—without a sympathetic understanding of its inner character; and the implicits on which it is based. Certainly this inner character is often difficult to recognize in its liturgic expression; and especially under the deformations which it so frequently endures through over-familiarity, hurry, indifference or popular misunderstanding. Both in the East and the West, its full significance, its deep interiority and vast metaphysical span, are far too great to be grasped by the average worshipper; who therefore easily tends to become an "assistant", rather than a true participant in that which is done. The muttered Low Mass, at which the Ministry of the Word is reduced to the semi-audible recitation of Latin lessons and the Ministry of the Sacraments to the Communion of the Priest—the congregation meanwhile pursuing their own devotions, reciting the rosary, singing hymns, or even listening to a discourse from a loud-speaker—or the Orthodox Liturgy which maintains its stately progress in complete isolation from the faithful whose oblation it should present before God, are mere caricatures of real Catholic worship. But those who judge this worship by its degradations and extravagances, its formalisms and atavisms, or the long rope it gives to popular religion, are gravely in error. Even within the most unfavourable appearances, and by the most unworthy of devotional methods, some souls may be caught into the great current of sacrificial love which is the essence of its life. Again and again that life emerges to redeem the religious situation and vindicate its claims ; as the great development of a living worship among the victims of the Russian revolution, and the liturgic revival now in progress within the Roman Communion, plainly show.

Catholicism is the result, not of any attempt to perpetuate that " simple Evangelical worship " to which the sects try again and again to return ; but rather of baptizing into Christ all the religious longings and religious desires of men. It can therefore absorb, and carry forward, many differing levels and strands of worship ; can offer a home to the crudest products of popular religion, yet can introduce the contemplative to the " wilderness where lovers lose themselves " ; gathering all unto its " great supra-national tidal wave of faith in God and love of Christ ".[1] It has five general characteristics which are enumerated for convenience here ; but are more fully discussed in the earlier chapters of this book.

(*a*) It is hallowed and penetrated by a sense of the Transcendence of God, Who is alone the cause and the goal of man's adoring worship. The *Sanctus*, which so early became the invariable introduction to the Eucharistic Mystery, at once sets the scene and accentuates the awfulness of that communion with the Incarnate, " holy, life-giving and terrible ", which is the culmination of the liturgy, and in which " it is vouchsafed to us to touch that God who dwells in unapproachable light."[2] This splendid emphasis on the

[1] Karl Adam, *The Spirit of Catholicism*, 2nd ed., p. 168.

[2] Simeon the New Theologian. Quoted by Heiler, *The Spirit of Worship*, p. 50.

Divine action—God alone the author and cause of that worshipping life, that awestruck feeding on the Eternal, in which man becomes truly real—is the heart of Catholic worship ; and the liturgies strike this note again and again. All the ceremonial acts of reverence with which the cultus is surrounded—genuflections and prostrations, incense and lights—are merely the outward signs of this ceaseless adoration of the Divine.

(*b*) Yet, since it is based on the Incarnation and acknowledges in the outward and visible the scene of the saving revelation of God, an unmitigated other-worldliness is quite foreign to the Catholic spirit. It is true that the worship developed here and now is a preparation for that unblemished worship which is the substance of Eternal Life ; and therefore it must never lose its transcendental reference. But its object is a God whose saving presence enters the natural world, and is discerned by means of natural things. Therefore it accepts, and consecrates to its purposes, the world of sense as well as the world of spirit ; showing a wide and unfastidious generosity in respect of all the outward instruments and expressions of human worship. Indeed, in its conservative use of naïve symbolisms—especially those which refer back to the ancient sacrificial cults—Catholicism is very like Judaism ; and, like Judaism, is able to make this archaic ritual pattern the vehicle of an intense experience of God, which spreads from the field of consciousness to transform and bring into the total act of worship the deep instinctive levels of the mind.

It follows from this that not sacraments alone but also sacramentals, and not only these but every image and sensible sign, are congenial to Catholic worship ; even though the natural tendency of popular devotion to lose itself in the concrete, requires (but does not always obtain) a carefu- discretion in their use. For it is the very nature of Christil anity to give supernatural value to the rhythms and events of our daily existence, to balance homeliness against awfulness, and draw into the life of adoration all the activities of man ; teaching him to sanctify the life of succession by that noble asceticism which is an element in every offering of love, and " add it to the Lord ". So, the rejection of the outward in favour of the inward is untrue to the spirit of Catholic Christianity. When the Eastern Church declared war on the iconoclasts, it did so, not because these were rebels destructive of Church order, but because their principles constituted a denial of the Incarnation.

(*c*) Catholic worship is essentially Christocentric: being the realistic continuance in liturgical form of the primitive Christian mystery of communion with the risen Christ, and in and through Him with the Infinite God. It is round this mysterious belief that the whole edifice of Catholic worship is raised. It is a shrine of the Presence. Emphasis and colour may differ in different parts of the Church, but the substance of the worship is the same. Here it is that mediæval emotionalism and Post-Reformation devotionalism have most gravely obscured the noble outlines of the ancient belief and experience ; where the emphasis lay, not on the private and often sentimental realization of the human Jesus, which has been popularized by the modern cult of the Reserved Sacrament and its derived devotions, but on the majestic presence of the Risen Lord " upholding all things by the Word of His power ".[1] Again and again this note is struck by the great liturgies ; though perhaps more clearly in the East than in the West.

Our God, our Lord, has appeared unto us ![2]

Behold ! I draw near unto Christ, our immortal King and God ![3]

[1] Hebrews i. 3. For a further discussion of this point see Dom Beauduin, O.S.B., *La Piété de l'Église*, and other Roman Catholic publications connected with the Liturgic Reform.

[2] *Armenian Liturgy*, Communion of the People.

[3] *Liturgy of St John Chrysostom :* Communion of the Priest.

In the sacramental system—and particularly in the central liturgic action of Catholicism, the Eucharist—the reality of this communion is or should be constantly re-experienced.

> The Worship of the Church is not merely a filial remembrance of Christ, but a continual participation by visible mysterious signs in Jesus and His redemptive might. . . . In Catholic sacramental devotion, Christ is faithfully affirmed and experienced as the Lord of the community, as its invisible strength and principle of activity. In the sacraments is expressed the fundamental nature of the Church, the fact that Christ lives on in her.[1]

(*d*) Catholic worship is fundamentally, though not exclusively, sacrificial. In it, the Church, the Body of Christ, again and again accepts her vocation ; offers herself to God by means of visible tokens in and with her Head, is consecrated to His redeeming purpose, and for that purpose receives her heavenly food. This great organic action is the very heart of her response to the Eternal. In it, she unites herself and each of her members—more, the whole created order—to the Cross. Hence her liturgic worship must have at least a sacrificial reference, and has in point of fact a strongly marked sacrificial orientation. Thus in the Roman Mass, the Offertory is followed by a solemn oblation of the Eucharistic elements—the "immaculate host" and the "chalice of salvation"[2]—and at the opening of the Canon the priest presents this oblation before God, and again and again begs the acceptance and transfiguration of the gifts for the good of holy Church, of the whole world, of all present, and as an earnest of the service of the whole family of Christ.

> Which oblation do thou O God we beseech thee, vouchsafe to make in all things blessed, approved, ratified,

[1] Karl Adam, *The Spirit of Catholicism*, 2nd ed., pp. 19, 22.

[2] Roman Mass : *Suscipe, sancte Pater* and *Offerimus tibi.*

reasonable and acceptable, that it may become for us the Body and Blood of Thy dearly beloved Son.[1]

All the great liturgies from the third century onwards speak in the same sense. No reduction of the Eucharist to a service of fellowship, a memorial of the Passion, or a means of communion, can therefore claim to be more than a mutilated expression of the Catholic ideal.[2]

(*e*) Last, Catholic worship is not only theocentric, incarnational, sacrificial. It is also thoroughly social and organic; for all its outward rites and symbols declare a hidden supernatural order, where all things are united in God. Here the individual, entering this order, always worships as part of the Church; and in his personal action is always implied the surrounding action of the Communion of Saints—the total adoring movement of all Christian souls living and dead. The Catholic Christian does not or should not go to the Eucharist on an individual errand, even of the most spiritual kind. He goes to take his small part in the total action of the single Eucharist, which the Church everywhere and at all times, in earth and in heaven, visibly and invisibly, offers to God. This too is the real significance of the Divine Office; the second great liturgical instrument of the Church. In its recitation the individual or group enters the ancient cycle of prayer, by which day by day and hour by hour that Church in the name of all creation adores and implores the Eternal God.

This intensely corporate spirit, for which " the household

[1] Roman Mass: *Hanc igitur*, and *Quam oblationem*.

[2] Cf. Karl Adam, *op. cit.*, p. 214 : " In the sacrifice of the Mass we are not merely reminded of the Sacrifice of the Cross in a symbolical form. On the contrary the Sacrifice of Calvary, as a great supra-temporal reality, enters into the immediate present. Space and time are abolished. The same Jesus is here present who died on the Cross. The whole congregation unites itself with His holy sacrificial will, and through Jesus present before it consecrates itself to the heavenly Father as a living oblation." Orthodox worship implies a similar theological basis.

of faith " is a vivid fact and real source of confidence and power, explains the great part played in Catholic worship, both Eastern and Western, by the veneration and invocation of the Saints ; the reliance placed upon their intercessions, their continued loving interest in the world of men. A saint is a human being who has become a pure capacity for God, and therefore a tool of the divine action : and it is consistent with the doctrine of incarnation that God should be adored, not only in His pure Being but also as present in these His instruments, and as the cause of their holiness and power. It is true that here popular religion has found its most congenial material, and that in actual practice the charge of " veiled paganism " brought against the cultus of the Saints—especially that of the Blessed Virgin in its more exaggerated forms—often appears to be justified. Nevertheless this cultus is, in origin, an acknowledgment of the corporate and totalitarian character of the Christian response to God, a confident appeal from the struggling members of the family to those who have achieved stability and peace. Further, the Catholic Christian finds and adores God's self-disclosure, not only at its focal point, but also in its total spreading radiance. Thus, gazing on the Saints in their manifest humanity, their heroic virtue and " spiritual persuasiveness ", he shares their trans-human experience ; and through, in and with them apprehends the divine charity and beauty tabernacled among men. Especially the Blessed Virgin, as the human agent of the Incarnation, must be for Catholic devotion the " saint of saints ", in whom the race aspires towards God, and abandons itself to His action. *Ecce ancilla Domini.* The provocative phrase " all through Mary " has therefore a certain theological significance. The dubious ancestry of some aspects of Marian devotion, its obvious Pagan affinities, the exaggerated position which it has occupied from the Middle Ages onwards, or the many phantasies, superstitions, and sentimentalisms of which it has become the core, must not blind us to the deep spiritual truth which it enshrines.

The organic character of Catholic worship—the fact that it is the worship of the whole Church, developed in different degrees and ways by souls of different types, and that each individual act of adoration contributes to the Godward life of the whole—is particularly seen in one of its greatest creations: the Religious Life. It is true that monasticism is not peculiar to Christianity: for it is the expression of a fundamental spiritual need, the longing for God, and for a life of unbroken communion with Him, which may be aroused within any great religion. But in Christianity that unconditional consecration and total oblation of personality, that death to the world, which is the essence of the religious vocation has a peculiar position and significance. God's total claim upon His creature here receives a total response; which transforms the whole life into an unbroken act of sacrificial worship, the *ne plus ultra* of adoring love.

The frequent and pitiful deterioration of monasticism, both in the East and the West, and the fact that only a few souls can in this life touch the level it demands, cannot affect the truth that this demand is the same as that of all full Christian worship—death to self, and unconditioned abandonment to the purposes of God. The prayer of St Ignatius Loyola, "Take, Lord, and receive all my liberty; my memory, my will, my imagination, all I have and possess", is an act of oblation which every Christian must try to make: and in this sense the ideal of monasticism is the same as that of any really theocentric life, and can be fulfilled anywhere and in any way by those who have sufficient courage and love. But in the solemn vows of religion, and the separation from the world which they require, that total oblation is given a concrete, dramatic, even sacramental form. And this sacramental life of worship, in which the *Opus Dei*, the common prayer, takes precedence of all else, is lived by those souls who are called to it, for and with the whole Church; not merely as an individual response to the all-demanding voice of God. This is especially true of the most austere and secluded contemplative orders, whose real vocation is so commonly misunderstood. For these are particular and hidden instruments, power-houses of prayer devoted to the increase of God's glory, and the furtherance of His hidden purpose. It is as a cell in one specialized organ of Christ's Mystical Body, obedient to the pressure of His Spirit and self-given for other souls, and not merely as an expression of her personal fervour or a means to her personal sanctification, that the Poor Clare or the Carmelite nun loves, suffers, and works. Thus she gives intercessory value, not only to her supplications, but to her life; subordinating all to the requirements of Pure Love.

II

The difference in tone between the traditional worship of Western and Eastern Catholicism is already seen when we set the antique Roman Mass—in so far as we are able to reconstruct it—over against its virtual contemporaries: the Liturgies of St John Chrysostom and St Basil. The Eastern Eucharist is a supernatural mystery, of which the most sacred actions are screened from view. Its devotional emphasis falls upon the coming into time of the Eternal Logos, the unworthiness yet adoring thankfulness of the creature, the awfulness of that which is done. The people are shut off from the sanctuary. Though they have their own litanies of supplication, led by the deacon,[1] they take little or no part in the real liturgic movement. Save for the lections, and some of the hymns, the service is invariable. The "Proper of Time" and "Proper of Saints", which

[1] Now very often by the Reader, who takes the Deacon's part.

give so much variety of tone and emphasis to the Eucharist and Divine Office in all Western rites, have no real equivalents in the service books of the East.

All this is in strong contrast with the genius of the true Roman rite, as we can find it in the earliest sacramentaries. Here the whole conception is more concrete, more dynamic, even though not less mysterious than in the East. The stress falls not upon the adoring contemplation of the Heavenly Sacrifice, but upon the due performance here and now of the Sacred Act, the Eucharistic sacrifice in which all take part. Further, the service is historically conditioned. It is concerned, not only with the Eternal Mystery, but also with the workings of that Mystery in the world of time. Though the Eastern Church celebrates with splendour all the great moments of the Christian Year, and the festivals of her greatest saints, it is in the West that this aspect of an incarnational worship has received full development. The Western Mass and Divine Office are flexible. They have prayers, antiphons, responses, and liturgical chants which vary with the seasons and are often chosen and combined with exquisite insight and skill; reproducing the successive notes of expectancy, joy, penitence, grief, and triumph which mark the Christian year, rising to a climax in the ancient and beautiful ceremonies of Holy Week and Easter, and celebrating with fraternal love and admiration the "heavenly birthdays" of the Saints.[1] Though many of the venerable prayers of the Missal, especially those associated with Holy Week, have come down to us from the infancy of the Church, and the Canon itself has hardly changed since the seventh

[1] Originally these commemorations were strictly limited; the solemn movement of the Proper of Time taking precedence over all but the greatest feasts of saints. But here the Western historical sense found its opportunity and has added to the Calendar more and more memorials; so that now the recitation of the Divine Office is orientated each day to some particular commemoration, and each Mass is given a particular intention and tone.

century, the steady development of these liturgical commemorations—not only of new saints, but of new devotions, and new lights[1]—witnesses to the essentially dynamic and factual character of Western Catholicism; the close contact which it seeks to maintain with the movement of life, as against the more static and other-worldly temper of the East.

Again, the general character of the early Roman worship was popular, democratic, even business-like. The Holy Sacrifice was offered by the priest and people, at an open altar in full view of the congregation. The emphasis lay on action, and the ceremonial detail was governed by practical considerations. The devotional tone was simple, moderate, and austere. The dignity with which the Roman gentleman conducted the affairs of life also controlled his intercourse with God. Psalms were chanted by cantors, choir, or people at the Introit, Offertory, and Communion. The Gregorian plain chant survives to remind us of the gravity and restraint of this early psalmody. The Gradual with its Alleluia was sung—perhaps to more elaborate music—before the Gospel was read.[2] The Prefaces and special prayers were short and pithy. The elaborate lists of God's splendours and mercies which we find in the Gallican and Eastern rites, are reduced in the Roman to a general phrase. The brevity and dignity of the ancient Roman collect or prayer of the day, which "asks for one thing only, and that in the tersest language",[3] is among the most distinctive characteristics of the service; and has given the universal

[1] E.g. the mediæval feast of Corpus Christi, or such late additions as those of the Holy Name, the Sacred Heart, the Immaculate Conception, Our Lady of Good Counsel, of the Rosary, or of Lourdes, the Seven Sorrows, Christ the King; and the ever-growing list of canonized saints. In fact Roman Catholic worship is now enfolded in a cloud of witnesses so dense that they almost hide the severe beauty of the original design.

[2] Cf. Cabrol, *The Mass of the Western Rites*, p. 212. For a vivid description of the Papal Mass in the seventh century, see W. H. Frere, *The Principles of Religious Ceremonial*, pp. 62 *seq.*

[3] A. Fortescue, *The Mass*, p. 249.

Church some of its most beautiful and best-loved devotional forms.[1]

From this severe, concise, objective, and dignified worship of the Gregorian Church, so stripped of symbolism and useless ceremonial, so aloof from direct emotional appeal, the rich sacramental edifice of modern Catholicism has grown, with its ceremonial elaborations, its many shrines and altars, popular devotions and emotional opportunities—the Rosary and Stations of the Cross, the Crib, the Crucifix, the Sacred Heart, and all the various aspects of the cult of the Blessed Virgin: much as its architectural embodiment grew from the austere simplicity of Romanesque to the last elaborations of fifteenth-century Gothic. Two factors seem to have controlled this evolution. First, the Catholic conception of the Church as a living organism, indwelt and guided by the Spirit, and therefore able to grow and change like all other living things; to expand and adjust her worship, and meet the needs of her children, giving fresh expression to the unchanging realities committed to her charge. Secondly, the concrete and practical character of the Latin mind, which prefers the active to the static and the declared to the mysterious; and is intensely conscious of the temporal order and its limitations and demands. Hence, whilst Orthodox worship is wholly bent upon the adoration of a timeless mystery, and keeps almost unchanged the characters of fourth-century religion, the West has transformed those characters by constant adjustments and developments: finding room within the fixed liturgical outlines for many grades and kinds of personal devotion, from the most self-interested to the most sublime. From this point of view the transformation of Eucharistic worship during and since the Middle

[1] Translations of some of the best of these ancient collects are in the Anglican Book of Common Prayer; especially those for the 3rd and 5th Sundays after Easter, and the 5th, 14th, 15th, 16th, 20th and 21st Sundays after Trinity—all of the fifth century. See for a full analysis W. Bright, *Ancient Collects*, pp. 197 *seq*.

Ages, by a shifting of emphasis from the total movement of the Eucharistic Sacrifice to the "Miracle of the Mass", with the accompanying cultus of the reserved elements in prayer before the tabernacle and in the services of Benediction and Exposition, can be defended as a legitimate growth —a means appropriate to man's requirements of actualizing the central mystery of the Church's being, the real Presence of the living Christ.[1]

In spite of its theological and historical unsoundness—for it is certain that before the Middle Ages no particular reverence was paid to the Reserved Sacrament in any part of the Church—this devotion has proved its worth as a carrying medium of the Supernatural, and an incitement to prayer; providing a focus of worship, a concrete and visible pledge of the invisible Presence, which can be appreciated by the most simple, yet can satisfy the needs of the deepest soul.[2] For the developed sacramentalism of the West, the whole Church is held to live a Eucharistic life. In her the Incarnation is continued. Within her own borders, in her tabernacles, the Object of man's worship and means of his sanctification is enshrined. Thanks to the central emphasis placed on the doctrine of transubstantiation, the altar is in a literal sense "a perpetual Bethlehem". The deepest implications of sacramentalism—the identity of humility and holiness, the self-giving of the Eternal by natural means

[1] "To say that because Christ ordained two uses for His sacramental presence, He excluded all other possible ones, is like saying that because the Incarnation was ordained in order that Christ might save us on the Cross, it excluded His playing with little children or going to marriagefeast s. Thus the Church, her Faithful waking up with delight, generation by generation, to the rich possibilities of the Eucharistic presence, permits processions, reservation, Benediction and so forth." (C. C. Martindale, S.J., *The Faith of the Roman Church*, p. 112.)

[2] "Though such devotion is not older than about A.D. 1340 (in the form of visits to the Blessed Sacrament) and not more than some eighty years older in the form of Exposition, Procession, or Benediction of the Holy Eucharist, yet the devotion has formed saints, and great saints." (Baron von Hügel, in an unpublished letter to the present writer.)

—are here, with relentless Latin logic, pushed to their term and given concrete expression. It would not be unfair to say that modern Roman Catholic worship is poised on these twin realities of Church and Eucharist, which are indeed obverse and reverse of a single reality—*Corpus Christi*, the continuing manifestation and incarnation of Christ under temporal accidents, and the response of humanity through and in Him to the all-demanding holiness of the Infinite God.

In spite of the rigidity of its institutional framework, and the intrinsically theological character of its worship, Roman Catholicism weaves into this great act of adoration all the varied responses and apprehensions of men. That thorough-going realism which takes man as he is and encourages him to worship as he can, is careful to provide on every level material adapted to his capacities, for the feeding and the expression of his Godward life. If the cult of the Reserved Sacrament trains him in loving adoration, no less do those frequent confessions of devotion, which are also acts of worship, keep him in mind of his creaturely weakness, and so tend to contrition and humility of heart; whilst in the Mass, considered as the Christian sacrifice, all the separate acts of self-oblation are carried up and presented in Christ to God. And beyond this, a wide and deep Catholicism is able to accept and redeem even the most primitive and concrete embodiments of man's religious instinct, his most sentimental devotions and self-interested prayers. The risks and disadvantages of such a policy need no emphasis. Its merits are less easily perceived; yet it is doubtful whether full Catholicity of worship could have been had at a lower price. For thus the Church can satisfy the childish craving of humanity for certitude, by attaching supernatural rewards to the obedient recitation of her formulas or generous contribution to her funds; can give simple souls the devotional variety which they need in ways that they can understand; and even makes the acceptance of these concessions to the popular level, a training in humility for her more enlightened members. Yet here, too, a path is opened along which the contemplative can pass with Nicolas of Cusa beyond that wall of Paradise where opposites are reconciled and "every blissful spirit beholdeth the Invisible God".[1]

So, too, in its progress through the centuries, the traditional character of the early Latin worship has been modified in some respects and elaborated in others. It has taken colour from the various cultures through which it has passed; especially that of the Middle Ages, which has given to it a particular character that it has never lost. If, in Orthodox worship, we re-enter the atmosphere of Patristic Christianity, in Roman Catholic worship we re-enter that of the thirteenth century; and recognize the peculiar temper of its religion, on the one hand so abstract and theological and on the other so concrete, personal, emotional and romantic. If we take the names of St Bernard, St Thomas Aquinas, and St Francis, as representing three complementary aspects of the mediæval passion for God, associate with these the intense mediæval devotion to the Holy Name of Jesus, to the Blessed Sacrament, and to the Cross, and place them within that atmosphere of adoration in which Dante's *Paradiso* is bathed, we perceive how large a part of specifically Roman Catholic worship—more especially the secret intercourse of loving hearts, and the deep mysteries of contemplative experience—still wears a mediæval dress. The personal, intimate, sometimes sentimental cultus of the Humanity of Jesus, which inspires such hymns as the *Jesu dulcis memoria* and its many derivatives, and the Christmas carols of the early Franciscan poets, is still living in the Church. It is the gift of the Middle Ages—a gift which is perhaps still most deeply appreciated by its direct inheritors, but in which the Protestant Churches too have shared. The vivid, realistically Christocentric worship which the Evangelical revival

[1] Nicolas of Cusa, *The Vision of God*, cap. XXI.

brought back into the religious foreground, and which the hymns of Wesley and the German pietists express, is substantially identical with that homely, personal, affective devotion which mediæval Catholicism poured out before the Crib, the Altar, and the Crucifix, and which gives a certain touching beauty to the more recent cultus of the Holy Family or the Sacred Heart. And this, in its turn, represents under its own symbolisms, and coloured by its own romantic temper, the realistic communion of the primitive Church with its invisible Lord: even as the stately Roman liturgy with its archaic constructions and grave impersonal movement "is the petrified form of the once-glowing lava of Early Christian enthusiasm".[1]

It is true that the long development of worship in the Catholic West—especially in the mediæval period—has involved loss as well as gain; additions, elaborations, adjustments and concessions to self-interest which can hardly be regarded as legitimate expressions of the Christian response to God. It is difficult to justify at the bar of Pure Love the juridical doctrines of merit and of indulgences, or the popular practices to which they have led. Especially the change of emphasis which stressed the propitiatory and sacrificial character of the Mass, to the exclusion of the oblation and communion of the people, spoiled the great rhythm of the ancient Eucharistic worship; and encouraged utilitarian religion by concentrating attention on a miracle performed and witnessed, and a benefit obtained.[2] The unfortunate development of the private and votive Mass, commissioned for a particular purpose and paid for at an agreed rate, brought with it a further degradation of the sacred realities of Christian worship. For here, the Eucharistic sacrifice was offered, not as a part of the total and disinterested oblation of the whole Church, "in and for all";

[1] F. Heiler, *The Spirit of Worship*, p. 69.
[2] Compare Pt. I, cap. VII.

but to obtain for those on whose behalf it was celebrated a remission of penalties or a granting of boons, which easily came to be regarded as dependent on the number of Masses said, and the amount of fees paid. All this, with its attendant and inevitable crop of popular superstitions and abuses, explains the horror felt by the early reformers for the "Sacrifice of the Mass"; and the fact that in their own liturgic constructions, the elements of communion and commemoration were so emphasized as almost to obscure in their turn the noble outlines of the Eucharist, to the great impoverishment of Protestant worship.

On the other hand, Roman Catholic devotion since the Reformation has tended more and more to a personal and individualistic piety centred on the Reserved Sacrament: also a departure from the Catholic ideal. Before the general revival of frequent communion which was effected by Pope Pius X at the beginning of the present century, Mass had almost ceased to be a corporate and organic act of worship; and Holy Communion—usually given from the tabernacle—was a private matter, a means of grace, but not the normal climax of the living Church's sacrifice of love. At present, we are witnessing the beginning of a movement for Liturgical Reform within the Roman Church, which seems destined to be of great importance. Its chief aim is the restoration of the primitive balance and integrity of the Mass, as the essential corporate act of Christian worship: the whole service being regarded as a single action shared by the faithful, presenting their self-oblation to God, and rising to its climax in their communion. In Churches affected by the Revival, the full co-operation of all present is assured by distributing translations of the Sunday Mass. The singing of the *Gloria*, Creed, and *Sanctus*, and even of the Proper of the day, is congregational; the Gospel is read in the vernacular as well as in Latin, the prayers are audibly recited. In some places, the ancient ceremony of the offertory-procession has been restored. With all this goes the severe limitation of extra-liturgical devotions, such as Benediction and Exposition of the Blessed Sacrament, the discouragement of the common practice of giving Holy Communion from the tabernacle outside Mass, and a general effort to draw back the devotion of the people from the periphery to the living heart of Christian worship.

III

The liturgical life of Eastern Catholicism will not be understood, unless its historical and cultural circumstances are kept in mind. Though here the abstract and the unchanging are more deeply realized and more passionately sought than in the West, here too the thoroughly incarnational character of Christianity, its acceptance and use of duration, have had a decisive influence. Orthodox worship, achieving its classic expression in the Patristic period, represents on one hand the spirit of the Greek Fathers in liturgical form ; their theocentric temper and cosmic outlook, their longing for the transfiguration of man, their deep and wide sacramentalism, their supernatural sense. The metaphysical element of religion, the transcendental reference, is more prominent than in the West : and it is this metaphysical element—the constant remembrance of the inaccessible light of the Godhead, "the unsearchable, incomprehensible Triune Essence, creating, embracing, and indivisible,"[1]—which gives their strange beauty to the Eastern rites. On the other hand, the ritual pattern of the Liturgy carries forward almost unchanged the gifts which the primitive Christian cultus received from the Hellenistic world. Entering its atmosphere, we part from the world of succession, and enter another order ; where, under symbols and in a mystery, the Eternal is apprehended and adored.

[1] *Armenian Liturgy :* Thanksgiving of the Priest.

Hence where Latin worship—true to the Roman genius—inclines to the concrete and the objective, is orderly, open, clear, and terse in expression, insists on definitions, factualness, exposes its sacred objects for veneration, and aims at realism in its sacred images, Orthodox worship is penetrated by an awed sense of mystery which resists definitions, and avoids naturalistic expression. Its most sacred things and actions are veiled, not declared: they signify, but do not represent. Its ikons are highly stylized, and deliberately avoid realism; for their function is to point beyond the world, and give access to invisible realities. Resting on a humble agnosticism in respect of the supernatural mysteries of God, save in so far as these are disclosed to the awestruck gaze of man in his worship, it refuses to define the nature of the change which is effected by Eucharistic consecration, or the moment in the total liturgic action at which it takes place: for this liturgic action embodies in a sacred drama an act which in its essence takes place outside time, and exceeds the apprehension of men. The developed Eucharistic doctrine and cultus of the Roman Church—Benediction, Exposition, the use of the Monstrance, the focussing of worship on Christ present in the reserved Sacrament—are therefore entirely foreign to the spirit of Orthodoxy.[1]

Orthodoxy, in fact, has retained much of the spirit and form of a mystery-religion in the best sense of the term; its symbolic yet realistic apprehension of the deep things of God, and the nearness yet otherness of the Eternal. Like other types of Catholic worship, it can fall to the level of a degraded formalism. But at its best it is one of the noblest of all embodiments of the Christian spirit of adoration; so deeply sensible of the mystery of the Transcendent, yet so childlike in its confident approach. Though there is a profound Evangelical strain in Orthodox devotion, and the Gospels are well-known, read, and loved by the devout, the

[1] Cf. S. Boulgakoff, *L'Orthodoxie*, p. 205.

tone and colour are Johannine rather than Synoptic. The liturgic emphasis lies more on the solemn truth of the Incarnation of the Logos, the mystery of the Divine Wisdom and Light coming into the world to save the world, than on the human method and cost of its accomplishment. Here the focus of adoration is not so much the suffering Redeemer on the Cross, as the majestic figure of the risen Christ living in His Church, as He is presented in the great creations of Byzantine art. The Crucifix is one ikon among others; and does not hold the unique place which it occupies in the West.

Thus the positive and affirmative note of Early Christianity, that conviction of the presence here-and-now of the Logos, the Living Christ in whom " all things consist ",[1] which is the essence of Pauline and Johannine realism, is central to Orthodox devotion. It is enshrined and constantly renewed in the highly stylized liturgical action which expresses the Church's life. The recitation of the Divine Office, whether in the form of the Vigils—i.e. Vespers, Mattins, and Prime—of Saturday evening, or of Mattins on Sunday morning, is regarded mainly as a preparation for the Holy Liturgy; which is the heart of Orthodox worship.[2] In the Liturgy something really happens. The presence of the Unmanifest Holy is manifest to the worshipping soul. This divine action and presence, the nearness of the supernatural, are felt in all parts of the service; and not at the moment of consecration and communion alone. The elements of time and sequence are negligible; because that which is done is entirely of the order of Eternity.

At the Great Entrance, Christ Himself " invisibly escorted by Angels " enters with the oblation into the Holy Place, and is welcomed by the choir in the people's name with the

[1] Col. i. 17.

[2] A full description of the Eastern Divine Office, by the Rev. R. French, will be found in *Liturgy and Worship*, edited by W. K. Lowther Clarke pp. 834–50.

Cherubic hymn.[1] Behind the closed doors of the screen, He offers by the hands of His priest the gifts of the people to God. At the *Epiclesis* the Paraclete comes, as to the Apostles; and makes of those earthly gifts a heavenly thing. The whole emphasis lies on the sacred wonder of that which is done; and the prevailing temper is that of a humble, contrite, and awe-struck delight. " He shall take the Holy Body in his hand, and he shall kiss it with tears ", says the Armenian Liturgy at the Communion of the Priest. Yet the compensating Christian element of intimacy and child-like trust is also present. It is seen in the detailed personal commemorations of the living and the dead in every Liturgy, in the individual gifts of little loaves for the sacrifice, which continue the primitive custom of oblation in kind, and in the homely distribution and sharing of the blessed bread at the end of the service, or the Agape of bread and wine still celebrated on the vigils of great feasts.

The arrangement of an Orthodox church is determined by the character of Orthodox worship. Everything here has symbolic significance, and contributes something to that church's Godward life. As the worship moves on two distinct planes—the heavenly and earthly, the veiled and the revealed—so the church is divided into two distinct parts by the screen or ikonostasis; which, like the wall of the Heavenly Jerusalem, hides the Holy Place and the sacred acts there done, and turns towards the worshippers on earth its ikons, the visible and sensible tokens of the invisible realities of the heavenly world.[2] The worshippers stand on the hither side of this mystical barrier: in the natural world

[1] See *supra*, p. 113.

[2] The chief ikons have doctrinal and liturgic significance, and are always arranged in the same order, i.e. those of Our Lord and the Blessed Virgin, as the human and divine instruments of the Incarnation, are placed on each side of the central or Royal Door, through which Communion is brought to the people; whilst the Royal Door itself, symbolizing the path by which the Eternal Logos enters time, bears an ikon of the Annunciation, and generally those of the Four Evangelists.

to which they belong, yet as it were in an enclave which is set aside for the purposes of God, and offers special means of access to the Holy. On its walls are other ikons of Christ and His Saints, like windows opening upon the supernatural order; offering a focus to personal devotion, and inviting a veneration which deepens into loving intercourse. Beyond the screen is the Holy Place, the "altar of the Lamb"[1] where the Divine Mysteries are celebrated. On its Holy Table are kept the Gospel Book, which is one of the most sacred objects of the Orthodox cult, the cross of benediction, and the arks containing the holy oils and the reserved sacramental elements. All this arrangement, every detail of which has symbolic as well as practical significance, forms the setting of that Divine Liturgy, in which the life and worship of Eastern Catholicism is summed up.

This Liturgy is in essence an act of adoration addressed to the Triune Being of God. It begins and ends with the ascription of glory to Father, Son, and Holy Ghost. The number three dominates its ritual design. It has three groups of suffrages, three antiphons, three lessons, a threefold Canon, three hymns of angelic praise. Retaining to a far greater extent than the Roman Mass the full character of a mystery-drama, the showing forth in time of an Eternal Act, it retains too the primitive Eucharistic sequence of the bringing of the oblation, the offering of the sacrifice of thanksgiving, and the distribution of the consecrated gifts; surrounding all this with a solemn and intricate ceremonial, and those songs of awe-struck adoration—the Trisagion, the Cherubikon, and the Seraphic Hymn or *Sanctus*—which are the glory of the Orthodox rite, and in which the Church on earth seems to share the exultant worship of heaven.

I have said that the liturgical action takes place on two

[1] The whole sanctuary in an Orthodox church is the altar; the Holy Table, where the sacrifice is offered and consecration takes place, being simply a part of the necessary furnishings.

planes at once; and this in quite a different sense from, e.g. the doubling of the parts in the Latin High Mass, where choir and people sing a Creed or *Gloria* which the priest has already recited rapidly to himself. Within the screen, as within the Eternal World, the Holy Mysteries go forward. At certain high points of the service, the doors are opened that the Lord may come forth to His people. He comes first (in the so-called Little Entrance) under the figure of the Book of the Gospels; next, in the Offertory or Great Entrance, as the Holy Lamb or prepared Oblation for the sacrifice; finally at the Communion, in the consecrated Eucharistic gifts, as the Risen Christ bringing to the faithful the food of Eternal Life. Outside the screen, in time, the devotion of the people, in litanies led by the deacon, follows that which is done. The deacon in his archaic vestment and prayer-stole occupies a peculiar position in Orthodox worship; linking those who stand without the Holy Place with that which is done within. He attends the priest, assists in the preparation of the elements, censes the ikons and the offering, carries the paten with the Holy Lamb at the Great Entrance, and directs the prayers of the people; "like an angel, flying from the altar to the people, and from the people to the altar, and gathering all into one spirit."[1]

The Liturgy, which sums up and expresses the Church's corporate worship, is from one point of view her perpetual sacrifice of love, sanctifying and confirming in love all who take part in it. But from another point of view that sacrifice is also a Mystery, in which she shows forth under symbols the life and death of the Incarnate Logos. Here the Gospel is seen in liturgic regard; not only as the biography of a divine friend and leader, but as a revelation of the Mind of God. Thus each great ritual act represents an episode in that revelation; and the worshipper, with this clue in

[1] N. Gogol, *Meditations on the Divine Liturgy*, p. 21. Unfortunately in modern usage the office of the deacon tends more and more to be suppressed.

mind, can follow in prayer the whole movement of the Christian cycle, from Christmas to Easter, under liturgic signs, and receive in contemplation its serial witness to eternal truth. In the "Liturgy of Oblation" or hidden preparation of the elements, he sees the humble birth and hidden childhood of the Incarnate ; in the bringing out of the holy Gospel Book to the people, Christ the Logos coming forth to teach him the Way ; in the Great Entrance of the Oblation into the sanctuary, Christ going up to the eternal sacrifice offered in, for, and with His Church ; in the laying of the holy gifts upon the altar, the laying of the Crucified in the tomb ; and in the bringing forth of the chalice at Communion the Risen Christ appearing to His disciples.[1] All this, then, provides an organic ritual action of inexhaustible significance ; within which the individual worshipper can see his own vision, and offer his own acts of penitence, adoration, and love.

In this Liturgy, Christian worship reaches its most perfect ritual expression ; but at a price. It is difficult for such worship to be truly corporate in the external sense ; and as a matter of fact in the Greek Church nearly the whole of the liturgic action is commonly delegated to priest, deacon, reader, and choir, even in monasteries the chanting of the Divine Office being undertaken in the name of the whole community by a choir of monks specially trained for this work. In the Russian Church, however, the ideal of full congregational worship is often achieved ; and none who have assisted under reasonably favourable conditions at a Russian celebration of the Holy Liturgy can doubt the intensity of spiritual co-operation obtained from those present, each of whom is standing on the frontier of mystery, and sharing by intention in the great sacrificial action of the

[1] Compare *supra*, cap. IV, p. 74. The whole of this symbolism is set out in N. Gogol's *Meditations on the Divine Liturgy* ; a book which gives remarkable insight into the spirit of Orthodox worship.

Church, her supreme rite of adoration. It is true that here, as in the Western High Mass, the worshipper is only on rare occasions a communicant[1] and to this extent the Eucharistic action is incomplete. Not only the length of the required fast, and severity of the preparation, but also the intense awe with which the Sacrament is regarded and consequent fear of unworthy reception, prevent the practice of frequent communion from becoming part of the normal Christian life of the laity.

> As thou dost approach O mortal to receive the Body of the Master
> Draw near with awe lest thou be scorched : It is fire.
> And when thou dost drink the Holy Blood unto communion,
> First be at peace with those who grieve thee,
> Then with courage receive the Mystic Food.[2]

In this acquiescence in the rarity of lay communion, Orthodoxy of course continues the common practice both of mediæval and of Post-Reformation Europe ; only recently modified in the West. Moreover, the elaborate nature of the ritual—for the Orthodox have no Low Mass—makes constant celebration of the Liturgy difficult. In most parish churches it is celebrated only once on Sundays, and on festivals ; though some—e.g. certain churches of the Russian exiles in Paris—have a daily Liturgy. In Cathedrals celebrations are more frequent, and in monasteries of strict observance they take place daily, at or before dawn. The Latin multiplication of Masses and altars is unknown to

[1] Usually three times a year, or in many cases at Easter only. The exceptionally devout may communicate as often as once a month. In the Greek Church, communion is sometimes given from the reserved elements outside the Liturgy, as in the Roman Church ; but this is regarded as a departure from the true standards of Orthodoxy, which never separates one moment of the Eucharist from the rest. Children " in a state of innocence " (i.e. under seven) are, however, brought frequently to communion by devout parents. There is at present a movement towards more frequent communion in some parts of the Orthodox Church.

[2] Preparation for Holy Communion, according to the Greek Orthodox rite. Compare with this the tone of equivalent passages in Western devotional literature : e.g. the 4th Book of *The Imitation of Christ*.

Orthodoxy; which regards the Eucharist as the sacrificial act of the whole Church seen and unseen, not of the individual celebrant, and prefers the ancient custom of con-celebration to separate celebrations by individual priests. The place which the private or votive mass occupies in Roman Catholicism is taken here by private services, called in Russian *molyben*; these usually consist of the Trisagion with hymn and Gospel, and a litany of intercession for the sick, the bereaved, the departed, those going on a journey, the newly born, or any others for whom the prayer of the Church is specially desired.

IV

It would be a mistake to assume from the elaborate ritual character of the cultus, that Orthodox worship has no place for the love and devotion of the simple, or fails to develop that inwardness, that secret and personal communion with God, which is the life-blood of institutional religion. A great reserve and a great freedom characterize the personal life of prayer in Orthodoxy; and for this reason it is difficult to form any clear conception of it. Eastern Catholicism is penetrated by the conviction that the true Object of its worship transcends all definitions. That which any one soul can apprehend is only a fragment; yet this fragment implies the whole mystery of that which we adore. Therefore within that total Godward life of the Church to which the Divine Liturgy gives ritual form, it is ready to allow great liberty of response to individual souls. There is something here for all levels and types, from the most naïve to the most sophisticated; and each must find their own place and make their own response. The disciplinary note, the analysis and ordering of prayer, the formal meditation and obligatory devotional rule, so characteristic of the Latin West, are hardly known in Eastern Christendom. Here the ideal of prayer is the free and secret intercourse of the soul with

God; a total supernatural act achieved by many means but transcending all means, and as much within the span of the simplest as of the most instructed soul.[1] Though here corporate worship may seem to touch the extreme of ceremonial and dramatic expression, personal worship has never lost that free spirituality and inwardness, that first-hand Evangelical quality, which is a direct heritage from the primitive Church. Both strands, the liturgic and mystical, are truly Orthodox; aspects of that "wholeness" which is an Orthodox ideal. Both enter into the individual life of worship; which is on the one hand closely bound up with the veneration of those ikons which play so great a part in the life of the Eastern Church, and on the other tends to a very intimate and realistic Christocentric mysticism. This finds a characteristic expression in the "Jesus-prayer"[2], which occupies an important place in Orthodox piety.

The position of the ikon in the Orthodox life of worship is hard for the concrete Western mind to understand. The ikon is far more than a mere focus of devotion, or a pictorial incitement to prayer. It is in the truest sense a sacramental: a visible instrument of communion with the invisible Holy. It was called by St John Damascene "a channel of Divine grace"; and in the Eastern Church its veneration takes the place now occupied in Western Catholicism by devotion to the Blessed Sacrament.[3] Easy enough to discredit if

[1] The anonymous *Way of a Pilgrim* (translated by R. M. French) and Tolstoi's parables of *The Three Old Men* and *Where Love Is* admit us to the very heart of Orthodox spirituality.

[2] *Infra*, p. 273.

[3] "According to Orthodox belief the ikon is a place where Christ is present by His grace. It is, so to speak, the site of an *apparition* of Christ (or the Virgin or Saints, or whomsoever it represents). . . . The veneration of the holy ikons is based not only on the nature of the subjects represented in them, but also on faith in that presence full of grace which the Church invokes by the power of the sanctification of the ikon. This rite of the benediction of the ikon establishes a link between the image and its prototype, between that which is represented and the representation itself. Thanks to the benediction of the ikon of Christ, a mysterious intercourse takes place between the worshipper and Christ." S. Boulgakoff, *L'Orthodoxie*, p. 196.

judged by appearances alone, and obviously capable of being debased to the purposes of primitive religion, the ikon is a means of bringing home to the simplest souls the here-and-now presence of the supernatural; yet can also become a genuine channel of the purest spiritual worship. Through it, thanks to the implicit Platonism of Eastern Christianity, the worshipper has access to that world of ideas, where dwells the Divine reality which it represents. It is "an act of contemplation clothed in colour and form".[1] In this sense the Gospel, with its pictures of the earthly life of Jesus, may be regarded as a verbal ikon, mediating contact between the Logos and the worshipping soul. The Western Catholic preparing his three-point meditation by making "a picture in his mind" of the subject on which he is to dwell, and the Orthodox standing in prayer before an ikon of the Life of Christ, are both reaching out to a certain sensible contact with supra-sensible truths; in one case by imaginative, in the other by pictorial means.

The Orthodox, then, coming into the Church and praying before its ikons, is seeking through them, a genuine communion with God and His Saints: and the deacon, censing the ikons of the saints at the beginning of the liturgy, salutes in and through them "guests come to the sacramental feast, as in Christ all live and are not separated."[2]

But the ikon is also personal: a special vehicle of grace to the particular person for whose use it is blessed, as is the crucifix or rosary in Western Catholicism. It occupies a unique position in respect of its owner's devotional life. Through it he addresses his requests and his thanksgivings to Christ and the Blessed Virgin; who is given in Eastern Catholicism at least as high a place as in the West,[3] and is the

[1] Boulgakoff, *op. cit.*

[2] N. Gogol, *Meditations on the Divine Liturgy*, p. 20.

[3] It is probable that the cultus of the Mother of God came from the Eastern Churches to Rome. The feasts of the Annunciation, and of the Nativity and Assumption of the Blessed Virgin, are of Eastern origin.

focus of much popular devotion, being specially invoked by those in trouble. Certain ikons—e.g. the ikon of Our Lady of Tenderness, beloved by St Seraphim—acquire spiritual reputations of their own. But all must be treated with deep reverence, as holy things indwelt and used by God.

Perhaps because of the atmosphere of adoration in which this liturgical worship is bathed, with its continuous reference to eternal realities and invitation to contemplative prayer, perhaps because the methodical and analytic temper of the West is absent from Eastern Catholicism, Orthodoxy seems never to have developed such an orderly technique of interior prayer, with its discipline of formal meditation, affections, and acts, as we find in the great spiritual teachers of the Latin Church. It has, nevertheless, a technique of its own, of a simple and beautiful kind, for the production and deepening of that simple, inclusive, and continuous act of communion with God, that humble "prayer of the heart", which is the substance of its mystical worship. This technique, so simple that it is within the compass of the humblest worshipper, yet so penetrating that it can introduce those who use it faithfully to the deepest mysteries of the contemplative life, consists in the unremitting inward repetition of the Holy Name of God; usually in the form of the so-called "Jesus-prayer"—"Lord Jesus Christ, Son of God, have mercy upon me!" This prayer has a unique place in the spiritual life of Orthodoxy. All monastic rules of devotion, and spiritual direction given by monks to the pious laity, aim at its development. It carries the simple and childlike appeal of the devout peasant, and the continuous self-acting aspiration of the great contemplative.

> It can, when needful, replace the Divine Office and all other prayers; for it is of universal validity. The power of this prayer does not reside in its content, which is simple and clear (it is the prayer of the publican) but in the holy Name of Jesus. The ascetics testify that in

> this Name there resides the power of the Presence of God. Not only is God invoked in it, but He is already present in this invocation . . . thus the Name of Jesus present in the human heart communicates to it the power of that deification which the Redeemer has bestowed on us.[1]

This prayer, then, is regarded as producing in the faithful soul supernatural effects. If the simplicity of its form be disconcerting, the doctrine which underlies it is profound. Orthodoxy is penetrated by the conviction of the need and insufficiency of man, and the nearness and transforming power of God. Therefore its truest act of personal worship will be a humble and ceaseless self-opening to that divine transforming power; which enters with Christ into the natural order to restore and deify the whole world. So the Orthodox communicant says as he approaches the Mysteries:

> The Divine Body both deifies and nourishes me;
> It deifies my soul, and strangely nourishes my mind.[2]

The Jesus-prayer, or rather the interior act which it embodies, is the simplest form in which this divine action is invoked. Beginning with the deliberate and persevering oral repetition known in the West as "forced acts", gradually but inevitably "the power of Christ which is hidden in it is disclosed;" and it takes on, more and more, the character of a ceaseless uplifting of the heart, which persists through the distractions of the surface-life. Finally, this adoring action involves the very substance of the soul, which finds itself transformed into a living act of worship, an organ of the Spirit. "The light of the Name of Jesus pours through the heart, to irradiate the Universe",[3] a foretaste of that final trans-

[1] Boulgakoff, *op. cit.*, p. 206.
[2] Preparation for Holy Communion according to the Greek Orthodox rite.
[3] Boulgakoff, *op. cit.*, p. 207.

figuration in which " God shall be all in all ". Thus the mystical and interior worship of Orthodoxy, true to its liturgical embodiment, is orientated towards that redemption of the created order in which the incarnation of the Logos finds its goal.

CHAPTER XIII

WORSHIP IN THE REFORMED CHURCHES

I

EVANGELICAL worship, as we find it in the two great Churches of the Reformation, was not originally intended as an innovation ; but rather as a restoration of the ancient Christian balance of Word and Sacrament, and with this, a bringing back into the religious foreground of that spiritual realism, that first-hand relation of the soul to God, which the elaborate ritual system of the later Middle Ages had obscured for all but spiritual specialists. The Reform on its nobler side meant the rejection of every possible substitute for realistic contrition and moral earnestness. Its attack on ritual worship, and especially the sacrificial aspect of the Eucharist, repeated the attack of the Old Testament prophets on the sacrificial system of their day. Thus it came into being not as an opposition to Catholic Christianity in its wholeness—for indeed Luther, like Wesley in another century, ardently desired to remain within his Mother-Church, and drew the substance of his teaching from Catholic sources—but as a correction, a rediscovery under the stress of great spiritual need, of the living truths which govern Christian worship. The saints, moving easily within the great Catholic system, had never lost contact with those living truths. But as far as the mass of believers was concerned, they had been buried under the ceremonial system which was designed to give them ritual expression.

These truths, these naked realities, which Luther and Calvin each in their own way rescued and emphasized, were: first, the absolute priority of God, the givenness of His revelation, and hence the sacramental authority of His uttered Word. Next, the creaturely status of man and his nothingness, poverty, and total dependence on that uttered Word for light, salvation, peace. The stress lay on God's holiness and man's helplessness; His saving and merciful movement towards man, and faith as the essential factor in man's humble and grateful response. It was the mystery of the Divine Charity seen from a fresh angle, and in the bright light of a personal need; and therefore seeming, to those who thus perceived it, a fresh thing and a fresh incentive to worship and love. To be "justified by faith" means, to be put in a right relation to that Divine Charity; the relation of a humble and confident worship. Faith, as Luther insisted, "is humility". It involves both *fides* and *fiducia;* the awed recognition of God in His utter distinctness, and the childlike trust in His mercy and grace. This is the living heart of Evangelical worship; and if that worship too easily becomes focussed upon man's need of personal salvation and assurance, this is perhaps no worse than the tendency of sacrificial worship to concentrate on propitiation and demand, and forget disinterested love.

The tempestuous personality and intense religious thirst of Martin Luther, his craving for that direct personal assurance so richly given in the Gospels, and deliverance from the haunting presence of metaphysical fear, gave its subjective tone and special colour to the devotional side of the Reform. Lutheran worship takes its departure from this situation, and still bears the marks of its origin. It was and remains a consoling presentation of the Divine Mercy, as offered to men in the Scriptures and in Christ. For it, the Crib and the Crucifix are still "mirrors of the loving Heart of God", inviting a loving, adoring, and grateful response in worship.

Luther had no Puritan designs. He retained the ancient surroundings of the cultus: the altar, the crucifix, pictures and images of saints and angels, vestments, ceremonial lights. The rich accessories of worship which we still find in many Scandinavian churches are true expressions of his mind; and throughout the seventeenth century, Lutheran worship was everywhere strongly Catholic in tone. But the devotional focus had shifted. The centre of all is now the constant proclamation of the Word; the vehicle of God's self-disclosure to men. The Word is for Evangelical worship something as objective, holy, and given, as the Blessed Sacrament is for Roman Catholic worship. Indeed, it is a sacrament; the sensible garment in which the supra-sensible Presence is clothed. Here, then, a genuine strand in the primitive Christian cultus, which had almost lapsed from the consciousness of the mediæval Church, is restored; and, as usual in such restorations, vigorously—even excessively—emphasized. For here, it is the prophetic strain in Christianity which dominates the worship; the acknowledgment of that Spirit "who spake by the prophets", still finding utterance through the preacher who has been called to be a channel of the Word and has accepted that great vocation. Preaching of this character enters the category of prayer, and is to be classed as a supernatural act: bringing all those who submit themselves to its influence into communion with God.

> "Such preaching", says Will, "not only brings the congregation into the Presence of God, but gives it, along with the sense of religious solemnity, that of Christian solidarity. Thus the sermon is not merely the personal prayer of the preacher, nor a personal prayer of each hearer. It is a truly corporate and ritual prayer, in the sense that each member of the congregation who opens his heart to the revelation, will perceive his neighbour's faith inflamed along with his own. The fire on each separate hearth will unite with all the others; till, like

a single flame upon an invisible altar, all this sacred ardour rises to God in one collective prayer."[1]

To this general and realistic restoration of the ancient Ministry of the Word, the prophetic element of the cultus, Luther attached primary importance. "One thing only is needful," he said, "namely, that Mary should sit at Christ's feet and listen to His Word daily", and, again, "Where the Word as the main matter goes right, there everything else goes right".[2] The Swedish reformer, Olaus Petri, was even more emphatic: "Without preaching, sacraments are of little use".[3] The essence of the Lutheran service, where its real spirit survives, is God's merciful Word coming to man in sermon and sacrament, and man's grateful response in praise and prayer. It originated in the religious experience of a soul; and never lost this subjective character. The congregational response is made chiefly through the singing of the hymns, which play an essential part in Evangelical worship. By these corporate acts of praise the democratic character of the Church, that priesthood of all believers which was a favourite Lutheran doctrine, is asserted; and through the suggestive and social character of choral singing, no less than through the more direct appeal of the preacher, the faithful are welded into a single instrument of worship. The preacher may scatter the Word; but "the chorale gathers the faithful together round the treasure of life which it contains, and breaks down as nothing else can do the isolation of the soul . . . one might almost say that the chorale creates the Protestant congregation."[4] The Lutheran hymn book is the people's real prayer book, and best guide to the temper of their Godward life. Indeed,

[1] Will, *Le Culte*, Vol. I, p. 318.

[2] Quoted by F. Heiler, *The Spirit of Worship*, pp. 78 and 85.

[3] Brilioth, *Eucharistic Faith and Practice*, p. 232.

[4] On Lutheran hymn singing in general, see Will, *op. cit.*, Vol. I, pp. 285–303. I quote from this section.

its rich collection of vernacular hymns, with their magnificent declarations of confidence, gratitude, and humble joy, must be reckoned the chief contribution of this Church to the common stock of Christian worship.

It is certain that Luther's aim was not the creation of a new cultus; but rather an evangelical revival of that which he conceived to be the ancient balance of full Catholic worship. Nevertheless the change-over from a ritual pattern which had become more and more centred upon the objective action of the Church in the name of her members, to a conception of worship based on the subjective response of each soul to the uttered Word, was complete. Lutheran subjectivity and romantic feeling re-made the liturgy in its own image. For him, even the Eucharist was a special presentation or utterance of the Word; a proclamation of God's saving love under the species of bread and wine. Its total movement was from God to man. The primitive element of oblation, the drawing near of man that he might offer his gifts to God, was ruthlessly cut out; and thus the real Eucharistic rhythm was lost.

The Lutheran rite is made up of dislocated fragments from the Roman Mass; the only liturgy which Luther knew. There is no Offertory, for this implies oblation. The ancient Trinitarian balance of the Canon is destroyed. At least in one order the *Sanctus* is placed after the consecration. Of the actual prayer of consecration with its memorials, only the Words of Institution remain. These Words are the essential features of the Lutheran rite: not because any supernatural change in the elements is conceived to be effected by them, but because they sum up the substance of the Gospel, its graciousness and given-ness, now declared in visible form. St Augustine, from whom all that is best in Luther's teaching derives, had called the Eucharist "the Word made visible", thus bringing together the eternal incarnation of the Logos and the oblation of the Cross;

and here we find our best clue to its significance for Evangelical worship. Communion was prized as an act of fellowship, in which the mysterious Presence of Jesus was truly experienced. In it, said Luther, " Christ with His Saints comes unto thee ". The stress lay, not on the total action of the Church, but on the communicant's individual experience.

From all this, it will be seen that it is unfair to credit Luther—or, indeed, any of the great Reformers—with an anti-Eucharistic bias; although, together with certain manifest abuses, much that was precious in Catholic sacramentalism was thrown away. On the contrary, had the Protestant Churches been true to the ideals of their founders, they would—in spite of the shortcomings in their doctrine—have led the Christian world in that practice of frequent communion which the Council of Trent sought in vain to bring back to the Church of Rome, which the decree of Pope Pius X finally established there, and which within the last century the Anglo-Catholic movement has fostered in the English Church. The infrequency with which in all countries the laity were given communion in the Middle Ages, and the excessive emphasis placed on the sacrificial and vicarious aspect of the Mass, were among the points most vigorously attacked by nearly all the preachers of Reform; who meant by Evangelical worship a return to the primitive synthesis of preaching the Word of God and breaking the Bread of Life. The Hussite movement had encouraged daily communion, and demanded the restoration of the chalice to the laity. The revolt of the Scottish Church from Rome was coupled on the part of many of its leaders with a demand for more frequent opportunities of communion for the laity. In the Lutheran churches, for the first two hundred years of their existence, the normal Sunday service was High Mass, with the primitive double climax of sermon and communion restored. It still retains this name and general character; even though the service is now seldom continued beyond the sermon.

Gradually, and especially during the eighteenth century, celebrations became everywhere less frequent. The whole service was more and more centred upon the preacher; as it had been from the first in Zwinglian and Calvinist churches. In Germany, eighteenth-century rationalism made havoc of the genuine Lutheran tradition. Its surviving Catholic features, including the ceremonial use of vestments, incense, and lights, its retention of Latin hymns, and in general its warm tone of realistic worship, were done away. By the end of the century the Eucharist, no longer recognized as the "bounden duty and service" of the Christian fellowship, but reduced to an occasional means of communion for pious souls, was separated from the chief service of Sunday and only celebrated on a few days in the year. This unhappy result was partly due to the deep awe with which the act of communion was surrounded. The necessary preparation lasted for several weeks, and there was great fear of unworthy reception. Institutional religion became in consequence more and more arid; and the spirit of worship, driven from the altar, took in the Pietists an ever more personal and subjective form.

Lutheran worship, originating in its founder's temperamental reaction to Reality, and conditioned by his historical and religious environment, still bears the marks of its descent. On one hand, Luther's subjective sense of sin and need, his craving for personal assurance, liberation, peace, his robust love of human life and revolt from monastic asceticism, are reflected in its emphasis on the Divine mercy and grace, the saving and releasing love of God; meeting His creature here and now on its own ground. Hence the tender and intimate devotion to the Person of Jesus, in which Lutheran piety continues the mediæval cultus of the Divine Humanity. Such worship is essentially receptive and responsive. In it one aspect of man's relation to the Holy—his humble and creaturely confidence—is given adequate expression ; though the other aspect of that one-sided relation, the adoring recognition of mystery, of the Inaccessible Light before which even the seraphs veil their eyes, is almost ignored. On the other hand, it was not in entire forgetfulness but trailing a few clouds of glory, that Lutheran worship came from its birthplace within the Catholic tradition. Luther had been a Catholic priest. His mind had been formed within the monastic system, and never quite lost the character it gave. He had learned to worship in the mediæval way and could not entirely dissociate the Eucharistic mystery from the liturgical sequence in which it was clothed. It was therefore from the Roman Missal and the Psalter that he took the material for his order of public worship ; and much of this material, fragmentary and out of order though it be, still remains embedded in the structure of the Lutheran High Mass. The successive attempts to revive the spirit of corporate worship and give it a richer liturgical expression, which have occurred from time to time—and especially in recent years in Scandinavia —within the Lutheran churches, have mainly consisted in a renewal of emphasis upon this liturgic material. This means the attempt to redress the lost balance between Word and Sacraments by more frequent, and more reverent, celebrations of Holy Communion as the proper climax of Sunday worship ; resulting, where this "High Church" movement has gained ground, in the creation or restoration of a service which conforms in general structure to the traditional Christian type.

The evangelical insistence on freedom—for any legalistic compulsion is foreign to the real spirit of Luther's reform —permits wide variation between "High" and "Low" in the theory and practice of worship in Lutheran churches. As in the Anglican communion, so here, Catholic and

Puritan influences live on side by side. We obtain one impression if we enter a bare German or Danish church of the old school; where the pulpit occupies the central position, the seats being arranged round it without reference to the altar or other effective symbol of the Godward direction of worship, and there is evidently no expectation that the congregation will wish to kneel in prayer. Here adoration has vanished, and information or attention takes its place. We obtain another and entirely different impression if we are present at the Sunday worship in one of the more living churches of Scandinavia; where the ancient church-order and rich cultural background which Luther retained have not been lost, and the sequence of the Christian year is observed. The beautiful and impressive Swedish rite has often been described.[1] It has passed through several phases on the way to its present form; which is that of a sung High Mass with variable collect, epistle, and gospel following the Western Proper of Time, congregational hymns and chants, sermon and communion. Where there are no communicants, the service ends with the sermon, prayer for the Church, and blessing.[2] But Lutheran worship reveals its quality and homely earnestness more fully in those wooden churches of the Norwegian valleys, till recently shut off from much contact with the outer world; where the Sunday service is still the centre of the local religious life. The church, with its carved and painted rood-screen, reredos and pulpit, its rows of dumpy and brightly coloured angels and saints, the great gilt candlesticks and sacred vessels on the altar, the hand-woven towels placed ready by the font, has a homely, hand-made, welcoming, curiously primitive air. It is in all its parts a local creation, made by a simple people and adorned according to their

[1] E.g. by Brilioth, *op. cit.*, pp. 260 *seq.*, where the text of the liturgy is given and critically considered.

[2] Separate services of Holy Communion are often held in the evening in the Swedish Church.

skill, for the worship of God and the dispensation of His sacraments. The service is at once traditional and Evangelical. The constant singing of hymns and psalms by the whole congregation gives it a strongly corporate character. It begins with a prayer to the Trinity, a hymn, and a confession of sin followed by the *Kyrie Eleison.* Then the *Gloria in excelsis* ; which here retains its rightful position as a welcome to the coming Lord. A rubric directs that the priest is to "sing it if he can". The rest of the Mass of Catechumens follows the common order, with the collect, epistle, and gospel of the day, and the sermon between two hymns as its high point. It ends with the great intercession, or prayer for the Church. Here there is a pause, and any children who have been added to the community are brought forward for baptism and received into the Christian flock. Thus the font and the altar are placed in their true relation ; and the first and greatest of the sacraments is given its proper place. The priest then retires, puts on a chasuble, goes to the altar, and prepares the elements for communion, while the "Supper-hymn" is sung. He proceeds at once to the Preface, *Sanctus*, and *Benedictus* ; when the communicants go to the altar, and kneel there during the rest of the service. The *Agnus* is now sung, and the Lord's Prayer is said. The Canon is replaced by a prayer for Christ's presence, leading up to the Words of Institution. There are no sacrificial references. No reverence is paid to the consecrated species : in fact, consecration in the Scandinavian churches appears to be regarded merely as a setting aside, and hallowing for the immediate purpose of communion, of the bread and wine, which become effective symbols for the time of the service alone. No objection is felt to the reconsecration, at a later service, of elements which have not been consumed. Communion is followed by a hymn, thanksgiving, and blessing.

The whole service has a touching simplicity and homeliness ; a deep and tender piety of its own. We re-enter the Evangelical atmosphere, and share the experience of Emmaus. Yet the specific quality of liturgy, its impersonal and objective character, its note of mystery, its other-worldly reference—the drawing-near of the Church to offer oblation, and the drawing-near of the Holy to sanctify and bless—are absent. The whole temper, in fact, is humanistic ; and here perhaps we find the word which sums up the special character of Lutheran worship.

II

We turn from this to the other, and completing, type of Protestant worship ; also originating in a temperamental reaction to religious truth. Luther, warm-hearted, vehement, uneasy, vigorously alive on every level, passionately desired to bring the supernatural grace and mercy within the reach of every needy soul. For him the message of the Gospel was liberation and assurance, and worship was man's grateful response. Loving confidence in the Divine generosity was its essential mood. This is the " faith " which is all-sufficient to adjust man's relation to God. For Calvin, on the contrary, the supreme religious fact was God's unspeakable Majesty and Otherness, and the nothingness and simplicity of man. In the type of worship which he established, we seem to see the result of a great religious experience—the impact of the Divine Transcendence on the awe-struck soul—and the effort towards a response which is conditioned by a deep sense of creaturely limitation, but deficient in homely and child-like dispositions ; and, with intrepid French logic, refuses the use of creaturely aids. Calvin desired, as so many great religious souls have done, a completely spiritual cultus ; ascending towards a completely spiritual Reality, and rejecting all the humble ritual methods and all the sensible signs by which men are led to express their adoration of the Unseen. God, who "hath no image", was the ultimate fact. Therefore a pitiless lucidity of mind, which ignored the mysterious relation between poetry and reality, and the need of stepping-stones from the successive to the Eternal, insisted that all which is less than God must be abjured when man turns to adoration. Unlike Luther, Calvin was really hostile to the mediæval embodiments of worship. He regarded them with abhorrence, and went to all lengths in the fury of his denunciation. Without Luther's first-hand knowledge of Catholic devotion, and interpreting Catholic theology in the terms of the crude popular religion of the time, he even felt able to say that in the Roman Mass "all that a criminal godlessness could devise is done".[1] Hence he cast away without discrimination the whole of the traditional apparatus of Catholicism; its episcopal order, its liturgy, symbols, cultus. No organ or choir was permitted in his churches: no colour, no ornament but a table of the Ten Commandments on the wall. No ceremonial acts or gestures were permitted. No hymns were sung but those derived from a Biblical source. The bleak stripped interior of the real Calvinist church is itself sacramental: a witness to the inadequacy of the human over against the Divine.

This austere Puritanism, utterly concentrated on the Eternal God in His unseen majesty, has a splendour and spiritual value of its own. It is a powerful corrective of humanistic piety; driving home the abiding truth of God's unique reality and total demand, and man's poverty, dependence, and obligation. The Word is the self-disclosure of the Eternal; and worship is man's abject but adoring response to the utterance of God. Karl Barth's "theology of Krisis", rooted in his acute sense of God's utter and qualitative distinctness and man's helplessness and sin, is a true child of the Calvinist tradition; and it is through him

[1] *Opera Selecta*, V., 239. Quoted by Brilioth, *op. cit.*, p. 171.

that we can best understand the powerful attraction which it possessed for devoted souls in its vigorous youth. The God whom it calls man to worship is the "Wholly Other"; to proclaim His awful majesty and to bow down in deep humility before Him is the fundamental religious act. Nothing else really mattered to Calvin; the homely, intimate, incarnational side of religion seems to have made little appeal to him.

Such a position, of course, is a subtraction from the total Christian outlook. Yet there is something magnificent in its uncompromising devotion to God's glory, its one-sided exaggeration of the creaturely sense, its total rejection of religious comfort and self-interested piety; its certitude of the priority of God's Will and inevitable character of His justice hardening into a doctrine of predestination so ruthless that it sees and adores in all things and events—even man's damnation—the inscrutable action of the Divine.[1] A Calvinist service is the solemn acknowledgment of God's sovereignty, as the one reality of life, made by His holy people, His elect. Publicans and sinners are hardly considered in such a scheme, which ignores His many-levelled disclosures and infinitely various dealings with weak and childlike souls, His delicate approaches in beauty no less than in goodness and truth; and this alone suggests how many Christian values pure Calvinistic worship fails to express.

Calvin, like Luther, had intended to bring back and make central to the worship of the Reformed Churches, the primitive Christian association of the "Liturgy of the Word"

[1] Those who are inclined to identify these harsh doctrines with the Protestant reform should remember that they represent a trend towards severity which was present in Christianity from the first; and can claim New Testament support. Calvin derived his predestinarian views from St Augustine, Doctor of the Catholic Church and master of adoring worship; and such loving souls as St Bernard and St Thomas Aquinas held that the contemplation of the sufferings of the damned would rank high among the joys of Paradise.

and " Liturgy of the Upper Room ". This is envisaged in the Form of Church Prayers which he issued in 1542 and described as being " according to the custom of the Ancient Church ". He desired that the Eucharist, with a general communion of the laity, should be celebrated at least once a week ; but in point of fact he never succeeded in establishing this.[1] At first these celebrations were monthly, and then four times yearly. The making of one communion only in the year, at Easter—at that time, the general custom of the laity in the Catholic Church—was violently condemned. In order to ensure the discouragement of this practice, Easter Eucharists, along with all other celebrations of the Christian year, were forbidden : the communion days being arranged without reference to ecclesiastical feasts.

Although the rite given in his Book of Common Order has the character of an Agape rather than a Eucharist, since there is no true consecration of the elements, Calvin's intense religious instinct is shown in his deep veneration for " ce sainct mystère " ; his conviction that it is " the holy meat and drink of eternal life ", and not only this, but a true declaratory symbol of the Divine Presence, brooding over the service though not " enclosed in the Bread and Wine ". After the thanksgiving, the communicants were directed to sing the *Nunc Dimittis* ; a real acknowledgment of supernatural experience. In the arrangements for the celebration of the sacrament, there was even an effort towards expressive ritual ; a reproduction of the primitive communion meal. Lutheran communicants, in the Catholic manner, knelt before the Holy Table to receive. In Calvinist churches they came forward, sat or stood at a table, and shared the one bread which was broken from hand to hand : thus restoring to Christian custom the ancient and precious symbolism of the One Loaf. This is the so-called Table Gesture : now generally and unfortunately abandoned in favour of a

[1] See W. D. Maxwell, *John Knox's Genevan Service Book.*

distribution of the elements to communicants seated in their pews.

At the present day, the Calvinist type of worship is chiefly to be found in the Reformed Churches of Switzerland, Holland, and France, and in the Presbyterian Church of Scotland and its offshoots. It has passed through many vicissitudes; sometimes becoming so entirely centred on moral and doctrinal exhortation that the responsive movement of adoring prayer is wholly lost, and sometimes allied with a harsh and excessive Puritanism. Though never entirely losing its austerely theocentric character, almost everywhere it shows a serious decline from its Founder's exacting and profoundly religious ideals. Since the liturgical quality of the worship in all Calvinist churches depends on the liturgical quality of the minister,[1] and the impersonal support and objectivity of a fixed and obligatory Church Order is only represented, at the most, by a "recommended" service, we might expect—and as a matter of fact we obtain —wide variation between the extremes of tasteless aridity and deep devotion, the stern rejection of all outward and visible signs, and the timid cultivation of the beauty of holiness. Many of the recommended services now in use, the result of successive attempts towards liturgic revival—especially those for the celebration of the sacraments—are based on a real understanding of the ancient liturgies, and fall into line with the great central tradition of Christian worship. Some even restore by implication that essential element of sacrifice, which the Reformers so ruthlessly cast away; and imply the fundamental importance of the Eucharist, and the duty and privilege of communion.

Such a liturgical revival is now in progress within the Dutch Calvinist Church: which has set up a commission

[1] It is strange that a reform which began as a revolt from sacerdotalism should have given such an overwhelming spiritual responsibility to an individual.

charged with the reformation of the public worship in a liturgical sense, and the bringing back into practice of Calvin's eucharistic ideals. So far, the supremacy of the Sunday morning service centred on the sermon has not been seriously threatened. But additional services of a liturgical type, together with a tendency to a greater dignity and beauty in worship—even the adorning of the communion table with flowers and lights—are creeping in; especially in connection with the Youth Movement. A great impoverishment of the material of daily worship in all the Evangelical and Reformed churches resulted from the casting aside of the Divine Office. In the Lutheran churches, a vernacular arrangement of Mattins and Vespers had continued for a time, but gradually died out. An attempt at the restoration of these offices and the compiling of a German Breviary was part of the programme of the abortive High Church Movement in Germany.[1] In the Calvinist churches also, the service of Vespers was at first retained; but failed to establish itself. The present liturgical movement in Holland includes the establishment of daily worship, and the introduction of an ordered evening service based upon Compline.

III

The living character of Reformed Worship, its powers of adaptation and growth, the fact that even in the most unpromising circumstances it has yet kept the spark of adoration alight, are now most easily studied in the Presbyterian Church of Scotland. This Church, of course, is not—any more than its sister the Anglican Communion—to be regarded merely as a Protestant creation of the sixteenth century: nor is its worship to be judged by its precise conformity with the uncompromising principles of

[1] See F. Heiler's article, "The Catholic Movement in German Lutheranism" in *Northern Catholicism*, pp. 478 *seq.*

Geneva. At the time of the Reformation, Catholicism had fallen on evil days in the North. The standard of the priesthood was low, the churches were often neglected.[1] In general, communion was given to the laity only at Easter. The desire of the first reformers, here as elsewhere, was not for mere destruction; but for a simplified and purified Catholic worship. The tendency of the changes they initiated was towards more, not less, devotion than had commonly prevailed; the bringing of the faithful to communion at least four times a year, the establishment in the larger towns of daily services and monthly celebrations of the "Great Mystery", the instruction of all men in Christian truth, and the dedication of the whole of Sunday to the worship of God.[2]

With this programme, the sacramental part of which was never fully realized, was unfortunately combined the dour Calvinistic contempt for beauty, incapacity for joy, and horror of ceremonial religion and sensible signs; the ruthless expulsion of symbols and ornaments, and the rejection of the feasts and fasts of the Christian year. Nevertheless the type of service which John Knox imposed upon the Scottish Reform in the place of the 2nd Prayer Book of Edward VI —which it had at first accepted—had a simple and austere dignity of its own. The minister preached in a Genevan gown, and read fixed prayers from the liturgy; but opportunity was also provided for the extempore and prophetic prayer in which it was his sacred privilege to lead his people out towards God. The reading of the Scriptures, the recitation by the people of the Lord's Prayer and Creed, and the

[1] C. L. Warr, *The Presbyterian Tradition*, p. 295.

[2] The Scottish Sabbath has come in for more than its share of ridicule and abuse: but its ideal—the setting aside of one-seventh of man's life for communion with the Divine and forgetfulness of the world—is one that we can hardly treat lightly. On the true Sabbath—Jewish or Christian—Creation pauses and contemplates the Face of its God. It is an act of adoration.

singing of appropriate psalms were all parts of this one concerted movement. In fact, the service reproduced with fidelity the main features of the primitive Christian Ministry of the Word.[1]

As regards the Ministry of the Sacraments, the deep awe with which Holy Communion is regarded, the fear of unworthy reception and the severity and length of the preparation required, have always been among the most noble characteristics of Presbyterian worship; which here preserves, as do the Eastern Churches, a supernatural realism, a holy dread, too easily lost where frequent communions become the general rule, yet a most precious constituent of the Christian response to God. In the old Scottish Church, the infrequent communion times had a deeply sacred and heart-searching quality.[2] All full members of the congregation were then visited by an elder. The Thursday preceding the celebration was known as the Fast Day; and was observed as a period of prayer and self-examination, with attendance at church. Monday was a day of thanksgiving. This ancient discipline has been considerably relaxed; but there is still, in many parishes, a service of preparation on the Friday before the half-yearly celebrations, and the admittance of young people to their First Communion is regarded as the crucial moment of the religious life, carrying with it a permanent obligation. The attitude here is entirely different from the way in which contemporary Catholicism puts before the growing child the privileges and gifts of its

[1] Dr W. D. Maxwell (*John Knox's Genevan Service Book*) has collected evidence that this morning service of the Presbyterian Church, which continues in general use, derives its structure through Knox and Calvin from the Roman Mass of the Catechumens.

[2] Annual communion was the early practice. Half-yearly communions became usual in the eighteenth century and are still the general rule. Even where more frequent celebrations are provided, the mass of the people make only two communions in the year. Thus here, the intention of the Reformers failed and the popular standard remains that of mediæval Catholicism.

spiritual home, and invites all to frequent communion as a sovereign means of grace.

As to the spirit of worship which this austere institutional framework can support and express, we can best discover its quality in the unflinching obedience to costly moral standards which in its golden age it demanded and obtained, in the heroism of those who suffered for it, and in the temper of those early Scottish Prayer Books, which were prepared for " Men in travel and being from their hame, quha glaidlie wald carie ane thin buik ". The prayers which these books provide, so serious and moderate in their demand upon God, so uncompromising in their implied ethical standard, so constant in their remembrance of that only consummation of worship in which " all thingis quhilk brethis with lyfe may praise thee, as the true lyfe of all creatures " are those which nourished the soul of the old Scottish Church. They show how near that soul, in its deepest moments, drew to the universal desire and experience of the Saints, and their selfless adoration of that God " quha surmountis all thingis in holinesse ".[1] This high standard of austere devotion seems to have been maintained through the controversies and persecutions of the early seventeenth century. But under the influence of a Puritanism introduced from England and superimposed on Calvinism, liturgical quality was gradually lost, preaching more and more vanquished worship; and in the bad years of the eighteenth century, the services had declined to a level of uncouthness and even irreverence which a sympathetic historian can describe as " unparalleled in Christendom."[2]

The general movement of the Church of Scotland in modern times, like that of the Church of England, has been

[1] See Dr Patrick Miller, *The Scottish Collects* (Church of Scotland Committee on Publications). These prayers, however, are not of Scottish origin: They are derived from those affixed to Beza's French Psalter of 1567 and written by Augustin Marlorat.

[2] C. L. Warr, *op. cit.*, pp. 296 and 343 *seq.*

towards the recovery of its best traditions ; especially in the ordering of its worship. At least in some quarters, the despotism of the pulpit is giving way, and the minister's "long prayer" is contracted and given liturgical form. Though parishes still exist where the Eucharist is only celebrated once a year, monthly communion services are becoming more frequent in the towns ; and there is a growing tendency towards daily services, and the opening of the churches on weekdays for private prayer. The chief commemorations of the Christian year have been restored ; especially Christmas, Epiphany, Easter, and Whitsuntide. In the admirable service book issued by the authority of the General Assembly in 1929, proper prayers for Advent and Lent are also given ; and there is provision for the commemoration of the Saints.[1] The order for Holy Communion in this book, based on ancient models and strongly influenced by the Eastern liturgies, has several points of technical superiority to the Anglican rite. The solemn bringing in of the elements, a ceremony which has always been observed in the old parish churches of Scotland, is preserved ; and is followed by the setting apart of the bread and wine for the purposes of the sacrament. The Eucharistic prayer includes a remembrance of the Passion, and ends with the *Epiclesis ;* which is regarded as the consecrating formula.[2] It is a peculiarity of the Scottish Eucharist, that the Words of Institution do not form part of the actual Consecration Prayer, but are said at the Fraction and Elevation ; one of the most solemn moments in this rite.[3] The consecration is followed by the

[1] *Prayers for Divine Service :* by authority of the General Assembly of the Church of Scotland. Edinburgh, 1929. The more recent manual *Prayers for the Christian Year*, published by the authority of the General Assembly in 1935, has complete services for all the principal festivals of the Christian year, including each day in Holy Week.

[2] Compare *supra*, cap. VII, p. 135.

[3] See Rev. J. W. Baird : "The Service for Holy Communion" in the *Church Service Society's Annual*, 1928–9, p. 35.

Pax and thanksgiving, with memorials of the living and the dead. The service has in a high degree the primitive characters of mystery and homeliness.

In those parts of the Presbyterian Church which are touched by this liturgical movement, some real progress has been made during the present century, especially in respect of Eucharistic worship. The Catholic tradition has always lingered in Scotland ; and in recent years has sprung to fresh life, to exert a quickening and supernaturalizing influence. It is true that at present this movement, like the Tractarian revival in its first phase, is chiefly clerical and urban, and hardly affects the practice of the country kirk, or the outlook of the average worshipper. Protestant feeling, too, is easily roused and views all change with suspicion. But in those whom this Catholic spirit has touched, there has been a true rediscovery of the meaning of sacramental worship. The Eucharist is more and more understood as at once a spiritual oblation of praise, a communion with the Living Christ who " comes sacramentally into the midst of the assembly of His faithful people " and a co-operation in His heavenly Ministry ;[1] and hence as the central act of the Christian cultus. With this go a renewed sense of the corporate life, historic continuity, and supernatural basis of the Church, a reverence for its saints, and a deeper cultivation of the life of prayer.

Nevertheless, Scottish worship as a whole retains its Biblical and prophetic emphasis, its severe ethical standards, and horror of sin. A great love of Biblical religion, and thorough-going conviction of the intimate connection between faith and works, and of the dedication of the moral life as the ultimate act of worship, have always been characteristic of the Scottish soul. These qualities are capable of unlovely and humourless exaggeration ; but at their best,

[1] See J. Macleod, *The Gospel in the Institution of Holy Communion*, p. 64, and H. J. Wotherspoon, *Religious Values in the Sacraments*, p. 24.

they represent the continuance of that prophetic and ethical strand, that emphasis on the moral will, without which the Christian complex lacks the noble element of costliness. Hence the worship of the Scottish Church, whether it be embodied in Puritan or Catholic forms, centres still on the proclamation of God's Word to man in its majesty and authority ; and man's duty of response. If we must not say that the *Ethos* is actually given priority over the *Logos*, at least it is chiefly here that the divine revelation is recognized and the divine Voice is heard. On this basic conviction of God's ultimate demand, and this sturdy sense of man's moral obligation, both Catholic and Puritan influences have played ; and each has contributed something to its expression in worship.

CHAPTER XIV

FREE CHURCH WORSHIP

I

THE great Protestant churches of Germany, Scandinavia, Scotland, and Holland have each developed a type of worship which retains a sufficient traditional and liturgical element to ensure stability, and even some continuity with the historic Christian cultus ; whilst leaving room for the expression of that prophetic, ethical, spontaneous element in the primitive Christian response to God, which every reform and revival seeks to restore. In these communions, some of the attributes of the Sect, its Biblical emphasis, its revolt from ecclesiasticism and re-assertion of simplicity, its passion for personal freedom, are combined with some of the attributes of the Church.[1] But this compromise has never fully satisfied the exigencies of that radical individualism, that appeal from tradition to experience—to the living quality of the Christian revelation in its first-hand impact on the soul, and consequent demand for an unhindered liberty of response—which has always been an element in the Christian outlook ; a valuable corrective of the special weaknesses inherent in stylized worship.

That " royally generous west wind " which blows through the Gospels,[2] with its freshness and freedom, its unlimited love and pity for sinners, yet positive demand for a life set towards Holiness, is of all constituents of Christianity,

[1] I use these terms in the sense given to them by Troeltsch, in *The Social Teaching of the Christian Churches*. See above Pt. I, cap. V.

[2] F. von Hügel, *Selected Letters*, p. 315.

one of the most life-giving, most precious, and most easily lost. It is this virile evangelical quality, this newness of life, which the Sect or Free Church at its inception, as seen in the ardent mind of its prophet-founder, always seeks to restore ; and this which—so long as it survives the corroding tendencies which make for the creation of a spiritual clique—gives its worship attractiveness, realism, and life. For the Sect represents the "little flock", the small company of keen believers ready to press the teaching of the Gospel to its logical conclusions ; ruthlessly rejecting all that conflicts with evangelical ardour and simplicity, demanding personal consecration, downright costly conversion of the whole life to God's purpose, repudiating all substitutes for the offering of the self. It restores to their original position of importance the charismatic and prophetic characters of primitive Christianity ; and hence is suspicious of set forms, and demands a spontaneous worship which shall be the devotional expression of a personal and subjective relation to God.

The responsibility and capacity of each soul, the "priesthood of all believers" the universal call to sanctity, are the central truths governing real Free Church worship. Here we find a deep conviction of sin and a serious pursuit of personal holiness, a passion for sincerity, a high standard of self-discipline, a strong sense of direct and individual relationship to God, often a profound and tender Christocentric devotion, as constituents of the worshipping life : but no organic conception of the Church, as a reality transcending and enclosing its members, living its own great sacrificial life in and for the world, and mediating supernatural grace by its sacraments. Holy Communion becomes the continuance of the primitive fellowship meal of the Christian group, in which devout souls may experience the Presence of their Lord. Psalms and spiritual songs are the nearest approach to stylized corporate worship.

Both the Church-idea and the Sect-idea, as Troeltsch saw,

lie "within the consequences of the Gospel". Indeed they are the completing opposites of that total Godward life which it reveals; and it is only the constant reassertion, both inside and outside its borders, of that vigorous spiritual realism from which Sects are born, which saves the worship of the Church from the crystallizing tendencies inherent in all formal religion.[1] In their extreme form, however, Sect and Church represent distinct and even incompatible conceptions of the life of worship; the one giving priority to corporate tradition and authority, the other to personal enthusiasm and experience.

Free Church worship, so greatly developed among English-speaking Christians that we tend to regard it as an Anglo-Saxon phenomenon, is at its best the devotional expression of the Sect-idea. Here we have the full Evangelical reaction from institutional and liturgical religion, its intense suspicion of ritual acts and outward forms, its demand for first-hand experience, its passion for simplicity and sincerity of expression.[2] The objective, artistic character of real liturgic worship, its transcendence of the individual, its power of conveying supra-sensible truth, of weaving together visible and invisible, history and poetry, symbol and prayer, to form one single response to God, are ignored. Hence, though devotional fervour and moral earnestness are here in full measure, we miss those intimations of the supernatural, that sense of the over-plus of Divine Being, the mystery of Eternal Life, so richly given in the higher forms of sacramental worship. The *Pilgrim's Progress*, which is the

[1] The Cistercian and Franciscan movements, as their founders conceived them, were really an assertion from within the Church of the evangelical and ascetical ideals of the Sect: the single-minded, realistic devotion to the adoration of God and the sanctification of life. So, too, the less fortunate revolts from accepted tradition of the Waldensians and other mediæval revivalists. Eastern Christianity also has its Free Church sectaries.

[2] The early Baptists even condemned hymns, as artificial compositions and therefore alien to the free motions of the Spirit of God. See H. Wheeler Robinson, *The Life and Faith of the Baptists*, p. 50.

Divine Comedy of Free Church Christianity, tracks out with deep spiritual and psychological insight the pathway of the individual soul "from this world to that which is to come". But the pilgrim soul and its necessities are always the centre of the picture; and its safe arrival on the further shore is all that concerns us. Nothing is here of the supernatural cause and goal of the journey: God, the magnet of the universe, drawing His creature, and that creature's craving for the Presence of God, in Himself and for Himself alone, fulfilled at last in the beatific vision of Reality—"the Intellectual Radiance full of love".

So, too, as regards cultus. The edifying is emphasized; the mysterious is refused. Though each of the three great Free Churches of the Anglo-Saxon world—Baptists, Congregationalists, and Methodists—accept the two major sacraments, these are scarcely regarded in the Catholic sense as covenanted channels of grace. By Congregationalists, Holy Communion is valued as "a token of faith and brotherly love".[1] Theoretically, though perhaps seldom in practice, any member of the congregation may be the celebrant. No need is felt for special preparation before communion. Though spiritual minds may hold that "all the bread and wine symbolize is actually received",[2] there is a general resistance to the whole conception of mystery mediated through things: and hence to the attribution of any special sanctity or quality to the Eucharistic elements. No reverence is shown to them outside the service. For the Baptists, baptism is not a sacramental imparting, from God's side, of the regenerating Spirit; nor is the water a visible instrument of the invisible Divine activity, doing something for man which he cannot do for himself. Baptism is a crucial act of surrender performed by the baptized, who is agent, not patient; a choosing of God, the seal of conversion, the

[1] *The Congregational Year-Book.*

[2] R. W. Dale, *Manual of Congregational Principles*, p. 155.

consecration of life, the solemn entry of the individual soul into the Church of regenerate men. Hence it is essentially an act of worship from man's side, a self-offering to the Holy; whereas infant baptism is an act of creative love from God's side, a free gift mediated through His Church.

No other Church has insisted, as the Baptists have done, on the centrality of the New Testament connection between baptism and personal faith, the importance of this great symbolic act of surrender to God; and on a realistic conversion of the whole life, inward and outward, as the condition of entrance into the Divine Society. Within that Society all are equal, and all are called to the worshipping life; the "priesthood of every believer" and the impossibility of substituting any liturgical act for personal communion with God and self-offering to God, are cardinal points of Baptist belief. This radical individualism and emphasis upon the moral will, when elevated into a standard of life, easily becomes harsh and rigoristic; yet how valuable is its witness to the heroic character of the Christian demand, the priority and total claim of God, the personal responsibility of the soul. Though the Baptists, with all other Protestant sects, have repudiated the sacrificial aspect of the Eucharist, for them—in so far as they accept the great ideals of their society—the very substance of worship is the oblation and transfiguration of life.

Baptist and Congregational worship derive from, and perpetuate, the ideals of seventeenth-century Puritanism; its prophetic and anti-sacramental temper, its passion for spiritual liberty, and impatience of ecclesiastical control. The Congregationalists, the modern representatives of the Independents, still keep the ancient organization of free assemblies; each a law to themselves, and varying much in their religious outlook and methods of worship. In principle this worship is non-liturgic, and indeed in early times was almost formless; the extempore prayer of the leader being punctuated by the "groans, sobs, and sighs" of the congregation.[1] In practice it now tends to an increasing use of liturgical forms; borrowing freely from the Anglican Book of Common Prayer, and combining a radical Protestantism and emphasis on the Ministry of the Word with the fervent singing of Catholic and Tractarian hymns.[2]

The third of the great Free Churches, Methodism, had in origin a different character from that of the seventeenth-century sects. It began, not as a revolt from institutional worship, but as an attempt to restore the continuity of the full Christian life of realistic adoration within the Anglican Church; and, had it achieved this aim, might have done the work which was afterwards set in hand by the Tractarian revival. The driving force of its founder was the driving force of the saints: the passion for Holiness, and the conviction that Holiness was the proper aim of every Christian life, the only standard of Christian perfection, and the supreme offering man can make to God. This is the explanation of the vigorous asceticism practised by the Oxford Methodists, and this is the note which is struck in the best of the early hymns:

> That I thy mercy may proclaim,
> That all mankind thy truth may see,
> Hallow thy great and glorious name
> And perfect holiness in me![3]

In spite of many changes, a great reduction in the theocentric temper, and a general approximation to the average

[1] E. R. Micklem, *Our Approach to God*, p. 142.

[2] The preface to the admirable *Book of Congregational Worship*, issued by the Congregational Union in 1920, mentions the "wide and increasing desire" for a book of services "providing for the use of liturgy". The book gives ten suggested orders for Sunday worship, and forms for the celebration of Holy Communion, for baptism, marriage, burial, etc., with a number of collects. It is chiefly based on traditional material, particularly the Anglican Prayer Book.

[3] John Wesley, *A Collection of Hymns for the People called Methodists* (2nd ed., 1781).

Free Church standards of worship, Methodism has never quite lost the special colour which was given to it by this tremendous orientation towards sanctity. Here the secret of primitive Christian worship in its fulness was caught again; the realistic certitude of God's transforming grace poured out on men, the light, life, and love of the Transcendent made accessible to every soul "in Christ". Hence the note of adoring gratitude and confident demand:

> Open faith's interior eye:
> Display thy glory from above:
> And all I am shall sink and die,
> Lost in astonishment and love![1]

We are not far here from the spirit of Faber's hymns. Indeed it is difficult to say whether early Methodism as its founders conceived it, impassioned and ascetic, democratic and transcendental, determined upon Perfection and yet sure of the Godward vocation of the simplest soul, was more Catholic or more Evangelical in tone. Like the Tractarians, John and Charles Wesley and the "three or four serious young gentlemen" who were their first associates were scholars; and learned through study of the past to recognize the religious shortcomings of their own day. A genuine knowledge of Christian theology, and of the mystical and devotional doctrine of the universal Church, lies behind their teaching. The writings of William Law—himself inspired by the study of the German mystics—were decisive in their influence on John Wesley's inner life; and Law has a certain right to be called the spiritual father of Methodism. The movement began in the souls of its founders, in their re-discovery of the reality of the worshipping life; and its "method" sought to organize the whole self for the purpose for which it was intended, the greater glory of God, by bringing back into practice the neglected

[1] *Op cit.*, Hymn 381.

disciplines of the Church. John Wesley restored the traditional duty of fasting to its place, and insisted on its spiritual value.[1] He provided in the Class and Band Meetings a means of close fellowship and mutual help, and a homely ministry of confession and reconciliation. Above all, he strove to bring back the Eucharist to its rightful position, and practised and taught frequent communion as the living heart of Christian devotion.[2] In all this he had no intention of promoting schism ; but rather of exercising the prophetic ministry to which he felt himself called, and creating a "little flock" of realistic Christians within the national Church. Unlike the majority of religious reformers, he had a strong belief in institutional Christianity, and a deep and instructed reverence for the great Christian tradition of worship ; here, as in so many other respects, anticipating the Tractarians.

In those early Methodist hymns which spread through England the forgotten treasures of Christian spirituality, expressed in language which the simplest worshipper could understand, we find reminiscences of all the masters of adoring worship, Catholic and Protestant alike ; from St Augustine to the Quietists. Though on the ethical side the Methodist standard was austere, all was penetrated by their passionate delight in God, the adoring abandonment to His Will and Purpose, the sense of a direct and enabling relationship with the living Christ. In the greatest of these hymns, especially those of Charles Wesley, we can recognize the fervour and realism which swept the country to re-kindle the smouldering devotional life. They constitute the true

[1] In the first period, the Oxford Methodists fasted with prayer every Wednesday and Friday. "And this has given occasion to such as do not approve of them, abusively to call them Supererogation Men". Roberts, *The Oxford Methodists*, p. 3. This practice was presently reduced to the observance of quarterly fast days. At the present time, even this degree of abstinence seems to have ceased.

[2] John Wesley received Holy Communion every few days and large numbers came to his early morning celebrations.

liturgy of Methodism; and in them, as in other liturgies, its essential spirit can still be found. They were, and are, greatly used both in public worship and private devotion; and though their exalted temper hardly represents the average religious level they have taught the deep secrets of communion with God to a multitude of humble saints. Like all the greatest creations of Christian devotional genius, they are both theological and personal; charged with dogma, yet so penetrated by the spirit of adoring and confident love that the firm outlines of the doctrinal framework are not at first observed.[1] But as a matter of fact, this doctrinal framework is seen on examination to imply so rich and deep a conception of the Godward life of man, that it requires for its full explication all the complementary aspects of Christian and Catholic worship; the expressive and sacramental, no less than the personal and interior. Thus Charles Wesley's Eucharistic hymns express with uncompromising directness the full Catholic doctrines of the sacramental Presence and the redeeming Sacrifice; and show the width of the gap which separates the ideals and conceptions of the founders from the reduced sacramentalism of modern Methodist practice, which does not greatly differ from that of the Baptist and Congregational Churches.[2]

All the Free Churches seem at the present time, as they move further from the inspiration of their prophet-founders, to be drawing towards an increasing use of liturgical forms; thus striving to elude the many difficulties of an unstylized cultus, and solve the situation created by the general decline in the "gift" of extempore prayer. In fact, modern non-

[1] Consider e.g. the theological implications of "Love divine, all loves excelling", "O thou who camest from above", "O thou eternal Victim slain", "Author of life divine!" and many others.

[2] A leader of contemporary Methodism estimates the frequency with which Holy Communion is now celebrated as once a month in towns, and once a quarter in smaller villages.

conformist worship, especially in the more important town churches, tends to become a working compromise between the ideals of order and spontaneity. Whilst retaining its own distinctive character, in the important place which is given to the reading and exposition of Scripture and the use of free prayer, it borrows without scruple from the general liturgic tradition of the Western Church ; one more example of the continuity in variety of Christian worship, and of the need which seems to be experienced sooner or later by all the separated parts of the *Corpus Christi* for resort to the central treasure-house of the Church. The Free Churchman of to-day, says E. R. Micklem, is indebted for his devotional material to " his mother the Church of England, his grandmother the Church of Rome, and his great-grandmother the Jewish Synagogue."[1] There is little difference in this respect between the services of the average Baptist, Congregational, and Methodist Church.

II

The reaction from liturgic to spontaneous worship, and from sacramental embodiments of spiritual action to pure inwardness, is carried to its extreme conclusion by the Society of Friends ; who stand alone among Christian communions in their thorough-going rejection of outward forms and sensible signs. Quaker silence goes behind all expressive worship to that which inspires it, and makes a direct metaphysical claim to communion with God in the inner deeps. The primitive, charismatic strain in New Testament religion, its realistic dependence on the " leadings of the Spirit ", is here brought back into the foreground and set over against all rites and sacraments as the very essence of the Christian worshipping life. Christ " did not design that there should be any rite or outward observance " of obligation in His

[1] *Op. cit.*, p. 148.

Church. The essence of worship is " the quiet gathering of souls together to share fellowship with God "[1] in a corporate silence which ensures the perfect freedom of each individual soul, yet is a powerful bond of union between all submitted to its influence.

These peculiarities set Quaker worship apart from all other types of Christian cultus, Catholic or Protestant; and give it an importance which is out of all proportion to the number of those who practise it. Here the mystical and inspirational element in Christianity, which had faded out of the public life of the Church—though always maintained in the secret experience of contemplative souls—is powerfully reasserted. In the records of the early Friends we seem to see a true prophetic disclosure of the Spirit, evoking a response marked by reverence, love, certitude, and above all unlimited trust; and in the corporate experience of those who waited together in confident expectation upon the Inner Light, we recognize again the spiritual realism of the New Testament. For Quaker worship is " rooted in ontology ". It " consisteth not in the words, neither in the silence, but in an holy dependence of the mind upon God ".[2]

Historically, Quakerism may be considered as the mystical wing of the Puritan movement; and, as regards its special practices, as a part of the general reaction from ritual observance and towards quietism, which was a feature of seventeenth-century religion in Europe. Here the intense Puritan suspicion of institutional worship, fear of formalism, and demand for a personal religious sincerity so drastic that no word may be said or sung which is not true for each individual worshipper, is pushed to its logical consequence; in the rejection of any kind of organized or premeditated service, even the use of hymns, as likely to involve the violation of " sensitive truthfulness ", in those who sing

[1] Yearly Epistles of the Society of Friends; 1880 and 1925.
[2] R. Barclay, *Apology*, 11th Part, § 9.

but may not always mean them.[1] Here all sense of the Church, as the worshipping unit whose action exceeds and embraces the individual experiences of her members, is lost.

This, however, is the negative and least attractive side of Quakerism. On its positive side, it is a noble experiment in corporate contemplative prayer : a passionate reassertion of the double truth of the transcendence of God and His loving penetration of life. A Quaker Meeting does not merely provide a suitable environment, within which individuals can follow in the silence their own devotional *attrait*. It is—if it be indeed a living Meeting—an organic and concerted act of recollection ; in which all the resources of group-suggestion come powerfully into play. In the silence the whole community " centres down ", as the early Friends were accustomed to say, to that ground of the soul which is the agent of contemplative prayer ; and thus achieves a common experience of communion with God, and with each other in His uncreated light. " Friends ", said George Fox, " meet together and know one another in that which is eternal." Here the practice of the Presence of God is found to involve also the practice of the Communion of Saints.

The living power of a meeting for worship, says the Yearly Epistle of 1925, depends " on united communion in the Presence of God, where each one passes the bounds of his individual self and knows a union of spirit with spirit ". Such a meeting, waiting on the Light, develops a spiritual sensitiveness and spiritual power which exceeds that of the units composing it, and may become an effective instrument of the Eternal Charity. Thus in the account of the conversion of James Sheppard in 1782 :

> Through the reverent attendance of the souls of those present upon Christ the best Minister, they were favoured together with His life-giving presence ; with the sense of

[1] J. W. Graham, *The Faith of a Quaker*, p. 181.

> which the said James was reached, and tendered into contrition in the sight of the self-denying path cast up to peace with God.[1]

The technique of Quaker worship is that which is familiar to all contemplative souls, and is described in countless manuals of the inner life. In fact, Friends have from the first appreciated this fact, and have willingly learnt from the Catholic mystics; developing this neglected strand in the texture of the Church's worship in isolation from the rest. Barclay, the determined enemy of all institutionalism, yet appeals to the authority of the *Golden Epistle* of William of St Thierry (which he attributes to St Bernard) and to the *Sancta Sophia* of Father Augustine Baker, for the excellence and validity of this silent recollection in God; and says with justice that "the best of men in all ages and sects have commended it". Moreover, there is a close parallelism between the ascetical methods of Catholic and of Quaker. The preliminary "gathering" of the attention from external interests and distractions, the establishment of "an inward silence of the mind from all its own imaginations and self-cogitations"[2] and the "centring down" of the self from the surface consciousness to the spiritual deeps—these are acts familiar to all contemplatives, and the necessary preliminaries to all practice of mystical prayer. The effort of will which this act of recollection requires is considerable, since nothing less is involved than a total change in the direction of consciousness and its dissociation from sensible experience; and this in itself is sufficient to defend Quaker worship from the charge of a lazy quietism.

> The silence of a religious and spiritual worship is not a drowsy unthinking state of mind, but a sequestering or withdrawing of it from all visible objects and vain

[1] Quoted by Violet L. Hodgkin, *Silent Worship*, p. 65.
[2] Barclay, *loc. cit.*

imaginations, unto a fervent praying to or praising the invisible omnipresent God in His light and love.[1]

Quaker worship is a powerful corrective of those faults to which Christian institutionalism has always been specially inclined: the tendency to ritualism and to formalism, to emphasize expressive worship, neglect the interior prayer which should inform it, and be satisfied with the routine exercises of the organized cult. It keeps alive the charismatic strain; that docile and realistic waiting upon the Spirit which was central to the life of the Primitive Church, but sank more and more into the background with its development. It points past all signs and symbols to the Invisible Holy, trusts the immanent presence with men of the Invisible Holy, and perpetually reminds us of the awe and humility, the pause, the hush, the deliberate break with succession, with which man should approach the great experience of communion with the living God: "not hurrying into the exercise of these things, so soon as the bell rings, as other Christians do."[2] St John Chrysostom demanding a deep silence at the awful moment when the Spirit descends upon the Eucharistic gifts, St Ignatius Loyola, always pausing with his hand on the latch, before he dared to enter the church for prayer, and countless others remind us that here the reverent practice of the Friends has always been the practice of the Saints.

Quakers, then, safeguard the truths of man's creaturely status and divine sonship: of the "deep ground of the soul" which is the true scene of his worshipping communion, where the Spirit dwells and may be found. They aim at the uncompromising application of spiritual truth everywhere and at all times; brushing away with a certain impatience all mediating symbols and sacraments, as hostile to the pure

[1] John Bellers (1718). Quoted by Braithwaite in *The Second Period of Quakerism*, p. 575.

[2] Barclay, *loc. cit.*

inwardness of Christian experience. In the silent Meeting, uniting the group in a confident waiting upon the spiritual Light, the Friend stakes all on the promises of the New Testament, and asserts the wholly supernatural character of prayer. " Friends everywhere," said Fox, " keep all your meetings waiting on the Light." The creaturely sense, man's utter dependence on an ineffable mystery, here takes precedence of all other elements in the religious complex. The recollective movement of the soul is fully emphasized ; and its possibility and value are claimed for all, and not merely for a spiritual élite. And indeed this deliberate retreat from the surface to the absolute levels of life, even though its real character may not be comprehended by the average worshipper, is yet strangely pacifying to the human spirit. To " sit down in meeting " may seem to mean no more than a pause in the rhythm of existence for tranquil attention to the things of God. Yet it is a pause in which the surface self is at a discount, and the transcendental self gets its chance. This is alone enough to account for the serenity, the recollected temper, so characteristic at least of the older type of Friend.

It is on the negative side that Quaker worship shows its weakness ; the unhappy Either-Or which creates a forced option between sacramental and spiritual worship, and repudiates the whole apparatus of visible religion in favour of an " inward retiring to the Lord "[1] instead of accepting as completing opposites these two great means of communion with God. For reasons which have already been fully stated, such an exclusive mysticism, making an arbitrary distinction between sense and spirit, could never be adequate to the generous realities of an incarnational faith ; or serve the religious needs of a creature poised between the worlds of spirit and of sense, and participating in both. Even though we find in Quaker history many convincing records of first-

[1] Barclay, *op. cit.*, 11th Pt., § xvii.

hand experience of God, yet it is significant that the Society of Friends, the only Christian communion which has made contemplative prayer the standard of worship, has produced no great contemplative or made any real addition to our knowledge of the soul's interior life. We cannot miss the authentic note of an overwhelming revelation of reality in George Fox, Elizabeth Fry, or Stephen Grellet; yet no Quaker teacher creates the impression which we receive, e.g. from St Augustine, from Ruysbroeck, or St John of the Cross, of the soul's entrance into a supernatural order "above reason but not against reason" which exceeds the resources of speech. The great masters of interior prayer seem always to appear within an institutional framework and practice, a sacramental and historical cultus; as if the energy of worship must overflow into sensible expression and orientate the whole life, physical and metaphysical, outward and inward, towards the Holy, in order to develop the full possibilities of the Godward life in man.

Nor as a matter of fact does Quakerism succeed in the total elimination of sensible signs. The bareness of the Meeting House is in itself sacramental; a positive witness to the otherness of God, which may be more impressive, more suggestive of the unseen Holy, than the veil before the tabernacle or the sanctuary lamp. So, too, Quaker silence is not merely the matrix within which individual recollection can develop. It means the deliberate subjugation of man's successive life to the Reality of the Abiding; a negative yet sensible acknowledgment of that immanent Presence before Whom all speech must fail. Here then Christian worship comes to full circle: and the still waiting of the Friend upon the Inner Light unites with the speechless adoration of the Catholic before the mystery of the Mass. For both, the Absolute is truly self-revealed under symbols: in one case, the negative symbols of ineffable Being, in the other, the homely and positive signs of a manifested and self-giving love.

CHAPTER XV

THE ANGLICAN TRADITION

I

WHEN we have considered the outward form and inward spirit of Catholic and Protestant worship, we are still left with the cultus which is, after all, of special interest to ourselves, and which refuses to make itself entirely at home in either of these classes—the worship of the Anglican Communion. The tangled history of its development has often been told ;[1] and need not be repeated, except in so far as it is necessary to demonstrate two points of cardinal importance.

The first point is this. Anglican worship is a special development of the traditional Christian cultus ; and not merely a variant of Continental Protestantism. The first rubric of the first Anglican Prayer-book, "The Priest being in the quier, shall begynne with a loude voyce the Lordes prayer called the Paternoster ",[2] at once establishes its claim to continuity with the past, and reminds us of the gradual stages by which the transition from the Latin to the English use was made.[3] The English Book of Common Prayer is not merely a permissive liturgy, like the Prayer

[1] It is excellently summarized by Dr F. E. Brightman and Bishop K. D. Mackenzie in *Liturgy and Worship*, pp. 130–200.

[2] An Ordre for Mattyns. 1st Prayer Book of Edward VI.

[3] Certain vernacular services—e.g. Prone, consisting of the Bidding of the Bedes with the Ten Commandments and a homily, all in English—existed before the Reformation ; and after the break with Rome, Mass continued for a time to be said in Latin, with an English office of Confession, Absolution and Humble Access, at the Communion of the People.

Books of the Lutheran and Calvinist Churches. It forms, with the Bible or Lectionary, the authorized Missal and Breviary of the English branch of the Catholic Church. Its use is obligatory, and its contents declare in unmistakable terms the adherence of that Church to the great Catholic tradition of Christendom and the general conformity of its worship to the primitive ritual type. Though simplification has involved some real liturgical loss, and many of the guiding lines which shape the whole of worship towards a total self-oblation have been obscured, the general sense of the Daily Offices and Eucharist, as we find them in that book, is that of an offering of all life for the service and glory of God. Thus it provides for the daily recitation of the Divine Office in a contracted and practicable form, dividing the Psalter in such a manner that it can really be—as in primitive times —the substance of daily worship :[1] and, requiring this devotion of every priest, reminds them that their first obligation is the praise or adoration of God.

> Priests are called *Angeli Domini*, and it is the Angel's office not only to descend to the people and teach them God's will, but to ascend also to the presence of God to make intercession for the people and to carry up the daily prayers of the Church in their behalf, as here they are bound to do.[2]

Thus to have restored the Divine Office to its true position as the daily prayer of the whole "household of faith",

[1] At the time of the Reformation, the Roman Breviary—so overloaded with Feasts, Commemorations, and variable parts that its total recitation had become impossible and the true rhythm of the Divine Office was lost—was already overdue for revision. Several efforts towards this had been made within the Church. As to the Missal, in 1549 over two hundred different printed Missals, representing various local uses, monastic and secular, were in circulation ; and as the preface to the Prayer Book reminds us, five such uses existed in England alone. See F. E. Brightman, *The English Rite*, pp. x *seq.*

[2] John Cosin. Notes on the Book of Common Prayer. Quoted in *Anglicanism*, p. 629.

uniting its corporate praise of God with the universal action of the Eastern and Western Church, is a chief glory of the Anglican rite; which has here been willing to run the risk of formalism in order to remain within the Catholic tradition of the Church. Indeed this ancient form of worship, Biblical in substance, theocentric in direction, sober yet fervent in tone, suits well the temper of the English mind. The tendency of some enthusiastic sacramentalists to discredit "Anglican Mattins" is strange: for here, in the solemn chanting of the *Venite*, the daily Psalms, *Te Deum*, and *Benedictus*, we have a genuine corporate act of adoring worship performed by the whole congregation in union with the whole Communion of Saints.

As to the Eucharistic liturgy, this too follows—though with certain unfortunate dislocations and omissions—the great lines of the classic ritual pattern. Its variable parts conform to the Western Proper of Time, and thus imply at least a weekly celebration of the Holy Mysteries. There is full recognition of the high points of the Christian year, with their seasons of penitential preparation, and a limited—yet according to ancient models, a sufficient—provision for the commemoration of the major Saints. The liturgical services for Baptism, Confirmation, Marriage, Churching of Women, the Visiting of the Sick and Burial of the Dead, witness to the continuing desire of the Church to sanctify and weave into her worship every circumstance of human life. The Prayer Book is therefore in itself a Catholic document; though a Catholic document which has been subdued to the penetrating influence of the Reform, and bears many marks of the vicissitudes through which it has passed.

The second point is this. The peculiar character of Anglicanism arises in part from the operation of history; the conflict within her own borders, both before and after her cultus took form, of Puritan and Catholic ideals. But it is also a true expression of certain paradoxical attributes of the

English mind: its tendency to conservatism in respect of the past, and passion for freedom in respect of the present, its law-abiding faithfulness to established custom, but recoil from an expressed dominance; its reverence for the institutions which incorporate its life, and inveterate individualism in the living of that life; its moral and practical bent. All these characters can be studied in any rural parish at the present day; and all spring to attention whenever either an innovator or an authoritarian threatens to disturb the ancient ways.[1] For the English mind will neither have too much authority nor too much novelty; it will love the past, and frequently turn back to it, but will insist on interpreting the lessons of the past in its own way. It will accept the duty of an ordered worship, but resist mere ceremonial for its own sake. It will listen with respect to its spiritual teachers, but will not tolerate interference with the liberty and deep reserve of the individual soul. The short treatise "On Ceremonies" inserted in the First Prayer Book of Edward VI and still retained in the Book of Common Prayer is here a matchless expression of the national mind; its conviction that "innovation and newfangleness . . . is always to be eschewed", that "order and quiet discipline" are desirable qualities conducing to the glory of God, its democratic demand that the ceremonies used in public worship shall be at no point "dark or dumb" but "so set forth that every man may understand what they do mean and what use they do serve", its desire to steer such a course between those "addicted to their old customs" and those that would "innovate all things", as shall "please God and profit them both"—a problem which the national Church has never perfectly solved.

Again, as this same document makes plain to us, the

[1] "I don't often go to church now", said a village woman to me recently, "it's so uninteresting. The vicar has put new tunes to all the hymns."

English mind is always inclined to assume that a primary object of ordered worship is the edifying of the congregation. Such worship chiefly exists to "stir up the dull mind of man to the remembrance of his duty to God"; for we tend as a race to give works priority over faith, to equate religion with goodness, and to estimate worship by its this-world effects in terms of the moral will, rather than by its power of lifting up the mind and heart unto God. This spiritual temper, which is still characteristic of the piety of rural England, did not spring into existence at the Reformation. It is fundamental to the national character; and Cranmer knew well what note to strike in recommending to his fellow-countrymen the edifying quality of his "godly and decent order" of daily prayer. Considering history, we gradually come to recognize this distinctive religious attitude, always seeking expression within the forms of its own day: in Catholics and Evangelicals, in Puritans, Methodists, and Friends; in the sturdy and disciplined faithfulness of those lives which it dominates, and the grave beauty and sanctifying power of the dedicated souls which it has formed. It is this characteristic response of the English soul to the demand of God to which Anglican worship at its best gives stylized expression; and to which in its periodic revivals it always returns. On the whole, it is a response which leans more to the prophetic and Biblical than to the liturgic and sacramental side of the Christian cultus. The hymn-singing and Bible reading, the moral emphasis, which the English mind considers to be essential parts of worship, are not mere legacies of the Reformation; nor is it by chance that the Church of England has been content to use for centuries a dislocated Eucharistic canon, but has carefully revised her lectionaries and constantly added to her repertory of hymns. Not the supernatural mystery, but the homely side of man's relation to the Transcendent, his here-and-now dependence and moral obligation, is developed here.

The one corporate vernacular devotion of Catholic times of which we have certain knowledge—the Bidding of the Sunday Bedes[1]—shows already this homely, practical, incarnational temper of English piety, its close and determined association of religion with all the events and anxieties of daily life. This devotion is really a detailed family intercession for the necessities of that daily life, and for all who have a claim on their fellow Christians' prayer; for "true tythers" and "true tyllers", for all the "grains and fruits sowed, set, or done on the earth" for merchants, seamen, and travellers, for all who have given to the Church for God's service "any behests"—"book, bell, chalice or vestment, surplice, altar-cloth or towel" and for the donor of that day's "holy bread"—for the sick, all "women in Our Lady's bands," and for all departed Christian souls. After each bidding, the people said the Lord's Prayer in silence. The Reformers, ruthlessly expelling the sacrificial element from the Mass, reducing with a heavy hand the symbolic setting of expressive worship, and in general stripping the mediæval colour from English religious life, yet left in such devotions as these the deepest roots of that religious life, the homely and filial dependence on the Providence of God, almost untouched.

Eucharistic devotion seems never to have had in England the primacy to which it attained in other parts of the Western Church: which perhaps explains the entire failure of the Reformers to restore frequent communion to its place in the life of worship. The vernacular writings of the English Catholic mystics[2] are curiously devoid of Eucharistic references; in this contrasting strongly with the contemporary mysticism of Italy, Germany, and Flanders. But these writings abound in Biblical citations and concrete moral

[1] Printed by Wynkyn de Worde in 1532 in *The Festyvall*: text in F. E. Brightman, *op. cit.*, Vol. II, Appendix I.

[2] E.g., Richard Rolle, Walter Hilton, and the author of *The Cloud of Unknowing*.

demands; insisting on the keeping of God's law as the essence of the worshipping life. "He praises all day that does all things well, and he stints not of praise while he holds his righteousness and errs not from God's love," says Rolle in his English Psalter:[1] and the celebrated passage in which Walter Hilton condemns the Christianity which is content to "adorn Christ's Head, but neglect His Feet"[2] is thoroughly English in teaching and tone. The Messengers of God who visit Piers Plowman are Do Well, Do Bet, Do Best. It is Good Deeds who saves the soul of Everyman. The roots of that sturdy, fervent, highly moralized Evangelical piety which is sometimes unfairly contrasted with the Catholic piety it should inspire and complete can be discovered in the earliest English religious works; which are coloured by an ardent and personal Christocentric devotion, closely connected with the mediæval cultus of the Holy Name of Jesus yet differing little in character from that which the Evangelical revival brought back into Anglican worship at a later day.

Even before it became articulate in the Lollard movement, the Biblical, anti-institutional temper was present in our religious life. Thus Richard Rolle, the father alike of English mystics and English lay preachers, combined a stern and Puritanical standard of ethics, a hatred of formalism and an anti-clerical bias, with a profound love and knowledge of Scripture, and an impassioned devotion to the Holy Name of Jesus his "tresoure and joy". He mentions the Mass seldom; but the Psalms much. To these characteristics he added another, always congenial to the English religious temper—a great love of music and song. Song was to him the perfect symbol of adoring love—"My heart Thou hast

[1] *The English Writings of Richard Rolle*, edited by H. E. Allen, p. lxii. Rolle (*c.* 1300–1349) was a hermit, lay-preacher, and contemplative, the first translator of the Psalter into English, and one of the earliest writers of English religious songs.

[2] *Treatise to a Devout Man*, cap. VI.

bound in love of Thy name and now I cannot but sing it ";—[1] and it is remarkable that in the many variants to the established worship which his fellow countrymen have set up, making melody to God has usually had a prominent place. Rolle and the Wesleys would well have understood each other; for they shared the same intense Christocentric fervour, the same evangelical passion for the awakening of souls, the same exacting moral standards, and would have enjoyed and approved each other's hymns. But the Wesleys, with their strong Eucharistic and doctrinal bias, and insistence on frequent communion—a subject in which Rolle appears to take no interest—might have seemed to an uninformed observer more Catholic in outlook than the Yorkshire hermit, with his independent spirit, and apparent aloofness from institutional practice.

We must not, then, suppose that the Tudor settlement merely evicted the ancient devotion; or introduced into England a new type of worship, a new Godward response, uncertainly poised between a reduced Catholicism and a stylized Protestantism, and seldom at rest between these extremes. It is easy to find superficial support for this view. But a more careful inspection shows us, that the separation of the English Church from Latin Catholicism—once the first period of acute and sometimes excessive revolt from mediæval conceptions and abuses was past—was the first stage in the formation of a real national cultus: vindicating in all essentials the continuity of Catholic tradition, whilst giving expression to the peculiar religious temper of the English soul. This Anglican cultus, uniting—though never without a certain tension—what are commonly regarded as the "Catholic" and "Protestant", i.e. the stylized, sacramental, and corporate, and the prophetic Biblical and individual, ideals of Christian worship, has endured many vicissitudes. Yet the spiritual temper which it expresses has

[1] Richard Rolle, *The Fire of Love*, Bk. II, cap. 12.

not varied much ; and at its best remains in harmony with our religious past. There is little fundamental difference between the pastoral ideals of St Aidan and those of Bishop Ken ; the dedicated life of St Gilbert of Sempringham's little flock, and that of Little Gidding, where " Mr. Ferrar and his happy family served God day and night " ; or the life of worship and service lived by a devoted country priest of mediæval times, and the " humble behaviour and visible adoration " of Mr. George Herbert of Bemerton " lifting up pure and charitable hands to God at the canonical hours of prayer " : whom the common people " did so love and reverence " that they would " let their plough rest when Mr. Herbert's Saints' bell rung to prayers, that they might also offer their devotions to God with him, and would then return back to their plough ".[1] Nor again is there any real divergence in religious outlook between the author of *The Temple* and the author of *The Christian Year* ; between the sober and reformed Catholic practice of the great Caroline divines, and that which the early Tractarians brought back to new life ; or again between the hidden life of worship which English mediæval books of devotion express and that which Mr. Pusey and his followers practised and taught. Along this line, we can trace an unbroken continuity between the " faith of our fathers " and our own, and between the English use as the First Prayer Book of Edward VI understood it, and that which is now the established custom in the great central body of the Church.

II

Anglican worship, then, seen in liturgic regard, is Christian worship according to the " English use " ; and this use, with its peculiar fusion of Catholic and Protestant elements,

[1] Izaak Walton, *The Life of Mr. George Herbert* (World's Classics edition, p. 302).

has been produced under historic pressure. Seen in religious regard, it answers to a special trend of the English character ; a trend which is already recognizable in mediæval devotion. The result has been the creation of a cultus which is true to the great lines of traditional Christian worship, yet capable of interpretation either in a Catholic or an Evangelical sense : thus making the ancient tradition of Christian ordered prayer available to the whole body of the faithful, and permitting the union in a common fellowship of those who lean either to the sacramental or prophetic, the " High " or the " Low ", the corporate or the individualist expression of the worshipping life.[1] Hence the puzzled student of Anglicanism can find within its borders, and using its liturgic books, an almost complete Evangelicalism: grave, Biblical, prophetic, devoted, based on the preaching and hearing of the Word, suspicious of ceremonial acts and sensible signs, emphasizing the personal relation of the soul to God, greatly concerned with man, his needs, problems, and duties, and hardly distinguishable in temper from the unstylized public worship of the Nonconformist sects. But he can also find, using the same books and obedient to the same authorities, a sacramental, objective, and theocentric worship ; emphasizing the holiness, authority, and total action of the Church, her call to adoration and vocation of sacrifice, reverencing her traditions and her saints, using all the resources of symbolic expression. Pressing eucharistic devotion to its logical term, in its more extreme forms this can hardly be distinguished from Roman Catholicism. No one who remembers the controversies aroused by the proposed revision of the Prayer Book in 1928 will doubt the existence of these contrasting tempers in

[1] " Our zeal ", says Jeremy Taylor, " was balanced with the consideration and the results of authority ; not like women and children when they are affrighted with fire in their clothes ; we shaked off the coal indeed but not our garments, lest we should have exposed our churches to that nakedness which the excellent men of our sister churches complained to be among themselves." " An Apology for Authorized and Set Forms of Liturgy " given in *Anglicanism*, p. 170.

the English mind. But it is somewhere between them that we must look for the peculiar synthetic genius of the Anglican Communion; that "liberal and Scriptural Catholicism . . . which is stable and in undoubted continuity with the whole movement of the Church in history,"[1] yet while stretching out one hand to the Church of the Western tradition, stretches out the other to the Evangelical churches of the Reform. This attitude maintains within the English Church a constant tension, and causes frequent reactions towards either the Protestant or Catholic pole. Moreover, it has inevitably its own spiritual defects. The *Via Media* eludes not only the extremes of Catholic and Protestant cultus, but also the heights and deeps of the spiritual life. The phenomena of individual conversion and the ardours of sacramental devotion are viewed with an equal suspicion. We do not find here the realization of an enfolding supernatural world as the environment within which the Church worships, and our entrance into that living world in communion and prayer, and close contact with its population, which is fundamental to a full Catholicism; or sense of the Church itself as a supernatural society, offering its very being as an oblation before God. On one hand that intimate relation of every soul to God which is the heart of Evangelical worship, though accepted, is hardly stressed. On the other hand, the more awful Mysteries of the transcendent order, with their unlimited demand on our worship, are not touched by this discreet formulation. We have only to open a Missal or an Orthodox service book, to realize how much spiritual treasure the Anglican reformers threw away, and at how many points they failed to carry through the deeper implications of Christian doctrine into expressive worship. Hence those who seek here for the "beauty of the Mysterious" will often be thrown back on themselves. Nevertheless, in spite of these difficulties and shortcomings and with all its inconsistencies

[1] C. Gore, *The Basis of Anglican Fellowship*, pp. 4 and 5.

—perhaps because of them—the Anglican compromise where administered with generosity and suppleness meets the average needs of the English soul: and the Church can hardly abandon it without a departure from her peculiar place in the Christian scheme.

The First Prayer Book of Edward VI, which sought to organize the national worship, was in all essentials a Catholic book. It provided an English version of those services which the English Catholic was accustomed to hear on Sunday in his parish church; namely, Mass preceded by Mattins or Prime in the morning, and Vespers or Evensong in the afternoon. It ordered a daily celebration of the Eucharist in the English tongue in all cathedrals and collegiate churches—a rule which was never abolished, but merely allowed to lapse, till its general restoration in our own times—and retained a sufficient number of significant ornaments and ceremonies, including Eucharistic vestments and the use of wafer bread, for the purpose of a dignified and reverent celebration of the Holy Mysteries. This standard of worship, the liturgical high-water-mark of the English Church, was reduced under pressure from Protestant extremists in the Second Prayer Book; and greatly marred by the breaking-up of the Eucharistic Canon[1] and the almost entire neglect of the element of sacrifice, in this and all subsequent revisions. Nevertheless, the great outlines and chief values of the traditional Christian cultus were faithfully conserved in it; and it developed under the religious leaders of the Caroline Church—Lancelot Andrewes, Laud, Jeremy Taylor, and their associates—that sober but Catholic

[1] In I Edward VI, the Canon included the Preface, *Sanctus*, Prayer for the Church, with a Commemoration of the Saints and of the departed, the consecration of the elements with Memorial of the Passion, the Prayer of Oblation, and Lord's Prayer. Thus it conformed closely to the pattern of the ancient Eucharistic Prayers. The detachment of the intercession for the Church, and the insertion of the subjective Prayer of Humble Access (from an earlier vernacular Preparation for Communion) after the *Sanctus* broke this total Godward movement of the Eucharistic Act.

English tradition, based on the Divine Office and the Eucharist, and faithful to the ancient disciplines of ordered prayer, fasting, and communion, which survived the disasters of the Puritan dominance and subsequent periods of reaction and of indifference, and is now again recognized as the classic norm of Anglican worship.[1] This persistence through many adversities is only understood, when we realize that the Anglican cultus was the institutional expression of a continuous and deep interior life, which survived even during the worst periods of decadence. The "faithful remnant" of worshipping souls never failed the English Church; and from Lancelot Andrewes to Simeon and Pusey these kept alight the secret fire of sacrificial worship. It is in the long series of devotional works which they produced, that this spirit lived on. We recognize it in such books as the *Preces Privatæ* of Lancelot Andrewes, the *Holy Living and Dying* of Jeremy Taylor, the *Mount of Olives* of Henry Vaughan, the anonymous *Whole Duty of Man*,[2] or the immensely influential writings of William Law. The great mediæval books of devotion, too, especially Thomas à Kempis, never ceased to be read by devout Anglicans; and those of the Counter-Reformation—e.g. St Ignatius Loyola, St Teresa, Fénélon, St François de Sales, and the *Sancta Sophia* of Father

[1] During the Puritan period, celebration of the Sacraments ceased in many parishes. Yet at the Restoration, Eucharistic worship at once revived and monthly and even weekly celebrations were eagerly attended. In the reign of Queen Anne, the Rector of St James, Piccadilly, could speak of "those multitudes that without superstition or Tumult, every month crowd up to the Altar." Though during the eighteenth century the average practice was poor, as indeed it was in most countries whether Catholic or Protestant, this devotional tradition never died out. See Wickham Legg, *English Church Life from the Restoration to the Tractarian Movement*, pp. 35 *et seq.*

[2] This book, probably the most popular devotional work in the English language, appeared in 1658; and continued to be published in countless editions till the beginning of the nineteenth century. At the beginning of Wesley's revival, it was chosen by the Oxford Methodists to be given with Bible and Prayer Book to those whom they sought to evangelize.

Augustine Baker—were mostly in circulation here by the end of the seventeenth century.

There was, in fact, no period between the Elizabethan settlement and the Tractarian revival in which spiritual books, recommending a high standard of prayer and self-discipline, and teaching a devout approach to Holy Communion which is hard to distinguish from that of continental Catholicism,[1] were not produced, and eagerly studied by a minority of faithful souls—even during the supposed "refrigeration" of eighteenth-century religion. It is chiefly by these books, which played their part in each successive revival of worship, that the continuity of the true Anglican spirit with its peculiar blend of reverence, sobriety, moral earnestness, and sturdy realism, was assured.[2]

III

Modern Anglican worship, whether Evangelical, Central, or Anglo-Catholic, is the heir of two great revivals of the God-ward life: the Evangelical and Tractarian movements. Now that the dust and heat of their beginnings have died down, and the realities which they brought back into English Christianity can be distinguished from the accompanying accidents, we see that they were in fact completing opposites; originating in a single impulse of the Spirit, which quickened first the dry bones of personal piety, and next the corporate religious life. Each began, as every real revival

[1] Even so Protestant a writer as Daniel Brevint (1673) could write of "the Lamb of God lying and sacrificed upon the Holy Table": and the use of the *Domine non sum dignus* and *Agnus Dei* was generally recommended to communicants, with prostration on approaching the altar. See Wickham Legg, *op. cit.*, pp. 69 and 60.

[2] Methodists, Evangelicals, and Tractarians have each in their turn acknowledged the magnitude of their debt to Jeremy Taylor and to William Law. The *Imitation of Christ*, which was edited by Wesley for the use of his followers, has had a formative influence on Anglicans of every type.

of worship must do, in a fresh realization of the Eternal, and of the poverty of man's response to the Eternal; a fresh contact through history and devotion with the spirit of Christ and of the Saints. If Evangelicalism at its best gave fresh vitality to that prophetic, Biblical, ethical strand, centred on the Ministry of the Word and on first-hand individual response, which has always existed in English religion; Tractarianism gave fresh vitality to its corporate and liturgical aspect, its Catholic quality, centred on the Church and the Ministry of the Sacraments. Each was a legitimate child of the Anglican tradition; and the revival still in progress, and within which we live and worship, is indebted to both.

The Evangelical movement represents that part of the spirit and fruit of Methodism which developed within the established Church. Indeed its leaders, such as Charles Simeon and his disciple Henry Martyn, were given by those who disliked their fervour the name of Methodist. Like Wesley, these Anglican Evangelicals were primarily spiritual realists; concerned to restore the living quality of Christian devotion to Christ. They deeply valued Holy Communion, and the "great and precious duties of secret fasting and prayer";[1] served the poor with love, and sought out sinners. They were in fact devoted to the single vocation of a costly, loving worship; and expressed this dominant passion in the traditional ways of devotion, self-discipline, and service. The emphasis lay upon the individual relation of each soul to Christ, the experience of conversion and assurance, and the consequent call to a total dedication of life. There was little sense of the Church's corporate action, but an ardent sense of personal response to God. In this respect the great Evangelicals rank, with Keble and Pusey, among those creative personalities who were the agents in the revival of the spirit of worship in the English

[1] David Brainerd, quoted by C. Padwick, *Henry Martyn*, p. 71.

Church. Such were the vigorous and eloquent Simeon, rising at four that he might spend the morning hours in meditation, or found murmuring again and again in self-oblivious rapture, "Glory! glory! glory to the Son of God!"[1] and the fragile scholar Henry Martyn, driven by the "mysterious glories of religion" from an academic to an uncongenial missionary career.

Save where it was influenced by this movement, or by rare survivals of old High Church ideals and practice, Anglican worship had fallen at this time to its lowest level. The infrequent celebrations of the Eucharist had little sacramental significance, and were often even irreverent.[2] Churches were bare, ugly and without devotional atmosphere. The comfortably furnished pews of the well-to-do contrasted disagreeably with those provided for the poor. The dignified beauty of Caroline ceremonial was forgotten, liturgical services were badly rendered, both Saints' days and days of abstinence were generally ignored. There was little or no consciousness of the life of the Church, the majestic character of the Christian revelation, or the supernatural reality of its sacraments. A level of institutional practice now expected of every country parish—e.g. a weekly celebration of the Eucharist—would then have seemed a remarkable, even an objectionable expression of fervour. This was the scene within which the Tractarian pioneers, at the cost of bitter suffering and misunderstanding, started the movement which has restored in all parts of the English Church the life of corporate worship. But they could hardly have done this without the influence and support of that Evangelical environment in which many of them had been reared;[3] and which gave both to their lives and to their

[1] C. Padwick, *op. cit.*, p. 64.

[2] Y. Brilioth, *Eucharistic Faith and Practice*, p. 215.

[3] E.g. Newman, Pusey and Manning. Keble and Hurrell Froude were sons of the old High Church tradition. See Y. Brilioth, *The Anglican Revival*, cap. III.

preaching the deep note of personal piety, the moral fervour, the bracing emphasis on man's own responsibility in character-building and the conquest of sin.

Thus many strands meet in the Anglican revival: for later events have proved that it was indeed this, and not merely a sectional movement within the Church. But it was, above all, a reassertion of the priority of God, and a revival of the spirit of worship; originating in a renewed contact with those realities of the eternal order which are alone the effective cause of adoration. Those external changes, that emphasis on institutional life, ascetic discipline, and ritual pattern which are sometimes mistaken for its substance, are merely the outward signs and necessary concomitants of an inner orientation. To breed saints, said Newman, is the proper task of the visible Church; here falling into line with Wesley, his fellow pupil at the feet of William Law. Though their appeal might be to history and theology and the witness of the early Fathers—for no revival of human religion, however supernaturally inspired, takes place *in vacuo*—the great Tractarians, as the sermons of Newman and Pusey make plain to us, were convinced, even impassioned transcendentalists. In them the Spirit, working as ever through minorities—and also, we may perhaps say, through the heads as well as the hearts of His faithful people—began again within the English Church the life of sacrificial worship. The restoration of a symbolic and sacramental cultus, the bringing back of beauty as an essential factor in full worship, and even the extravagances and absurdities of the later ritualists, all had their origin in a movement inspired by "the severe and lonely spirit of the Cross".[1] The greatest thing which they did for their Mother Church is not to be found in the sphere of expressive ceremonial; but in the restoration of this other-worldly temper, and with it the essential link between adoration and sacrifice. The spiritual

[1] H. E. Manning, quoted by Y. Brilioth, *The Anglican Revival*, p. 263.

world to which they looked, and which they believed to be revealed in sacramental experience, was a world charged with mystery and awfulness; and made an unmitigated demand upon the soul. Not Calvin himself shows a keener sense than Pusey of the majesty and holiness of God. Hence the austerity, almost the grimness, which we feel in the early Tractarian preaching. It brought back that remembrance of the august realities of faith and the total claim of the Eternal God on man, which contemporary Christianity had almost lost. This lofty ethical standard, this demand for self-discipline, and close interlocking of moral effort and worship, attracted serious English Christians to a movement which might have seemed on the surface to make its chief appeal to the devotee. "Surely," said Pusey, "our conflict is, to uproot everything which interferes with the love of God, and the thought of God, and the likeness of God in our souls", and again, "Seek the glory of God alone; desire to be indwelt by God, because He is Love and the object of all love, and in His Love is all."[1] The high value which the Tractarians set on the doctrine and writings of the Patristic Church seems at least in part to be due to the profoundly theocentric temper of the early Fathers, their uncompromising standards and realistic hold on the unseen.

It is important to recognize the massive spiritual stature of the first leaders: the greatness of their vision, the faithfulness and the courage, continued over many years, by which they won for English Christianity victories which they did not live to see, and the deep sense of vocation under which they suffered and worked. The utmost demands of adoration, contrition, and sacrifice were fully met in their own lives; and these are of course the only conditions under which a genuine revival of Christian worship can take place. Pusey, the true prophet of the movement, was by temperament an ascetic and contemplative. His inner life,

[1] E. B. Pusey, *Parochial Sermons*, Vol. II, pp. 153 and 254.

disciplined by much suffering, was nourished by the writings of the great Catholic mystics, whose influence can constantly be detected in his sermons, and sometimes breaks out in passages of sustained splendour. Indeed, the modern recognition and restoration of the mystical element in religion, in so far as it is a factor in the Anglican revival, began with this scholar-saint. Further, his *Spiritual Letters* reveal Pusey as a great director of souls, devoted, wise, and gentle; the first in a series of teachers who have brought back into the English Church the secrets of the interior life of prayer. Without the dangerous literary gifts of Newman, he gives the impression of a more self-oblivious holiness, a greater spiritual power. He had no love for ritual excesses: or any great interest in the externals of religion save in so far as they expressed inward realities, or ministered to the good of souls.[1] His real spirit and the source of his power is most fully revealed to us in his prayers.

> Let me not seek out of Thee what I can only find in Thee; peace and rest and joy and bliss, which abide only in Thy abiding joy. Lift up my soul above the weary round of harassing thoughts to Thy Eternal Presence. Lift up my soul to the pure, bright, clear, serene, radiant atmosphere of Thy Presence, that there I may breathe freely, there repose in Thy Love, there be at rest from myself and from all things that weary me; and thence return, arrayed in Thy peace, to do and bear what shall please Thee.[2]

It is here, not among the vestments and candles and the discussions provoked by them, that we find the inspiring cause and enduring spirit of the Anglican revival of worship: and it is consistent with this, that those who saw Pusey in the last years of his life did not see a brilliant preacher or a

[1] The moderation and sanity of his remarks on these subjects in the *Spiritual Letters* make sad reading for many of those who regard themselves as his successors.

[2] E. B. Pusey, *Private Prayers*, 12th ed., p. 39.

determined controversialist, the leader of a Movement destined either to wreck or to revive his Mother Church; but a quiet man of God, inured to opposition, anxiety, failure, and weariness, "speaking in the calm power of the Holy Ghost, not as the head of a party, but as the somewhat saddened but irrepressible instrument of the Divine Will".[1]

The character of the Anglican revival, as fundamentally a re-awakening of worship, a renewed response to the Holy, is fully realized when we come to the second phase of the movement, with its intense concentration on the details of corporate devotion. This impassioned ritualism is easily discredited; and in its extreme forms often became ridiculous. But it was in fact the outward expression of a deeply-founded life of worship and self-oblation; which could not be content with less than perfection in all that belonged to the service of God. The incarnational and sacramental spirit was here applied to the details of the cultus; sometimes with more enthusiasm than common sense. But it did not stop short with the cultus. The most convinced ceremonialist was often in fact the most undaunted and loving of slum evangelists; carrying through the implications of his sacramental worship and self-offering to the lifelong and devoted service of Christ in His poor.[2]

But the fullest expression of this spirit of adoration, and perhaps the greatest achievement of the Anglican revival when seen in spiritual regard, is the restoration of Religious Orders within the English Church. For the religious life sums up, and expresses in a living symbolism, the ideal consummation of all worship; the total oblation of the creature to the purposes of God.[3] No Church within

[1] R. M. Benson, *Letters*, Vol. I, p. 73.

[2] Thus Father Wainright, who ministered for fifty years at London Docks, began each day by an hour of silent worship before the altar, and spent the rest of it in the service of the sick, the destitute, the sinful and the dying.

[3] Cf. above, cap. XII, p. 252.

which these sacrificial dispositions are not produced, and which does not possess its hidden power-house of surrendered personalities, the consecrated channels of its adoring and redeeming love, has risen to the full possibilities of the Christian call; or proclaimed, in the only language which carries conviction, the unlimited demand of God upon the soul. This was the knowledge by which the founders of the Anglican orders were inspired, and this is the truth which those orders continue to declare.

> Whatever the life of religion may be externally, it must be a life of worship, all its acts pointing towards God with constant elevation . . . we come out of the world for that purpose alone. We do not come out of the world merely under the idea that by association we may be able to accomplish certain plans which commend themselves to our hearts. We come out of the world in order that we may give ourselves to the worship of God . . . yield up both soul and body with all their faculties, one vast combination of activity, in the great complex act of worship.[1]

IV

The new life which entered the Church of England with the Tractarian movement, changing its appearance as it grew and spread, has now penetrated and transformed in varying ways and degrees the whole temper of her worship; and brought it back into harmony with Catholic tradition. This achievement is not seen at its best on the extreme right; where a deliberate mediævalism, and an excessive use of Italian ornament, obscures the liturgical outline and fails to express the peculiar *ethos* of English religion. It has won its greatest triumphs at the centre. There, a dreary and undistinguished institutionalism of which here and there the frowsty relics still remain, has been generally quickened and transformed; and the true ideals of the Tractarians have been realized in

[1] R. M. Benson, *Instructions on the Religious Life*, pp. 10, 17.

an ordered worship, which is faithful to the spirit of the Book of Common Prayer. That worship, at once Biblical and Sacramental, carries through all that is best in the spirit of the past; yet preserves the flexible and synthetic character of Anglicanism. Here, there is an increasing recognition of the organic life of the Church, and the duty and meaning of her common liturgic worship, especially the Eucharist; and a serious concern for the beauty, dignity, and objectivity of her services, which was hardly known a century ago.

This new life, which is not to be equated with definite Anglo-Catholic practices, is specially seen in the Cathedrals; once little better than badly-kept museums, where the spirit of prayer was sternly discouraged,[1] lumber—or sometimes fuel—was stored in the altar-less chapels of the Saints, and a brisk tour of inspection under a competent verger effectively destroyed any suspicion that the building existed for the praise and glory of God. Though much remains to be done in this sphere, the Cathedral is now once more recognized as a sacred shrine, and the Mother Church of the diocese; the visible sign and gathering point of its adoring prayer, where its interests, needs, and activities are remembered before God, and the daily celebration of the Eucharist and the Divine Office maintains the ancient tradition of worship. The setting up of nave altars, the restoration of the chapels, and their dedication to special interests and intentions, the bringing back of every part of the building into the current of liturgic life, is all part of this movement; which does or should sum up that total life of worship in which every parish takes it part.

The peculiarity of the Anglican tradition is the equal emphasis which it gives to the Divine Office and the Eucharist; that is to say, to Biblical and to Sacramental worship.

[1] "Young woman," said the pre-war verger of a great Cathedral to a visitor caught reading her New Testament, "only guide-books may be read here."

Where this balance is disturbed, its special character is lost. The common worship of the Roman and Orthodox Churches is predominantly Eucharistic, and gives priority to the Ministry of the Sacraments. The Divine Office is the devotion of priests and "religious" in the technical sense; and with the exception of Saturday Vigils in the East and Sunday Vespers in the West is almost unknown to the laity. On the other hand, the common worship of Continental and English Protestantism is predominantly Biblical, and emphasizes the Ministry of the Word and the ethical demands of Christianity. Here the celebration of the Eucharist is a special occasion, and not the heart of the Church's life. The *Ecclesia Anglicana* alone—though "Protestant" and "Catholic" extremists may tend to cultivate one strand to the detriment of the rest—is true to the twofold primitive pattern; and along both these paths leads out her people towards God. This is a fact not lightly to be set aside; for it creates a special liturgical formula, in which are united just those elements of worship most deeply valued by the English soul. The Scriptural quality, the grave theocentric temper, the common singing of psalms and spiritual songs, and the dependence on Providence which is expressed in the prayers for the community and the common needs of daily life, exactly fit the Morning and Evening Prayer of the English Church to the religious temper of her children. Here, too, that Church keeps in touch with the Evangelical tradition of worship, based on the Ministry of the Word and the corporate singing of hymns.

Over against this, the great work of the Anglican revival has been the bringing back to its ancient place of the Eucharist, and a gradual disclosure of the meaning of its liturgic sequence. Here, Anglican worship takes up its Catholic heritage; but in its own manner, and clothed in a sober English dress. The elaboration of music and ritual, the importation of Latin ceremonies and mediæval devotions, is no real part of this sacramental revival; which has in its best expressions something of the austere dignity, the simple and practical ceremonial, the corporate character and concentration on the business in hand, of the ancient Gregorian rite.[1] It is, I believe, by the balanced and instructed development of these two great instruments of Christian worship—carrying them forward without deflection from their supernatural orientation, yet keeping them flexible to the changing spiritual needs and spiritual insights of the world—that the Anglican Communion will best fulfil its liturgical office within the Body of Christ. Here support and stimulus is given to the Godward life of the individual, while the solemn objectivity of true Catholic worship is preserved.

The really corporate parish Eucharist, in which all take part in the Church's movement of contrition, oblation, intercession, praise, thanksgiving, consecration, and communion, bringing to the altar and transforming in God all the homely interests of life; the common recitation of the Divine Office, and hearing of the Word; the sanctification and blessing of each great phase in our human experience; the open church and opportunity of access to the sacraments; the children's corner, the mission service, the encouragement of personal devotion and training in prayer, and the realistic development of Christian fellowship: this mixed and many-levelled life of worship, so clearly in the spirit of historic Christianity, should surely be the normal means by which that historic Christianity permeates the people's life. Perhaps the renewed sacramental devotion, which is so generally characteristic of the revival of worship,[2] will never appeal in its fulness to more than that minority of English Christians decisively called to interior and supernatural paths.

[1] Cf. cap. XII, p. 255.

[2] E.g. in the Roman and Orthodox Communions; and also in various degrees in the Scottish, Scandinavian, and Free Churches.

Yet theirs is not a solitary spirituality, but avails for the whole Church; and it is significant that those shining examples of holiness which the revival has produced have all found here the focus of the life of worship.

The second factor in the restoration of Anglican worship has been the re-discovery of the realities of the interior life, the re-opening and exploration of ancient devotional paths, and the fresh emphasis placed upon personal training in self-discipline and prayer. This began with Pusey and his followers; to whom we owe the restoration to currency of many ancient treasures of the spiritual life, and the reassertion of the Church's duty of directing souls. The result has been the creation of a nucleus of ardent and spiritually educated Christians; and the production of a vast literature upon which they can feed. Closely connected with this is the gradual domestication of the once-dreaded practice of confession, and increasing recognition of its religious and psychological worth; and the more recent growth of the Retreat movement, with its opportunity for spiritual instruction and undisturbed communion with God.[1] These practices are no longer regarded as marks of an extreme Catholicism. They are accepted, and even recommended, by that sober Anglicanism of the centre which traces its descent from the Caroline Church; and their value is more and more recognized by those who have little affection for their place of origin. The existence and growth of this economy of the supernatural life means that underneath appearances which are sometimes disconcerting, the true business of the Church goes forward; and the reasonable, holy and living sacrifice is still offered for the whole created order by a company of faithful souls.

[1] In 1913 the Church of England had one retreat house. In 1932 it had twenty-two Diocesan Houses and over thirty belonging to religious communities. Some of these houses receive over one thousand retreatants yearly.

CONCLUSION

CHRISTIAN worship is a supernatural action; and more than a supernatural action, a supernatural life. It is the response of the human creature to the besetting charity of God: a response in which man moves out towards Reality, sheds self-occupation, and finds the true basis of his life. Nor is this merely one form of that general recognition of the Holy which is the basis of natural religion. Christian worship is a distinct response to a distinct revelation; God's self-disclosure to His creature at a particular point in time and space, under particular human accidents, entering the time-series to illuminate and save—a disclosure which spreads, to interpret and transform the whole of human experience. With those who are historically minded, we may think chiefly of this revelation in its human aspect, in close connection with the earthly life, death, and continuing presence of Our Lord; and make of this the focal point of worship. Or with those who seek always for the Absolute and Eternal, we can "pass through the Humanity to the Divinity" to dwell upon the outpouring of the Divine Wisdom through this narrow door, and the gathering up of creation in Him. Both these responses lie within the span of the Christian cultus. But whether our outlook be towards the personal or the transcendent, it is here, in this movement of the abiding God towards His creature, that the incentive is given to man's deepest worship, and the appeal is made to his sacrificial love: and all the kinds and degrees of Christian devotion, in prayer and in action, are ways in which he replies to this utterance of the Word.

The true life of the Church, that *Corpus Christi* "whose feet are on earth and whose head is in heaven," is, then, to be thought of as one continuous Godward stream of adoration, supplication, and sacrificial love. Within this, all separate acts of sacrifice and worship—whether of individuals or of groups—are events subdued to the total action; yet also making their own essential contribution to the life of the whole. Christian worship, therefore, is patient of many kinds and degrees of expression. It must carry forward many strands of devotion, from the most crude to the most sublime, and find room in its choir both for sinners and for saints. It is at once fully personal and fully corporate; requiring the utmost individual action from every member of the Body, yet the giving of every small movement and act to the great movement and act of that Body's total life, as a dancer is fully concentrated on his own action yet perfectly subordinated to the movement of the whole. So in worship, the soul poured out in its solitude to God is yet subordinated to the great rhythm of the Divine Society, going up to the altar and offering itself for the purpose of His undeclared design.

This adoring, sacrificial life of the spirit-filled Body, having as its nucleus the "blessed company of all faithful people" with their liturgical and actual responses to God in Christ, must spread till its periphery includes all loving acts, all sacrificial dispositions, all life outpoured: for liturgical worship has no meaning, save in so far as it shows forth under tokens the ultimate realities of man's Godward call. That instinctive offering of life which, at the dawn of worship, is represented by the primitive sacrificial rites, already acknowledges the truth which is proclaimed by the Cross, and set forth in the Christian liturgy; the fact that only in and by self-offering man triumphs over his own successiveness, and achieves the absolute action which is the substance of eternal life. Thus the full life of worship requires as its prevenient cause and constant support the self-disclosure and self-giving of the Transcendent God to the creature, within that creature's order: that is to say, Incarnation, with its corollaries of the uttered Word, of prophecy, and of sacramental grace. Only this act of love can wake the creature's love, and call forth the self-offering of that creature to the Transcendent; in self-oblation, consecration, and sacrifice. This truth is the very heart of the Christian mystery. It is fully declared on Calvary, and again set forth in every Eucharist.

If this be so, and Christianity be indeed the disclosure of the Eternal God to men, it follows that the Eucharistic principle—the free offering and consecration of the natural life, that it may become the sensible vehicle of the Divine life—must radiate beyond its ritual expression; gradually penetrating and transforming all the actions of humanity. This will mean that every sacrificial life, whatever its apparent incentive, is woven into the garment of the Church's worship. Thus it is entinctured by the Incarnate Life, and in virtue of this given absolute worth; for even where such lives seem to achieve little, yet they are sacramental disclosures of the presence and authority of Pure Love. Christian worship, then, both personal and corporate, as it achieves consciousness of its full vocation, will expand to bring within its ever-widening radius and lift towards God more and more sacrificial material from every level of life; thus bit by bit achieving that incarnation of the Eternal in the temporal, which is the Divine creative goal. Into such a conception of worship the Cross must enter deeply: since its ultimate agent is the purified and dedicated will. Christian devotion, reaching out through liturgy and sacrament, or by the way of contemplative prayer, to adoration of the Perfect, may find the deepest secret of its relation to Reality disclosed in the simple abandonment of the Crib, or in the entire self-oblation of Gethsemane and the Cross. Christian action, striving for the healing and transfiguration of the natural, will find that secret, wherever life's failure to correspond with the requirements of Pure Love asks for the costly redemptive efforts of men. Yet these two paths are really one ; and it is by the recognition of this, and not by any choice between them, that the spirit of worship will respond to the incitement of God, and the Church will rise to the full meaning and possibilities of her call.

The devotional and liturgical path is at once Evangelical and Eucharistic. Here the renewed emphasis on the person of Christ and the centrality of the Eucharist, found in various ways and degrees in all parts of the Christian Church at the present day—the tendency to more frequent communion, the deeper and wider significance which is attached to the Church's sacramental life—all point to a fresh recognition of the close dependence of man on the Divine self-giving, and of the Eucharistic rhythm as the supernatural theme of human life. The active path is that of a devoted co-operation with the creative purpose within the temporal world, a striving for perfection : and this, subdued in its own manner to the supernatural theme and pursued in direct dependence on the supernatural power, is also in its own measure sacramental. Here, the selfless spirit of worship pours itself out in that sacrificial effort which seeks to transform the material order, and especially the human scene—cleansing, healing, saving, reconciling, and making of it a fit vehicle of the divine indwelling Life —giving, in fact, concrete and social expression to the Eucharistic ideal. Nor without such concrete and costly expression, carried to its utmost limits, can Christian adoration be complete. For since God in His Logos is revealed to man in expressive and creative acts within the visible world—through history, and through human personality—so man's response in worship also needs expressive and creative acts; weaving every aspect of our human personality, physical, mental, and spiritual, into its adoring recognition of the beauty and perfection of God. For worship is not merely an expression of the technically religious life. It *is* the religious life, and so, conterminous with life itself: Creation's response to its Origin and Lord.

The Christian hope of the future is that this, the true meaning and message of the Incarnation, will come to be more deeply understood: and the demand on man's worshipping love and total self-offering, will receive a more complete response—a response stretching upward in awe-struck contemplation to share that adoring vision of the Principle which is "the inheritance of the saints in light", and downwards and outwards in loving action, to embrace and so transform the whole world. When this happens, Christian sacramental worship will at last disclose its full meaning, and enter into its full heritage. For it will be recognized as the ritual sign of our deepest relation with Reality, and so of the mysterious splendour of our situation and our call: the successive life of man freely offered in oblation, and the abiding life of God in Christ received, not for our own sakes, but in order to achieve that transfiguration of the whole created universe, that shining forth of the splendour of the Holy, in which the aim of worship shall be fulfilled.

INDEX

I. INDEX OF SUBJECTS

II. INDEX OF PERSONS

THE BOOK

This book is meant to explore those primary realities of man's relation to God which are expressed by his devotional actions. It presents an enduring study on the nature and principles of worship and the foremost forms in which they are articulated in Christianity. The Author contends that though it may be possible that there is diversity in the expressive worship of each of the member of a Christian family, but they all are directed towards the single revelation of the Divine.

Inter-alia, this solemn presentation is divided into two parts. The First part encircles the fundamental characteristics of Christian worship. The methodology in which ritual, symbol, sacrament and sacrifice become part of worship is also examined. The Second part presents descriptive and historical studies that are intended to illustrate the principles of worship, as embodied in the chief type of cults.

It provides a thoughtful introduction on the subject of Christian worship and its interrelation with specific rituals and ceremonies. Also, a separate 'Index of Subjects' amplify the value of this handy presentation. This book is a must buy for Christian Laity, Church Clergies, Researchers, and all those Church ministers who want to enrich their understanding on the subject for further impartation.

THE AUTHOR

Evelyn Underhill (1875-1941) was one of the most widely read English Anglo-Catholic writer in the first half of the 20th century. In 1913, she became an honorary fellow of King's College of Women and in 1927 fellow of King's College; in 1939 she received the honorary degree of D.D. from the University of Aberdeen.

She was the author of well renowned books like: *Mysticism* (1911), *Ruysbroek* (1914), *The Mysticism of Plotinus* (1919), *Worship* (1936). While working on *Worship*, written for the Library of Constructive Theology, she became deeply interested in the Greek Orthodox Church and joined the fellowship of St. Alban and St. Sergius. Besides writing books, she also wrote reviews and special articles for the 'Spectator' (of which she was for some years the theological editor), and later for 'Time and Tide'.